Religion and Culture in Indian Civilization

Religion and Culture in Indian Civilization

Essays in Honour of Prof. C.N. Venugopal

Edited by
Amit Kumar Sharma

D.K. Printworld (P) Ltd.
Publishers of Indian Traditions

Cataloging in Publication Data — DK
[Courtesy: D.K. Agencies (P) Ltd. <docinfo@dkagencies.com>]

Religion and culture in Indian civilization : essays in honour of Prof. C.N. Venugopal / edited by Amit Kumar Sharma.
p. cm.
C.N. Venugopal, b.1939, Indian sociologist; contributed articles.
Includes bibliographical references (p.).
ISBN 13: 9788124605639
ISBN 10: 8124605637

1. Religion and culture — India. 2. India — Civilization. 3. India — Religion. I. Venugopal, C. N. II. Sharma, Amit Kumar.

DDC 306.60954 22

First published in India, 2011
ISBN 13: 978-81-246-0563-9 (HB) ISBN 10: 81-246-0563-7

Published and printed by:
D.K. Printworld (P) Ltd.
Regd. office : *'Srikunj,'* F-52, Bali Nagar
Ramesh Nagar Metro Station
New Delhi - 110 015
Phones : (011) 2545 3975; 2546 6019; *Fax* : (011) 2546 5926
E-mail: indology@dkprintworld.com
Web: www.dkprintworld.com

Preface

THIS book is a collective endeavour to honour Prof. C.N. Venugopal. Prof. Venugopal joined the faculty of the Centre for the Study of Social Systems, Jawaharlal Nehru University (JNU), New Delhi in 1971. He retired from JNU in October 2001. In JNU he taught several courses at the MA and the MPhil levels but he is usually remembered for his lectures in sociological theory and sociology of religion. Although he wrote a number of scholarly articles on different aspects of religion, ideology and Indian society, he is primarily remembered as a teacher, seeker and thinker of the highest order. He was born in the year 1939 at Hassan Town, Karnataka. After completing MA in Sociology in 1964, he spent a few years working on research projects conducted by University of Mysore and TISS, Mumbai during 1964-71. After retirement he has settled with his wife at Bangalore. He is a great scholar but he is also a great human being. When his turn came he declined chairpersonship of the centre in JNU. When he approached 62 years of life, he did not seek three years extension as a Professor of JNU. Unlike many others of his generation he never tried to get the limelight or seek power or privilege. He remained a true believer in the Sanātana Dharma of Indic tradition and practised what he taught to his students. He tried to synthesize sociology and Indology in his own way. A.K. Coomaraswamy, G.S. Ghurye and Radhakamal Mukherji were his main inspirations. Among the three Coomaraswamy's influence was most decisive in his personal domain and Ghurye's influence was decisive in his public domain. The writings of Radhakamal Mukerjee on religion, art and culture have exerted a benign influence on his thinking. In his personal life Jainism and some aspects of the Liṅgāyata Sampradāya influenced him. Given his Vaishnavite background these influences were very productive both as a Sanātanī Hindu and a Professional Sociologist associated with JNU.

As a sociologist, religion and culture were his core concerns. He always regarded India as a civilization. When Prof. Venugopal was about to retire, Prof. J.S. Gandhi, Prof. Anand Kumar, Prof. Avijit Pathak and myself organized a seminar with the assistance of DSA, CSSS/SSS. We expected to bring out a volume in his honour. We requested the participants for their written papers. Prof. Gandhi, Prof. Pathak and I were to edit this volume; unfortunately the participants were preoccupied in their other works. In the meantime Prof. Gandhi retired from the Centre and Prof. Pathak was preoccupied with his other concerns. Therefore, I was left alone to handle this project. In the last five years I have received some good contributions from the academic community. The contributions were given as an honour to Prof. Venugopal but every contributor had his or her own views and concern. The articles were not related with the writings of Prof. Venugopal. Unfortunately, most participants of the Felicitation Seminar have not given their contributions so far. I have arranged the received articles in two related volumes:

(1) Religion and Culture in Indian Civilization: Essays in Honour of Prof. C.N. Venugopal.

(2) Religion and Society in India: Essays in Honour of Prof. C.N. Venugopal.

The present volume is concerned with the civilizational dimensions of religion and culture in India. The other volume is primarily concerned with the sociological aspects of religion and society in India as a nation-state.

In the making of the volume Prof. Anand Kumar, Prof. Avijit Pathak, Prof. M.N. Panini, Prof. E. Haq, and Prof. J.S. Gandhi have been a constant source of inspiration. Prof. Satish

Jain (Economist) and Dr Wagish Shukla (Mathematician), have added new dimensions to the collection. Vinay Srivastava, Tiplut Nongbri, Susan Visvanathan, Rabindra Ray, Roma Chatterji, Nita Mathur, Anand Kumar and Avijit Pathak have enriched the volume by their valuable contributions. I am grateful to all of them. The DSA had provided the initial assistance. Shaswat Bharati, Kautilya Institute and SITA members were always enthusiastic to help in time. Serva Chetan Katoch, Dependra Pathak, Rakesh Kapoor, Ashok Malhotra, Mithilesh Kumar Tripathi, Prabhat, Nishant, Rajshree, Subrat, and Basil have given their valuable time in the preparation of the volume. Vandana has been inspiring and helping whenever I needed her help. I thank them all.

11 August 2010 **Amit Kumar Sharma**

Contents

Introduction

SOCIOLOGICAL theories of religion and culture are marked in a variety of ways by presuppositions about the nature, meaning, function and significance of religion and culture in the Western civilization in general and Abrahamic traditions of the West in particular. This proves to be a serious handicap in the study of non-Western civilizations in general and Indian civilization in particular. Often, keywords derived from Western civilization have been used as cues to explore the repertoire of beliefs, rituals, cultural processes and institutions of non-Western civilizations. This has led to unintended consequences. The same cannot be said about the concept and framework of civilization itself. Every civilization evolves over a longer period as a product of a dialectical process between nature, culture, religious beliefs and everyday practices. In this way every civilization is unique and provides a broad framework in a given space and time to its people. In the social sciences "civilization" occupies the same space which paradigm holds in the natural and the physical sciences. Each civilization is constructed, preserved, and transmitted in a number of ways such as oral narrative, iconic constructions, monuments, literary texts, customs, folkways, mores and institutions. It is also mediated by saints, seers, martyrs, shamans, mystics, technical experts, artists and craftspeople. The defining feature of any civilization is continuity. It grows gradually and sometimes changes radically. However, only the structural framework of the civilization changes (i.e. the elements of the civilization and their relationship) but the organizing principles and the underlying values, to a large extent, remain the same. The organizing principles and values, thus, require a comprehensive understanding (Inden, 2006; Dumont, 1971; Ghurye, 1962; Mukherjee, 1960; Marriot, 1990; Sharma, 2005).

The defining feature of Western sociology is that it is rooted in the European enlightenment of the eighteenth century, and regards modernity as a great rupture in space and time. Perhaps, therefore, it seems to be baffled by traditional civilizations like Indian and Chinese. Moreover, it is hostile towards the non-modern elements of Western civilization itself. This volume tries to articulate some of these anxieties in a more nuanced understanding of religion and culture in Indian civilization. This volume underscores that, arguably, religion and culture are important elements of all civilizations, but it is their interplay that has given a unique feature to Indian civilization.

According to Indian sociologists like T.N. Madan, J.P.S. Uberoi, A.K. Saran and C.N. Venugopal, a creative synthesis of the structural sociology of Claude Lévi-Strauss and Indology of A.K. Coomaraswamy can be helpful in understanding some crucial aspects of religion and culture in Indian civilization. This volume implicitly shares the need to go beyond Western sociology of religion, culture and civilization but different authors evolve their own strategies to capture the unique aspect of their chosen study. The diversified opinions presented by different contributors have resulted in some looseness of structure, but it has preserved the seminal ethos of Indian civilization. What is presented here is a volume with a unifying theme, namely, religion and culture in Indian civilization. They also articulate the Indic orientation in their own way. There is, however, diversity and not uniformity in their approaches, treatment and orientation. Individually they do not present a coherent or consistent picture of a homogeneous viewpoint about religion and culture in Indian civilization. The volume as a whole however, represents the new thinking about religion and culture in India today.

Amit Kumar Sharma in his essay, "Unity and Diversity in Indian Civilization," interrogates the various Western sociological discourses on civilization and articulates the alternative conceptualizations available in Indian sociology. He also underlines the unity and diversity in Indian civilization. Civilization is an umbrella term that has been variously defined by sociologists. For Durkheim, civilization helps to conceptualize the relationship between society, culture and the individual. The learning of culture takes place through the process of civilizing. He claims that human being is a symbolizing animal, and therefore, the civilizing process takes place through symbolization. Marcell Mauss argues that civilization is a social entity in which cultural forms are co-present and co-extensive, yet non-reducible to one another. Civilization constructs its own identity, and has an organic passage of time. Civilizational process refers to art, philosophy and religion. Civilizational discourse of the Chicago School was rooted in Malinowski's anthropology and American philosophical pragmatism. In the Western discourses, we find that civilization has had a linguistic turn. It took an objective form from the works of Saussure, Barthes, and others. Human world is symbolically constructed. Symbols in the Western tradition are arbitrarily chosen to represent the signified objects. Coomaraswamy claims that symbols are not chosen arbitrarily in Indian civilization. He also claims that modern industrial civilization is a great rupture in the Western tradition in itself. In the same way, G.S. Ghurye holds that civilization is a collective endeavour of humanity and that India represents a pagan civilization. Indian civilization is rooted in broad universalism and integral cosmopolitanism, human tenderness and compassion. Ghurye says that the cultural unity of civilization is based on complementarity, reciprocity and exchange. Accommodation without assimilation has been the characteristic of Indian civilization. A civilization includes both folk and classical cultural traditions. Tribal cultures on the other hand are characterized by a common territory and shared sentiments. The classical, folk and tribal represent three types of cultural streams which interact within Indian culture. There is peaceful coexistence of different religions in India and most festivals are celebrated by the majority of the regional cultures. The salient features of Indian civilization are a cosmic vision, a sense of harmony, order and beauty, tolerance, emphasis on duty, sacrifices and altruism, joint family, theory of *karma*, diversity and plurality and *kāla cakra*. Various political, economic and geographical factors have led to the unity and diversity in Indian civilization.

According to W. Norman Brown (1973) the most enduring element of Indian civilization is tolerance,

> . . . a tolerance of the new, the unusual, and the different, a capacity to reshape itself in changing conditions, a quickness of comprehension and a willingness to seek for solutions to new problems. Certainly her history from period to period has revealed a kind of flexibility. She can keep the old, if it is useful because she can uncomplainingly give up the old when it is no longer useful. She does not have to experience a violent conversion, get rid of her past at once and suddenly become something different. She can, instead, progress by successive steps, even by the steps taken in quick succession. She can always be adapting herself, without experiencing the feeling of guilt for doing so.
>
> — "Foreword," M. Singer, ed., *Entrepreneurship and Modernisation of Occupational Cultures in South Asia*, 1973.

Western scholars have long been fascinated to notice how occupations are embedded in complex social and cultural systems in South Asia. In South Asian countries occupations are more than jobs; they are the ways of life or occupational cultures, that is, distinctive sets of beliefs, values and social institutions that have become associated with occupations. For many modern writers, at least India and South Asia have replaced ancient Egypt as the archetypal long-enduring traditional history, a society of long duration, stability, and slow-changing character of the social and cultural system. Given such a picture of the Indian society a major question of debate among social scientists was whether it is possible for Indian society to modernize. There have been three dominant schools of opinion in question: that modernization of Indian society is impossible because of the strength of its traditional social institutions and beliefs, that modernization is possible only when traditional system is eliminated or transformed into a modern system of nuclear families, social classes, free markets, rational bureaucratic organizations and an achievement-oriented scientific world-view; and that the classification of traditional and modern societies was largely a definition of ideal type concepts and not description of empirical realities. Traditional institutions like *varṇa*s and Ashrams were not empirical realities rather they are normative models derived from scriptural texts and cultural traditions, and are emulated in different ways by different groups in different regions.

Wagish Shukla conceptualizes on the idea of world religion and centrally talks about the idea of harmony. It seemed that Pythagoras theorem threatened the harmony of world dynamics that was governed by the celestial harmonies. He says that world religion is an ambiguous concept. The term "religio" retains a moral bond, anxiety of self-consciousness, etc. World religion is extended to all forms of social demonstrations in connection to the sacred. Earlier it related to the worship of gods and later it talks about the bond of piety that binds to God. The discipline of comparative religions has taxonomized some of the religions as monotheism. The concept of demons did not exist before Christianity. Christianity renamed all the gods of polytheistic people before conversion as demons. Hindu Dharma in India represents the pre-Christian pagan systems which refused to be integrated into the Christian genealogy of truth. Wagish Shukla points out that co-dwelling of diversity is preferred in Indian paganism. Global religion is universalistic. In contrast some anti-pagan systems tend to regard Africa as a spiritual focus, a true home and the heaven on earth. The Hindu category is an identity label and geographical marker from the past that is hated by the colonial rulers. The question of harmony was solved in an affirmative way in India by two religious differentials in a practical fashion. While a superficial and elusive unity of thought was never pushed out of the picture, there was an agreement based on economic and humanitarian ground realities, and a kind of working consensus was evolved.

There are at least three clearly identifiable strands in the contemporary discussions about civil society: the Scottish enlightenment, French enlightenment and the German strand running through Marx and Hegel. The idea of "civil society" passed into the political literature of European colonies in the nineteenth century. The idea of a civil society is usually contrasted with the institution of state on the one hand and the notion of citizenship on the other. Introduction of the modern state everywhere disrupted and transformed earlier distributions and arrangements of social power. Actual political processes in the non-Western civilizations have been mostly very different from political life in the West; yet, strangely, the language used to describe, evaluate and express the experiences of power, culture and civil society is the same everywhere. For historical reasons, nearly every former European colony speaks a Western language of power, culture and civil society. It is a language which identifies states and civil societies, speaks of distributive justice, human rights, bureaucracies, political parties, parliaments, formal democracies, rationalization, secularization and globalization (Kaviraj and Khilnani, 2002; Chandhoke, 1995; Civilcus, 2005). Many non-Western societies have alternative cultures of power, civil society citizenship or political agency (Uberoi, 1999; Kaviraj and Khilnani, 2002). According to Uberoi (1999) India has a highly developed vernacular tradition of civil society and a very effective way of dealing with the excesses of the state. The educated intelligentsia, however, tends to express the Indian experience and Indian trajectories. Anand Kumar deals with some of these issues in his conceptual essay.

Anand Kumar claims that the idea of civilization is usually conjoined with the idea of civil society. The idea of civil society is related with the concept of culture and it gets legitimacy in religious, linguistic and ethnic movements. Civil society generates a debate regarding tradition and modernity. It is linked with the idea of decentralization and communitarian democracy. Civilization is a framework of cultural behaviour that points out to man the path of duty. Gandhi found that Indian *swarāj* system was based on genuine freedom and it is an Indian contribution to the idea of civilization. It facilitates the creation of universalistic conduct on the part of human beings and togetherness across nationalistic and linguistic communities. Community sentiment is a genuine basis of group identity. According to Gandhi, *swarāj* may be attained by any of the fourfold means: self-control, passive resistance, *svadeśī* and violent means; but the first two are favourable for a genuine civilization.

Culture embodies characteristic forms of collective self-expression as well as ideas and ideologies which influence social life, whether religious or otherwise.

To a considerable extent social facts can be adequately explained with reference to other social facts alone. However, in many instances social facts can only be properly understood with reference to the natural environment within which humans live, survive and reproduce. The ecological infrastructure powerfully conditions the evolution and direction of human economic life, political relations, social structure, and ideology.

At the same time, human intervention itself reshapes the natural environment in its own image. However, the intricate linkages of cause, effect and feedback in nature can produce many unintended consequences of human intervention. Social ecology rests on the awareness of the interdependence of the biophysical and sociocultural domains.

The folk cosmologies and art present various representations of nature. Local communities have different kinds of knowledge about natural environments.

World religions and religious philosophies have developed their own theories of environment and development (Dwivedi, 1989). Most economists and sociologists have taken the independence of the natural world for granted. In contrast, anthropologists studying small-scale societies have traditionally exhibited a greater interest in ecological questions in different religious groups or cultural systems (Guha, 1994, 2006; Banawari, 1992; Dwivedi, 1989; Gadgil and Guha 1995). From an ecological point of view, Indian society is, perhaps, the most complex society in the world. The relentless transformation of the natural world into the world of artefacts has the most asymmetric implications for these different constituents of Indian society. As the natural world recedes, the capacities of local ecosystems are increasingly shrinking. It has adverse implications for the four-fifths of India's rural poor. The remaining one-fifth of India's population, however, is the real beneficiary of this growth of the artificial at the cost of the natural.

These beneficiaries are bigger landowners with access to irrigation; these are modern entrepreneurs in pockets of industrialization and the workers in the organized sector; these are the urban professionals rapidly gaining in wealth and prestige; and these are the ever-growing numbers of employees in the government, semi-government and government-aided organizations. Not only do they have the money to pay for these commodities, but they have the clout to use the power of the state to ensure that the goodies come to them cheap, if not altogether free. They enjoy the produce of the entire biosphere, in contrast to the ecosystem people, who have a very limited resource catchment (Gadgil and Guha, 1995). As a result, India is divided on the issues of development and ecological crisis. The ruling elite and the middle classes (one-fifth of India's population) are, by and large, the supporters of development at any cost, whereas the rest of India is, by and large, a supporter of ecological balance and sustainable development. This volume is also sensitive to this issue of ecology and environment. Satish Jain, an economist, has interrogated the relationship of culture, institution and contemporary ecological crisis at the conceptual level. Vinay Kumar Srivastava has dealt with the relationship of religion and environment in the ecosystem of Bishnoi community of north India. Tiplut Nongbri's article also touches some of these issues in the context of Khāsī religious beliefs and practices.

Satish Jain is concerned with the ecological crisis in the modern world. The ecological crisis is becoming more severe day by day. Jain feels that the very concept of modernity is flawed from the point of view of ecological rationality. The modern market is the chief factor that propels this crisis. He asserts that the value perspective is important to the study of culture. Market, like other institutions, fosters values and preferences in a particular direction. Individuals will be motivated by their values and preferences and will act in accordance with them. Institutions are required for the articulation of values and preferences. Market articulates values and preferences related to the economic life. Institutions are sets of rules and embodiments of values. Individual preferences and values are mediated through societal institutions. The dominance of the market has implications on the non-market situations. Symbiotic relations between institutions and individual values and preferences do exist in the present day. Market is leading to environmental and ecological crisis. Market filters values that cause environmental destruction and ecological crisis. The dominance of the market weakens pro-environment values among many other things. Most values associated with any culture can be applied to widely differing domains of the same civilization. For determining the domain of values, a meta-principle (civilizational) is required. Non-modern cultures differed in their attitude towards non-modern beings. The culture underlying modernity is unique not only from the perspective of all non-human life forms as resources. This also does not put value to ecological integrity. Non-modern cultures attribute intrinsic value to ecological integrity. The culture of modernity finds expression in the context of intra-humanity interactions. Mahatma Gandhi's idea of Hind *swarāj* was a rejection of the idea of modernity. This article of Satish Jain implicitly echoes the spirit of Coomaraswamy, Ghurye and Mukherjee. But as a professional economist he does not contextualize his argument within the sociology of civilization. Together these essays complement each other and set the texture of conceptual arguments of the volume.

Religion in India

The relationship between religion and culture changes from civilization to civilization. Religion is not only related with social events like birth, initiation, marriage or death but it also regulates the everyday life of the individual. The everyday life of the individual is conceptualized by Durkheim as profane whereas the collective life of the members of a community is called sacred. The sacred and the profane are always set apart in every civilization but the mediation between the two (i.e. the sacred and the profane) is always culture-specific within a civilization. In other words, there is possibility of diversity within the cultural mediation between the sacred and the profane but there is a structural homology in these mediations at the civilizational level. The sacred is identified by the intensity of emotions experienced and the unconditional acceptance of its value. The sacred is usually unchanging at the structural level of a community, while the members of the community may go through emotional upheavals at the cultural level. Within the same civilization different communities may conceptualize the sacred and the profane in different cultural discourses but at a deeper structural level there is a unity in diversity (or homologous relationship) between different mediations in all the cultural discourses within a civilization.

The second part of the book refers to the discussion on the various aspects of religion in India or rather it deals with the empirical dimensions of the sociology of religion in India.

Historic religions which originated in West Asia share a common ground, that is, they all believe in monotheism and the transcendentalism of divinity. Cultural factors such as migration, physical proximity, diffusion or other forms of contacts mitigate the religion followed in a particular place. Normative, that is ethical, perceptions provided for the values in religions. Prof. Venugopal believes that the Sana Mahi cult provided for the shamanistic practices of the pre-conversion phase. Manipur classical dance draws from the *bhakti* cult. Christianity has a powerful impact on the tribes of the north-east, south-west and south-central India. Islam has not extended influence to the tribes on a large scale. Popular Hinduism has absorbed certain tribal elements in it. Therefore tribal culture has had a constant interaction with various forms of interaction. Sherpas have drawn a lot from the Hindu religion and the caste system. Religious activities are bound by feelings or emotions. When we look at pilgrimage we find that it accommodates a variety of practices. There are two patterns of religious behaviour that are in a dialogue with each other. First, the institutional, in which solidarity is established through rituals. Secondly, charismatic, in which a person is invested with magical authority that guides individuals in crisis. Shamanism is prominent in Hindu religion. Priests and *gurus* are prominent allegories and spirituality is dependent on the personal experience of divinity. The living *guru* is a warm and affable person. At the micro-level hierarchy, each priestly caste is responsible for guiding others. Religious authority depended on a supernatural source. The subjective interpretation of signs provides the key to religious behaviour. The Indian religious scene is characterized by heterogeneity and interaction among various diverse elements. There is religious pluralism and Indian culture results out of the interaction between these religions.

According to Dalton (1973: 57) the Khāsī have no temples or idols connected with their ancient faith. But they are much addicted to consulting auspices, especially in the appearance of eggs on being broken. In a similar vein, Mathur expresses the opinion that, magic, medicine and religion are interlinked in the religious system of the Khāsī. Tiplut Nongbri strongly denies the idea that Khāsī religion is spirit worship. To the Khāsī, religion is a set of beliefs and practices that are designed to restore their link to God. The belief centres on the covenant that governs man's relation to God. The Khāsī believe that originally humankind had direct interaction with God but due to man's sin the direct link between them was broken. Hence to find their way back to God the Khāsī had to take recourse to prayers and sacrifices. This is the *raison d'être* of their religion. In the Khāsī language this idea is conspicuous in the very content of the word religion. When the Khāsī speaks of religion it is always accompanied by the imitative *ka rukom* (custom or practice). The Khāsī say *ka niam ka rukom* (the religion the practice) to underscore the fact that an idea cannot attain the status of a belief unless it has the force of a custom which is put into regular practice. In the conception of the Khāsī a belief that is not acted upon is a dead belief and would have no chance of survival even for a single generation. While the Khāsī have a clear conception of God, He is an abstract entity with no physical representation or form, but reveals Himself through his creations. The Khāsī also believe in spirit worship. Belief in spirits also helps the Khāsī to infuse moral and ethical values in the minds of the people. By eluding that the souls of wrong-doers turn into evil spirits the Khāsī indirectly seeks to control the adverse consequences of evil ways, which inevitably lead to instability and anomie in the society. By personifying the souls of such persons as evil beings that are in the clutch of demons and must forever remain estranged from God the imagery exerts a powerful influence especially in the minds of the young and the impressionable about the horrifying results of sinful lives.

According to Rabindra Ray, India is home for a diversity of religions, like Buddhism, Islam, Hinduism, and so on. However, we find that India primarily remains a Hindu state.

There is difficulty in separating Christianity from the Western. Caste practices have changed over the years after exposure to Christian and Western ideas. Christian ideas have been Indianized. Hindu spiritual tradition remained superior to the Christian ones. Swami Dayanand Saraswati of the Arya Samaj chose to do away with the superstitions and traditions. The chief instrument of the modernization process is the education system. Curriculum and syllabus have undergone change and Western ideas are specifically subject to change. Western scholars feel that individualism and individualistic ideas are a characteristic of the modern West. The arrival of Christianity and the Europeans in India has led to the growth of communitarian sentiments to the extent that religious pursuits and personal salvation are taken in communitarian tastes. Life cycle rituals are very common and practised in India but they have been modified by Christian influence. Rabindra Ray talks about the way in which Christians have been portrayed in Indian cinema. Christians are considered as the "significant others" in Indian cinema. Their religion is portrayed as separate element in Indian culture and Christianity invokes God as a collective. The Christians are always portrayed as good Christians in terms of Ten Commandments. Gradually traditions are excluded and academicians are becoming secular. The Christian influence on the left is a deep and complicated issue. These influences and inclinations are prominent in the historical ideas of the left. The issue of earthly realization indicates the second aspect of Christian influences on the leftist sensibility. There is Christian impact on the ideational and intellectual system of Hindu India. In the debate between D.P. Mukherjee and Andre Béteille we find that the essence of Hindu learning is exemplified. Heterodox sects like Rastriya Swyamsevak Sangh (RSS), Arya Samaj, Ramakrishna Mission and ISKCON have responded to the social responsibility with their missionary urges.

Vinay Kumar Srivastava begins by pointing out that Durkheim's ideas were developed by many sociologists to explain the unanticipated consequences. He brings in the ecological dimension whereby he explains why some religions bury their members while some others cremate their members. Nature, he argues, has the strength to annihilate species and today a lot of activism concerning nature has taken place. This ignites sentiments and also leads to protests. Man is seen to control nature. Nature is given female attributes and religion does not arise from the materialistic conception of nature. Spiritualism is the core value of the East. Among the Bishnoi community of north India religion is born out of environmental convictions and compulsions. Their religion is promoted by 29 principles. The life of Bishnoi revolves around the idea of cleanliness. They practise strict vegetarianism, thereby expressing their love for living beings. *Pūjā* forms an integral part of the life of the Bishnois. Their personal habits are supposed to follow certain proscriptions. These practices have led to environmental preservation. Environmental conservation and development are political agendas but it is in-built in the life of the aforesaid community. This aspect of the practice shows how the various religious practices are socially constructed and this leads to environmental conservation.

In the article, "Religious Philanthropy in India," Amit Kumar Sharma discusses the concept and history of religious philanthropy in India. According to Sharma religion is a concept that binds individuals. Sanātana Dharma is central to Indian tradition and man is divine by nature. Philanthropy demonstrates love for mankind, benevolence and so on which in turn reflects some kind of charity. In this way often the welfare of people is brought about. *Dāna* refers to the voluntary endowments whereas *dakṣiṇā* refers to the things that are given to the priests by his *yajamāna*. *Bhikṣā* refers to the *dāna* given to the *saṁnyāsī* by the householder when he visits the householder. Sanātana traditions forbid begging. The philosophical motives of *puṇya*, *prāyaścitta*, *aparigraha*, and *karuṇā* are well recognized. All this refers to the benevolence and charitable aspect of the Hindu religion which is common in India. Even in Islam he points out that there is reference to voluntary offerings. *Sadāqat* is prescribed by the Qur'ān. *Dharmaśālā, pāṭhaśālā,* and *madrasa*s were traditional expressions of religious philanthropy. *Dāna* could be of three forms, namely: *anna-dāna, jñāna-dāna* and *kriyā-dāna*. Ramakrishna Mission and Belur Math were established in 1987 and these were doing all welfare activities. Religious philanthropy meant building up a moral community and it also provided an alternative to state intervention. There is the mediating role of religion. There are different negative aspects of religious philanthropy induding misuse and misappropriation of religious funds. Secondly, the nature of religious philanthropy is *ad hoc*. Lastly it has little impact on the unequal social structure. This shows how the various aspects of society are linked with each other. Indian tradition has always supported the idea of the general welfare of the people and this has led to the idea of religion and social welfare being linked together.

In her article, "Travellers and Pilgrims," Susan Visvanathan says that pilgrimage is a cultural activity, which, in many respects, has wholeness. Many aspects of societal existence fuse to contribute to the multidimensional nature of pilgrimage. Basically it is connected with a surviving tradition. It is the result of the historical process of change and transformation. Though rooted in a tradition, it has assimilated diverse trends and influences to assume its present form. Pilgrimage is a living and vibrant phenomenon in India, which maintains its basic nature amidst different currents of change. Every religious community, sect or cult articulates its own discourse about the nature, function and goal of pilgrimage. Most pilgrims and travellers follow the traditional routes to their chosen pilgrimage destinations. Traditionally such destinations are called *tīrtha*s or sacred destinations. The *tīrtha*s bear testimony to the unfolding and growth of different faiths in all its richness. Sacrifices, meditation, recitation of religious texts, devotional songs, *kīrtana,* and shaving of hair, bath, and charity and all other religious rites and rituals are performed at the *tīrtha*s. Installation of images, buildings of temples, mosques, churches and gurdwaras were necessary follow-ups resulting in the development of art, architecture and iconography. Before the coming of the industrial economy and modern systems of transport and communication the *tīrtha*s occupied a pivotal role in the economic life of ancient and medieval society. The important routes, both land and riverine, passed through the *tīrtha*s, which, thus, were important centres of trade and industry. Some of the *tīrtha*s were the centres for hosting annual or periodical fairs or business *melā*s for the sale of diverse commodities on a vast scale. The *tīrtha*s also acted as important seats of education, training and patronage of arts, crafts and traditional sciences. *Tīrtha*s are a microscopic representation of the cosmos of the community and pilgrimage is a unique cultural behaviour of any traditional civilization. During pilgrimage the barriers of linguistic and regional differences are effectively surmounted for communicating with other people. The differences of sects and creeds or caste and gender become secondary during such travelling (Gopal and Dubey, 1990; Bhardwaj, 1999). Susan Visvanathan has dealt with some of these issues in her article.

Stories in the form of travel accounts of anthropologists form the backbone of anthropological discourse. Diverse questions and aesthetic dimensions have been dealt with. Very extensive and vivid accounts of cities and social life are given by anthropologists. Often these descriptions have visual contents. Susan Visvanathan points out that in the pilgrim town of Tiruvaṇṇāmalai a temple is dedicated to Śiva and Pārvatī in their consummation as *ardhanārīśvara*. There is too much of garbage in the pilgrim towns but gradually it is becoming cleaner with subsequent visits. Garbage and noise are chief detriments to meditation. Travellers' account refers to an objective gaze. Old order gives birth to the new but something of the old remains. For meditation a lot of tranquillity is required which is not possible in a bustle. Anthropologists record details regarding the different ways of life. Observation and classification also take place as to what is recorded. Revitalizing aspects of people's life is brought out. A pilgrim is considered as the best of traveller because he carries a clear idea of the place. Ideas about the Ashrams come through the accounts of travellers and pilgrims. The data elicited through these accounts gives rise to the study of cultures and therein lies the primacy of the data. Anthropological accounts embody subjectivities of the researcher. Stories become an important understanding feature of the civilization. Civilization has developed on the lines of societal chord and harmony.

In the next article, Tiplut Nongbri has discussed "Khāsī Religious Beliefs and Practices." Here she notes that, though the structural positions of kin groups and affinal groups differ from each other, it's very interesting to find out how the bond of alliance demands kin and affines to co-operate with each other on all ritual occasions. She also talks about the dominance of the ancestral cult in Khāsī religion.

Culture in India

Part three of the book deals with essays on the issue of culture in India. To begin with, C.N. Venugopal believes that Indian culture is composite by nature. India has sheltered not only different religions but also different sects within these religions. There are amidst us Hindus, Buddhists, Jains, Sikhs, Muslims, Christians, Pārsīs and Jews. Many of these religions are divided into sects. For example, Hindus have Śaiva, Vaiṣṇava and Śākta sects and sub-sects. Muslims have Sunnī, Śiā and a variety of sub-sects. Christians too are divided into sects. Sometimes, there is more friction between two sects of the same religion than between two different religions. Frictions in religious life have arisen from ideological, institutional, historical and cultural factors. These frictions have been overcome or made less explicit by the expansion of the mental horizon of tolerance. Two anecdotes given below will illustrate it.

When Pārsīs arrived in a boat (*c.* eighth century CE) on the coast of Gujarat they sent an appeal to the king for providing them shelter. The king sent an emissary with a pitcher of milk to which the Pārsī leader added sugar and sent it back to him. When Guru Nanak was camping in the north-western area of Punjab in the *c.* fifteenth century CE, a Sūfī saint who was dominant in the area sent him a vessel of milk in which the milk was up to the brim. Guru Nanak floated a few flowers on the milk and sent it back to the Sūfī saint. In both instances the message was clear. The new creed was not superfluous but could thrive with the existing religion without turmoil. Both the above instances bear ample testimony to the spirit of accommodation.

Swami Vivekananda has emphasized that sects in India did not *per se* contribute to religious disharmony. They merely expressed different viewpoints on divinity. They shared the common heritage of Vedānta although they argued from different perspectives. Further, they gave rise to different patterns of reform in Indian society. The Buddhist and Jainas did not express total opposition to the Vedic path but only to certain beliefs and practices which were not conducive to a humane outlook. Thus animal sacrifice was a point of contention. The Vedic rituals were often engrossed with materialistic desires, for example, desire for progeny or prosperity. Instead they focused attention on the knowledge content of the Vedas: their spirituality. In sum, the sects did not detract from religious pursuit in spite of their differences. In fact, the *ṛṣi*s, *muni*s and *sādhu*s associated with various sects modified the meanings of original texts (Vedas, Upaniṣads, Dharmaśāstras, etc.) in order to develop a more pragmatic outlook. Hence, instead of setting aside the heritage of the past, the sects contributed to a dynamic awareness of India's religious philosophy. Among the Indian religions Hinduism, Jainism, Buddhism and Sikhism have mutually enriched each other. Sri Aurobindo's writings on Vedas have made some striking observations. Firstly, if we go to the Vedas on the verbal level mostly they are not intelligible or at least they are susceptible to multiple interpretations. Secondly, the European Indologists Max Mòller onwards systematically distorted the Vedic message by focusing on philology or the purely textual interpretation. Thirdly, India's own academic researchers in Oriental studies vied with each other to excel in the European type of scholarship. It is a matter of concern that today a political interpretation of what a particular religion stands for has led to a biased thinking. As a matter of fact both Islam and Christianity have been an integral part of India for a long time. The spirit of India is essentially manifested in religious tolerance.

The cultural diversity within the Indian society in terms of inter-regional, inter-caste, inter-tribe, inter-sect or community differences are so great that any general statement is a suspect. We must, however, endeavour to look beyond the enormous variety of cultural forms which through mutual reinforcement or limitation bestow on all of them a civilizational distinctiveness. Amit Kumar Sharma in his introduction and C.N. Venugopal in his essay in part III have tried to underline some major themes, nature, structure and direction of Indian culture.

The Whole in Indian culture is a transcendental concept which encompasses contraries but belongs to a higher level than them. There is a sense in which contraries are complementary (Madan, 1987). For example, the concept of caste and renunciation are antithetical and complementary. While caste provides a broad social framework for individual and group actions in a world of social relations, renunciation is its repudiation as both value and empirical condition. Similarly, renunciation is undoubtedly a remarkable value orientation which permeates the world-view of even the worldly householder. It does not bestow its distinctive character upon the everyday life of Hindus. Renunciation has been traditionally regarded as not an arbitrary annulment of the life of the man in the world but as its culmination (Madan, 1987).

In contemporary times culture is no longer practised as a social phenomenon; rather it is perceived or imagined by the individuals under the influence of print media, television, cinema and electronic capitalism. Culture today is not that inner refinement, the grooming of a deep enriching sensibility with which the Indian concept of Sanskrit is associated. Increasingly culture has come to be associated with the theatre of politics and rhetoric which is affected profoundly by outer influences which shape the way we speak, educate our young, and profess allegiance to national icons (Sen, Geeti, 2003). In this volume Rabindra Ray and Avijit Pathak deal with some of these issues in their respective essays.

Avijit Pathak has provided an illustrative contribution on the culture in Bengal. There was life energy amidst decay and destruction. The culture of *aḍḍā* was also very common and there can be poetry in culture and this is inherent in the culture. Again innovation has taken place with regard to Bengali music. Book fair is another sensitive phenomenon in Bengal. There are continuous festivities and thereby growth of magazines. The *aḍḍā* culture of Bengal cannot be conceived without the phenomenon of *aḍḍā*. This refers to the relaxed communications and reflections. *Aḍḍā* disobeys the discipline of time. The environment is a relaxed environment and this *aḍḍā* is often used for productive purposes. Another striking feature of contemporary Bengal is its ethos of communal harmony. The local clubs arrange for the celebration of festivals. Pāṛā is an important component of Bengali culture. Pāṛā symbolizes many things — intimacy, informality face to face interaction, shared memory and a sense of belonging. The club culture is undergoing a lot of transformation. Bengali culture cannot be imagined without Kālī temple and in the contemporary times the local youths arrange festivities around the Kālī Goddess. There is too much investment in Bengal. There was also phenomenal growth of nursing homes in Bengal which implied that the health facilities were ameliorating gradually. The education system in Bengal has undergone change. The children are being sent to engineering and medical colleges. Previously Bengalis had contempt for capitalism but gradually it is assimilating into the culture of Bengal. In Bengal the culture of protest and *bandha* is very strong. However, this is counter-productive because the culture of protest was becoming self-destructive and easy. The Bengali psyche is gradually becoming cynical, it debunks and condemns. This is expressed through different dailies like *Ananda Bazar Patrika*. Bengal has become stagnated due to the rising unemployment. The manifold problems confronting Bengal have to be removed by a process of self-reflection and analysis.

According to L. Dumont what one is in the habit of calling Indian thought is for the very great part the Hindu thought of the *saṁnyāsī*. The renouncer of the world (*saṁnyāsī*) has been identified by him as the creator of values in Indian religion and culture. Dumont also claims that renunciation is a sort of universal language of India (Dumont, 1970).

T.N. Madan, however, does not agree with Dumont's viewpoint. He says that the renouncer is by no means the only actor on the Hindu stage of life. The central figure in Indian (primarily Hindu) society is the householder. It is the ideal of his life to live in the world in the renouncer's philosophy. He hopes to mediate between total indulgence and total renunciation. He lives a disciplined this-worldly life as the good life. He seems to be convinced about the glory of the *gṛhasthī* (householdership) who religiously discharges the traditional debts to gods, *gurus*, and ancestors (1987). The ideal of good life is complemented by the idea of good death. The definition of good life and good death varies in different communities and sects. It also changes over the years. New values emerge and adaptations are made. For example, the modern Indian adapts himself to the new values of the modern West although his personality retains the seminal values of the Indian culture. This adaptation is not always smooth. As a result the modern Hindu suffers from the strain of fragmented consciousness. Rabindra Ray in his article in part II deals with some of these issues.

The *bhakti* movement in medieval India reformulated the ethos of Indian culture. It gave birth to new sects. Basava

(1125-70), Nanak (1469-1538), Vallaba (1479-1531) and Caitanya (1485-1534) were some of the most influential personalities of the *bhakti* movement. In the sects founded by these seers song, dance, art and craft became very sacred forms of worship. It led to the revival of arts, crafts, music, dance, drama and popular narratives in vernacular languages and folk idioms.

According to Coomaraswamy (1909/1989) Indian culture represents certain features of pre-industrial life in the East. It is a product of a traditional society and traditional guild organizations. This culture was manifested into art and crafts. Art and crafts were vocations or calling or *svadharma*. It was based on the principle that "one cannot put more into one's work than one has in oneself." In traditional context personal desire for gain was definitely not a major consideration in entering a craft or a trade. One's vocational disciplines were integrally tied to the loftier disciplines of personal and ascendant interiorization, under the guidance of men who themselves had successfully trod the same path. Time was available for ample training, for learning one's craft and related skills to the point that they became fully integral to the man, under years of patient apprenticeship to master craftsmen. The principles and activity of one's professional calling, its theory and practice, concepts and rituals, formed an organic whole with one's primary spiritual and intellectual endeavour, so that quite literally one earned one's living and at the same time, in the same activities, and with the same thoughts and the same gestures, one worked out one's salvation. Remuneration for services was usually in kind; or in the case of larger undertakings or of outstanding artisans, a grant of land might be the form of payment. A lust for gain and the concomitant spirit of competition were practically unheard of before the advent of modern Europeans in South Asia. Honest work, one's reasonable best, was taken for granted by all concerned and, if required, enforced by the guilds. The guilds set and enforced standards of workmanship, of quality in materials, and of qualifications for practitioners of the crafts and they fulfilled other professional, civic, religious, and political responsibilities. The guild determined the qualifications and criteria of craftsmanship by birth, by training, physical and mental aptitude, moral harmony, and intellectual potential, in short by caste, sect and *dharma* (Coomaraswamy, 1999).

In modern as well as contemporary India occupations have taken the place of vocations, trade unions and professional associations have taken the place of traditional guilds. The qualification of the modern worker is determined primarily by the demand in the concerned industry or the market, and by the wishes of individuals who may or may not prefer such activity to other employment — but in any case for purely contingent reasons. Beyond the exigencies of the modern trade, the modern work is entirely subject to economic forces which determine quality, ends, materials, and methods, as well as the time allowed for the tasks. In this case time is not available for "good work." There is no time for linking the elements of one's craft with concepts and forces of the cosmological and ultimately metaphysical orders. The rhythms are determined by machines and the average worker comes from his tasks with no benefit other than his wages (Coomaraswamy, 1909). But as Milton Singer has shown Indians in general and Hindus in particular have shown tactical adaptability and cultural resilience (Singer, 1972). Others have also noted the simultaneous existence of the traditional with the modern in Indian civilization.

Throughout its history India has been under national rule for more than four relatively brief periods. The unity and continuity in Indian civilization has been primarily cultural. Scholars like Coomaraswamy, Mukherjee and Lannoy have asserted that it is the artistic expressions and crafts which reveal the organic development and patterns of continuity more clearly and more tangibly than any other activity, visual arts, crafts, and narratives exhibit the natural creativity of Indian culture in the most intense form (Coomaraswamy, Mukerjee, Lannoy, 1971). Roma Chatterji and Nita Mathur, have presented the dialogical relationship between artistic expressions and cultural praxis.

Roma Chatterji points out that Hinduism as a folk religion coexisted with little traditions that were non-Sanskrit in nature. The most crucial aspect is the divine presence. Gods and Goddesses were accessible in the form of *mūrti*. The corporeality of the deity is the central feature of Hindu religion. The telling of sacred stories helps in understanding the divine presence. In Puruliā there is narration of *kathā*s which discusses the truth. The utterability of a *kathā* is a sacred event with respect to cosmic life. *Kathā* takes a different form in the *pūjā*s and it is related to the others in the world of discourse. *Karma* took place in the different *yuga*s. The narration of *kathā* is ritualized. In the sacred texts *kathā*s are compiled as they are related to the sacred. Human activity is a part of the cosmic design. History is revealed through the epics and myths. Folklore mythicizes the mundane. Thus the sacred events become a part of our being.

Nita Mathur quotes Durkheim by referring to the sacred as something which is forbidden and set apart. Baidyanath Saraswati denies the idea of the profane in Indian thought. Sacred ideas get articulated through dance. It is a ritual that demonstrates reverence, worship and honour to the deities. Vedas talk about dance as the integral aspect of religion. In the dominant Hindu psyche we find that there is mention of the *apsaras*es dancing in the court of lord Indra. Fire, water, energy are depicted through the ideas of dance. Dance of gods established the cosmic order. Bharatnāṭyam marks together emotions, melody and rhythm. Dance in religion is found through the *devadāsī* system. Therefore art forms get accumulated into the idea of culture. This would ensure prosperity and destroy evil. Dance also performs an important aspect of cultural identity. The world of the supernatural and the humans are mediated through dance.

It is a humble attempt to compile the emerging concerns in the recent studies by the relatively younger generation of social scientists. It is a befitting tribute to Prof. C.N. Venugopal who devoted his life as a student and teacher of religion and culture in Indian civilization from a sociological perspective.

References

Adorno, T.W., 1991, *The Culture Industry: Selected Essays on Mass Culture*, London: Routledge.

Adorno, Theodor, 1964, *The Jargon of Authenticity*, London: Routledge.

Ali, M., Athar, 2006, *Mughal India: Studies in Polity, Ideas, Society, and Culture*, New Delhi: Oxford.

Appadurai, Arjun, et al., 1994, ed., *Gender, Genre, and Power in South Asian Expressive Traditions*, Delhi: Motilal Banarsidass.

Appadurai, Arjun, 1981, *Worship and Conflict under Colonial Rule: A South Indian Case*, Hyderabad: Orient Longman.

Banawari, 1992, *Panchavati: Indian Approach to Environment*, New Delhi: Sri Vinayak Publications.

Basham, A.L., 2004, *The Wonder that was India*, London: Picador.

Béteille, Andre, 2002, *Sociology: Essays on Approach and Method*, Oxford University Press.

Bharadwaj, S.M., 1973, *Hindu Places of Pilgrimage in India*, New Delhi: Munshiram Manoharlal.

———, 1999, *Hindu Places of Pilgrimage in India*, New Delhi: Munshiram Manoharlal.

Borden, C.M., 1989, ed., *Contemporary India: Essays on the Uses of Tradition*, Delhi: Oxford University Press.

Bose, Nirmal K., 1996, *The Structure of Hindu Society*, New Delhi: Orient Longman.

Bruce, Steve, 1996, *Religion in the Modern World: From Cathedral to Cults*, New York: Oxford University Press.

Carstairs, G.M., 1957/1968, *The Twice-Born: A Study of a Community of High-Caste Hindus*, London: The Hogarth Press.

Chandhoke, Neera, 1995, *State and Civil Society*, New Delhi: Sage.

Civicus, 2005, *Civil Society at the Millennium*, USA: Kumarian Press.

Connarton, Paul, 1989, *How Societies Remember*, Cambridge: Cambridge University Press.

Connolly, Peter, 1999, *Approaches to the Study of Religion*, London: Cassell.

Coomaraswamy, A.K., 1909/1989, *The Indian Craftsman*, New Delhi: Munshiram Manoharlal.

———, 1989, *Time and Eternity*, Bangalore: Select Books.

———, 2004, *The Transformation of Nature in Art*, New Delhi: Munshiram Manoharlal.

———, 1999, *Introduction to Indian Art*, New Delhi: Munshiram Manoharlal.

Das, Veena, 1999, *Critical Events: An Anthropological Perspective on Contemporary India*, New Delhi: Oxford University Press.

Dumont, L., 1970, *Religion, Politics and History in India*, Paris: Mounton.

During, Simon, 1993, ed., *The Cultural Studies: Reader*, London: Routledge.

Dwivedi, O.P., 1989, ed., *World Religions and the Environment*, New Delhi: Gitanjali Publishing House.

Eaton, Richard M., 2006, *Themes in Indian History: India's Islamic Traditions, 711-1750*, New Delhi: Oxford University Press.

Erasov, Boris, Yogendra Singh, 2006, *The Sociology of Culture*, New Delhi: Rawat.

Forward, Martin, 2006, *A Beginner's Guide: Religion*, London: One World.

Foucault, Michel, 2003, *Society Must Be Defended*, New York: Ricardor.

Fruzzetti, Lina & Sirpa Tenhunen, 2006, *Culture Power and Agency: Center in Indian Ethnography*, Kolkata: Stree.

Fuller, C.J., 2003, *The Renewal of the Priesthood: Modernity and Traditionalism in a South Indian Temple*, New Delhi: Oxford University Press.

———, 1992, *The Camphor Flame: Popular Hinduism and Society in India*, Princeton: Princeton University Press.

Gadgil, Madhav & Ramchandra Guha, 1995, *Ecology and Equity : the Use and Abuse of Nature in Contemporary India*, New Delhi: Penguin Books.

Gellner, David, 2003, *The Anthropology of Buddhism & Hinduism: Weberian Themes*, New Delhi: Oxford University Press.

Gopal, Lallanji & D.P. Dubey, 1990, *Pilgrimage Studies: Text and Context*, Allahabad: The Society of Pilgrimage Studies.

Gottlab, Michael, 2003, *Historical Thinking in South Asia: A Handbook of Sources from Colonial Times to the Present*, New Delhi: Oxford University Press.

Guha, Ramchandra, 1994/2001, ed., *Social Ecology*, Delhi: Oxford University Press.

Guha, Ramachandra, 2006, *How Much Should a Person Consume? Thinking Through the Environment*, New Delhi: Permanent Black.

Hall, Peter, 1999, *Cities in Civilisation: Culture, Innovation and Urban Order*, London: Phoenix.

Heelas, Paul, 1998, ed., *Religion, Modernity and Post Modernity*, Blackwell, Oxford University Press.

Horkheimer, Max and T.W. Adorno, 1944/1973, *Dialectic of Enlightenment*, London: Allen Lane.

Inden, Ronald B., 1990, *Imagining India*, London: Hurst and Company.

Judith, Anodea, 2004, *Eastern Body, Western Mind*, Kolkata: Alchemy.

Kakar, Sudhir, 2003, *Culture and Psyche: Selected Essays*, New Delhi: Oxford University Press.

Kaviraj, Sudipto and Sunil Khilnani, 2002, ed., *Civil Society: History and Possibilities*, New Delhi: Cambridge University Press/Foundation Books.

Khare, R.S., 1976, *Culture and Reality*, Simla: Indian Institue of Advanced Study.

Lange, Nicholas De, 2000, *An Introduction to Judaism*, London: Cambridge University Press.

Lannoy, Richard, 1971/2004, *The Speaking Tree: A Study of Indian Culture and Society*, Delhi: Oxford University Press.

Lechner, Frank J. & John Boli, 2006, *World Culture: Origins and Consequences*, Noida: Blackwell.

Lenzen, V.F., William R. Dennes, 1959, *Civilization*, London: University of California Press.

Madan, T.N., 2004, ed., *India's Religions*, Delhi: Oxford University Press.

———, 1992, ed., *Religion in India*, Delhi: Oxford University Press.

———, 1987, *Non-Renunciation: Themes and Interpretations of Hindu Culture*, Delhi: Oxford University Press.

Maheed, Sheema, 2005, *Culture and Identity: Selected English Writing of Faiz*, New Delhi: Oxford University Press.

Mannheim, Karl, 1953, *Essays on Sociology and Social Psychology*, London: Routledge.

———, 1956, *Essays on the Sociology of Culture*, London: Routledge and Kegan Paul.

Michaels, Axel, 2005, *Hinduism: Past and Present*, New Delhi: Orient Longman.

Midgley, Mary, 1985, *Evolution as a Religion*, London: Routledge.

Misra, Vidya Nivas, 2004, *Strands of Indian Thought*, Delhi: Ocean Book.

Momensen, W.J. and J. Ostelhammel, *Max Weber and His Contemporaries*, London: The German Historical Institute.

Mukerjee, Radhakamal, 1960, *The Philosophy of Social Science*, London: Macmillan and Co. Ltd.

Murty, K. Satchidananda and A. Dasgupta, 1995, *The Divine Peacock: Understanding Contemporary India*, New Delhi: New Age International Limited.

Nandy, Ashis, 1998/2002, ed., *The Secret Politics of Our Desires: Innocence, Culpability and Indian Popular Cinema*, Delhi: Oxford University Press.

———, 1989, *The Tao of Cricket; on Games of Destiny and the Destiny of Games*, New Delhi: Viking.

Narayanan, Vasudha, 2004, *Understanding Hinduism*, London: Duncan Baird.

Oberoi, Harjot, 1994, *The Construction of Religious Boundaries: Culture, Identity and Diversity in the Sikh Tradition*, New Delhi: Oxford University Press.

Oomen, T.K., 2004, "Futures India: Society, Nation State and Civilisation", *Futures* 36 (2004).

Poonawala, I.K.H., 2006, *The Pillars of Islam*, vol. 1 : *Ibadat: Acts of Devotion and Religious Observances*, New Delhi: Oxford University Press.

Prabhu, Pandharinath H., 1998, *Hindu Social Organization: A Study in Socio-Psychological and Ideological Foundation*, Mumbai: Popular Prakashan.

Pramanick, S.K., 2001, *Sociology of G.S. Ghurye*, Jaipur: Rawat.

Radhakrishnan, S. and P.T. Raju, 1956/2000, *The Concept of Man: A Study in Comparative Philosophy*, New Delhi: Harper Collins.

Raman, N.S.S., 1998, *Methodological Studies in the History of Religions: With Special Reference to Hinduism and Buddhism*, Simla: IIAS.

Rao, Vijayendra and M. Walton, 2004, ed., *Culture and Public Action*, Delhi: Permanent Black.

Renou, Louis, 1953, *Religions of Ancient India*, New Delhi: Munshiram Manoharlal.

Robinson, R., 2004, *Sociology of Religion in India*, New Delhi: Sage.

Rogers, J.M., 2006, *Makers of Islamic Civilization: Sinan*, New Delhi: Oxford University Press.

Saraswati, Baidyanath, 1985, "Sociology of Religion," *Survey of Research in Sociology and Social Anthropology*, vol. 2 (pp. 1-35), New Delhi: Satvahan.

Schuon, Fritjhof, 1998, *Language of the Self*, Pondicherry: Select Books.

Sen, Geeti, 1993, *Perceiving India: Insight and Inquiry*, New Delhi: Sage.

———, 2003, *India: A National Culture?*, New Delhi: Sage Publications.

Singer, Milton, ed., 1973, *Entrepreneurship and Modernization of Occupational Cultures in South Asia*, Duke University Press.

———, 1972, *When a Great Tradition Modernises*, London: Pall Mall Press.

Singh, Y., 1973, *Modernisation of Indian Tradition*, Delhi: Thomson Press.

Swarup, Ram, 1992, *Hinduism vis-à-vis Christianity and Islam*, New Delhi: Voice of India.

Tanner, Jeremy, *The Sociology of Art: A Reader*, London: Routledge.

Tim, J.R., 1992, ed., *Texts in Context: Traditional Hermeneutics in South Asia*, Albany: State University of New York Press.

Trautmann, Thomas R., 2004, *Aryans and British India: New Perspective on Indian Past*, New Delhi.

———, 2005, *The Aryan Debate: Debates in Indian History and Society*, New Delhi: Oxford University Press.

Uberoi, J.P.S., 1999, *Religion, Civil Society and State: A Study of Sikhism*, New Delhi: Oxford University Press.

Vatsyayan, Kapila, 2005, *Bharata: The Natyasastra*, Delhi: Sahitya Academy.

Vaudeville, Charlotte, 1996, *Myths, Saints and Legends in Medieval India*, New Delhi: Oxford University Press.

Veer, Peter Vander, 2001, *Imperial Encounters: Religion and Modernity in India and Britain*, New Delhi: Permanent Black.

Venugopal, C.N., 1998, *Religion and Indian Society*, New Delhi: Gyan.

Weber, Max, 2000, *The Religion of India*, New Delhi: Munshiram Manoharlal.

Wittgenstein, Ludwig, 1921, *Tractatus Logico-Philosophicus*, London: Routledge.

Part I
Conceptual Essays

1

Unity and Diversity in Indian Civilization
A Sociological Perspective

Amit Kumar Sharma

SOCIOLOGISTS have conceptualized the "Unity and Diversity" in Indian society and culture from the European idea of civilization. The European idea of civilization usually includes a power centre, territorial expansion of a particular culture as well as cultural continuity at a particular period, over a long period of time. Thus, culture and civilization are related concepts in sociology. All societies have cultures but all societies are not civilizations. In modern sociology, the concept of civilization is reserved for a special aspect of advanced cultures. In modern Western discourse the term civilization is usually invoked in three different senses: first, region-specific, second, religion-specific and third, based on a specific mode of production (Rundell and Mennell, 1998). In traditional social thought and Indian sociology, however, the concept of civilization is conceptualized differently. Let us have a detailed analysis of the two perspectives on civilization.

THE MODERN CONCEPT OF CIVILIZATION

The modern concept of civilization is a product of European enlightenment. Although there is a common thread between different intellectual traditions of European enlightenment, there are subtle differences as well.

The French Tradition

In the writings of Auguste Comte, civilization is considered as a special feature of only developed cultures; however, in the later writings of Emile Durkheim, the concept of civilization serves a triple purpose. First, it enables him to conceptualize more deeply both the relation between society and the individual and between the different levels of social reality. He argues that the human being is a mixture of both beastly and divine qualities and that human being requires a rich or thick medium of learning culture through a civilizing process. Furthermore, for Durkheim, this civilizing process does not occur at the level of everyday life, which is characterized by fragmentation and heterogeneity; it is constituted rather through a society's collective ethos, which is gathered, condensed, and represented in symbolic forms. For Durkheim, humankind is a symbolizing animal, and it is through symbolization that a civilizing process takes place that anchors each individual in society. For Durkheim civilization is an inclusive category, integrating both the processes of identity formation and symbolic creation (Durkheim, 1915).

Extending the Durkheimian notion, Marcel Mauss says that civilization is a social entity in which states and cultural forms are mutually co-present and co-extensive and yet irreducible to one another. Their coherence is achieved in an unstable, yet enduring combination of cultural factors and forms of political association, which are not contained within the parameters of state formation only. For him, the common characteristic of all civilizations is their arbitrariness (Mauss, 1954; Lévi-Strauss, 1987).

In a slightly different perspective Lucien Febvre and the Annales School have conceptualized civilization as the intersection and long history (long duree) of the multiple forms of human life within specific (although often extensive) geographical settings. Febvre sees himself as part of the Durkheimian legacy and claims that historical "facts" are not events but abstractions, inventions or constructs, which have their own genealogies and histories that are quite specific and local (Skinner, 1985; Stoianouich, 1976).

The German Tradition

According to Spengler each civilization constructs its own identity and has an organic passage of time. He says that West is one of the many civilizations at the verge of extinction (Spengler, 1959; Horkheimer, 1979; Toynbee, 1947). In contrast to Spengler, Alfred Weber critically engages with the morphological approach in which world history is broken down to become the continuous organic birth, growth and decline of great cultures. For him, the task of civilization analysis is to identify the processes through which civilizational formation and development can be theorized. It is also essential to account for both social innovation and historical continuity without invoking a principle of universal history from the vantage point of the particular history of the West (Weber, 1921/1998).

Alfred Weber has differentiated civilization process from social and cultural processes. Each has its own "logic" of development and each is unique historically and socially. By social process, he refers to the material world in which human beings work, co-operate and establish institutions, which make social continuity possible. The civilization process, on the other hand, refers to art, religion and philosophy. It also refers to the intellectualization of the world, increasing domination over nature through the development of cognitive-rational means and the development of practical skills. In other words, for him, civilization process refers to the internal historical development of cultural forms. According to Alfred Weber, social, cultural and civilizational processes are interrelated and constitute the cosmic or global condition of humankind. For him the "cosmic" process is a metaphor for the self-perpetuating or self-transforming capacity of humankind (Weber, 1921/1998).

Norbert Elias points out that German sociology continues

to be trapped within either ontological (particularly Hegelian) or transcendental (Kantian) assumptions. For Elias, there are two escape routes — both Nietzschean; one which emphasizes power and another which entails the examination of the Nietzschean image of humankind as the animal that undergoes a civilizing process as the outcomes of power struggles and strategies of inclusion and exclusion between groups. These entail as a long-term historical process transformations in the regime of affects. There is a link between transformation of power and transformation of affects during a civilizing process. (Elias, 1994, 1996).

Elias says that there is a link between the long-term structural developments of societies, especially state formation, and change in people's social character, typical personality make-up or habitus. The basic proposition is that: if in this or that region the power of central authority grows, if over a larger or smaller area the people are forced to live in peace with each other, the moulding of affects and the standards of the drive economy are very gradually changed as well. State formation involved an "elimination contest" between numerous rival territorial magnates, a violent competitive process with a compelling sequential dynamic through which successively larger territorial units emerged with more effective central monopoly apparatuses. State formation, for Elias, is only one process interweaving with others to enmesh individuals in increasingly complex webs of interdependence. It interweaves with the division of labour, the growth of trade, towns, the use of money and administrative apparatuses, together with increasing population, in a spiral cumulative process. Furthermore, the gradually higher standards of self-restraint engendered in people contributed in turn to the upward spiral of gradually more effective and calculable administration. (Elias, 1994).

American Tradition

Martin Bulmer has noted that the civilizational discourse of Chicago School was rooted in Malinowski's anthropology of culture and American philosophical pragmatism (Bulmer, 1987). He argues that there are four things that typify American civilization: mechanical invention, mass education, suffrage and mobility. Put together, this gives fluidity and restlessness to the American city. It is the benchmark of the modern world and ultimate characteristic of American civilization. The city air makes one free but alongside its liberating qualities, the city is also a place of disaffection, alienation and violence. Adam Ferguson, Schiller and Simmel were ambivalent towards modern civilization; Nietzsche was overtly hostile to it.

The contemporary perspective in the Western Tradition: The linguistic turn

Following Herder's (1969) basic insight, language rather than culture *per se* was viewed as the repository of human creativity and self-reflexivity. In this perspective, language itself was viewed as the paradigm and the model through which the multiple processes of human and social life are made possible and take objective form. Saussure, Lévi-Strauss, Wittgenstein, Habermas, Heidegger and Gadamer systematized this perspective in the Western discourse on civilization and culture. In this perspective, the notion of culture is extended to embrace all aspects through which the human world is linguistically and symbolically constituted, from speech acts and utterances, to signs and symbols. Thus, language is a constitutive image; it embraces the way in which culture is learnt, transmitted, valued and embodied. In this perspective symbolic structures are constituted by the arrangement of signs that give shape to an apparent bricolage of forms, which were arbitrary (Fekete, 1984; Skinner, 1985; Guenon, 1999).

Indian Concept of Civilization

According to Ananda Coomaraswamy, the root in "civilization" is *kei*, as in Greek, *keisthai*, Sanskrit *si*, to "lie," "lie outstretched," "be located in." In Plato's thought, there is a cosmic city of the world, the city-state, and an individual body politic, all of which are communities (Gr. *Koinonia*, Skr. *Gaṇa*) (Coomaraswamy, 1989: 1). Quoting Plato he also says that the human city of God contains within itself the pattern of all other societies and of a true civilization.

The man will be a "just" (Gr. *Dikaios*) man when each member of a society performs its own appropriate task and is subject to the ruling reason that exercises forethought on behalf of the whole man; and in the same way the public city will be just when there is agreement as to which shall rule, and there is no confusion of functions but every occupation is a vocational responsibility. Not, then, where there are no "classes" or "castes" but where everyone is a responsible agent in some special field. A city can no more be called a "good" city if it lacks this "justice" (*dikaiosyne*) than it could be where it could be wanting wisdom, sobriety or courage; and these four are the great civic virtues. Where occupations are, thus, vocations "more will be done, and better done, and with more ease than in any other way" (Republic, 370C). But "if one who is by nature a craftsman or some sort of businessman be tempted and inflated by wealth or by his command of votes or by his own might or any such thing, and tries to handle military matters, or if a soldier tries to be a counsellor or guardian, for which he is unfitted, and if these men interchange their tools and honours, or if one and the same man tries to handle all these functions at once, then, I take it, you too hold that this is a sort of perversion and being jack-of-all-trades will be the ruin of the city"; and this is "injustice" (Republic, 434B) (Coomaraswamy, 1989: 5).

Thus the ideal society is thought of as a kind of co-operative workshop in which production is to be for use and not for profit, and all human need, both of the body and the soul, are to be provided for. Moreover, if the command is to be fulfilled, "Be ye perfect even as your Father in heaven is perfect," the work must be perfectly done. The arts are not directed to the advantage of anything but their object (Republic, 432B), and that is that the thing made should be as perfect as possible for the purpose for which it is made.

This purpose is to satisfy human need (Republic, 369B, C); and so the perfectionism required, although not "altruistically" motivated, actually "serves humanity" in a way that is impossible where goods are made for sale rather than for use, and in quantity rather than quality. In the light of Plato's definition of "justice" as vocational occupation, one can better understand the words, "seek first the kingdom of God and his justice and these things shall be added unto you" (Matthew, 6: 33) (Coomaraswamy, 1989: 5).

The Indian philosophy of work is identical. Act thou, according, with a view to the welfare of the world; for whatever the superior does, others will also do; the standard he sets up, the world will follow. Vocations are determined by one's own nature. Man attains perfection through devotion to his own work. He who performs the task that his own nature lays upon him incurs no sin; one should never abandon his inherited vocation. It is fundamentally the incubus of world trade that makes of industrial "civilizations" a "curse of humanity," and from the industrial concept of progress "in line with the manufacturing enterprise of civilization" that modern wars have arisen and will arise; it is on the same impoverished soil that empires have grown, and by the same greed that innumerable civilizations have been destroyed. The machine age and the world trade have made the possession of civilization difficult. Agriculture and handicraft are the foundations of civilization.

In this way, Coomaraswamy equates the Indian concept of civilization with the traditions of Greece, and Eastern Christianity, among other traditions of the ancient and medieval times. It is interesting that Mahatma Gandhi also shares a similar viewpoint about civilization. He says that civilization is that mode of conduct, which points out to man the path of duty. Performance of duty and observance of morality are convertible terms. To observe morality is to attain mastery over our mind and our passions. So, by doing, we know ourselves. The Gujarati equivalent for civilization means "good conduct" (Gandhi, 1938: 55). Coomaraswamy and

Gandhi are usually recognized as major traditional theoreticians in Indian social thought; however, they are also significant in Indian sociological debates about civilization. Ramkrishna Mukherjee and T.N. Madan recognize the importance of Coomaraswamy, whereas N.K. Bose and J.P.S. Uberoi underscore the significance of Gandhi as non-Western theoreticians of our time (Mukherjee, 1979; Madan, 1995: 139; Bose, 1977; Uberoi, 1999).

G.S. Ghurye, the father of Bombay School of Sociology, holds that civilization is a collective endeavour of humanity and that behind the rise and fall of civilizations, there has occurred a "steady growth" of culture. He has noted that amidst the vicissitudes of civilizational growth, there are certain values, which are regarded as final and sacrosanct foundations of cultures. He found five such foundational values of civilizations — 1. Religious Consciousness; 2. Conscience; 3. Justice; 4. Free Pursuit of Knowledge and Free Expression; and 5. Toleration. Like Toynbee, Ghurye believed that a civilization in its growth period produces a creative minority, whereas in its disintegration period, it fails to do so (Ghurye, 1965).

Radhakamal Mukerjee, another towering figure of Indian sociology, also opines that modern sociology has usually underestimated the sickness of modern civilization and the strength of Indian or other traditional civilizations. As a result, the meaning and values of civilizations have become difficult to define or conceptualize in one unified theoretical framework. At the macro theoretical level all civilizations have three components — Man, Values and Nature. All the three are elusive, free and unpredictable. Civilization comprises the dynamic interchange or "transaction" between these three open entities. Civilization denotes the emergence or transcendence of human nature, values and environment over a period of time. Civilization is fundamentally open, emergent or transcendent, issuing forth into totalities, continuities and potentialities and cannot be causally explained. The mansion of civilization is represented by the aspirations of mankind (Radhakamal, 1964, 1964b).

Thus, from the Indian perspective civilization and tradition are synonymous terms. By tradition, more is meant than just custom long established, even if current usage has tended to restrict it in this way. Here the word will always be given its transcendent, which is also its normal, connotation without any attempt being made, however, to pin it down to a particular set of concepts. It is only because tradition, being formless and supra-personal in its essence, escapes exact definition in terms of human speech or thought. All that can usefully be said of it at the moment is that wherever a complete tradition exists this will entail the presence of four things, namely: a current of influence or grace issuing forth from divine source and transmitted without interruption through a variety of channels; a way of "verification" which, when faithfully followed, will lead the human subject to successive positions where he is able to "actualize" the truths that Revelation communicates; and finally there is the formal embodiment of tradition in the doctrines, arts, sciences and other elements that together go to determine the charters of a normal civilization (Pallis, 1994; Swaroop, 2000; Guenon, 2000; Mukerji, 1979; Saran, 1998; Frawley, 1993; Renou, 1987).

There are only three civilizations out of many that have so far survived the shock and collision of historic forces. First, Indian civilization that has continued and thriven for more than fifty centuries; second, Chinese civilization that has shown a span of thirty centuries; and, third, European or Western civilization that is still vigorous after twenty-five centuries.

Western civilization has rooted itself in the Greek discovery (belief) of man as the measure of things or the absolute value of individual self or ego. From this stems the notion of the universality of the individual, and of the inalienable subjective rights of the free citizen in democracy, who contains society or civilization in himself. In this framework, the perennial quest for the dignity and majesty of the human individual is regarded as the ultimate goal and supreme reality.

In Indian civilization the central reality consists of the order, beauty, transcendence and mystery of the cosmic process. The individual seeks a personal, immediate cognition of the one-and-real and the cosmos. The highest spiritual goal sought empirically is the complete identification of self with the transcendent, incomprehensible, cosmic being in non-theistic mysticism on the one hand and a vivid and fruitful sense of the worth and majesty of the individual, and of the reality of the ideal community of persons as full and complete persons in practical social life and relation on the other. The first is termed the goal of "God-realization" and the second is called the goal of "self-realization."

The Chinese civilization regards the unity and solidarity of the race, the human-cum-divine community of Heaven (the common father) and Earth (the common mother) as the highest goal. The Chinese practice of ancestor worship emotionally integrates the love, affections and reverences of the present with those of the past and the future without any dogma or supernatural doctrine and gives salutation without God or divine saviour.

There is a remarkable similarity between the Indian concept of *dharma*, the Chinese concept of Zen and the Socratic concept of justice. Yet there is a profound difference. Both *dharma* in India and Zen and its moral expression Yi (righteousness) in China stress duties (rather than rights) and mutuality in human and trans-human relationships. In Western ethics, the Socratic justice is based on rights (rather than obligations) and the metaphysical supremacy of individual self or ego (Radhakamal, 1964).

It has been noted by the historians that institutions of higher learning usually play a decisive role in moulding the destiny of civilizations. For example, *gurukula*s like Nalanda and Taxila had played an important role in shaping the ancient Indian civilization. Although the Arabs had developed a higher institute of learning in Spain (Saragosa University), in the medieval period, the interest of Muslim rulers in India was more into dance, music and fine arts, than in the institutionalization of science and technology. The oral tradition and vocational education, however, remained intact up to eighteenth century, but the Muslim rulers were not sufficiently interested in maintaining central universities. On the other hand, Europe was reawakening from the thirteenth century. By fifteenth-century Europe had institutionalized centres of learning at Oxford and Cambridge in England, at Paris in France and Leipzig in Germany. In a way, universities like Nalanda, Taxila, Saragosa, Oxford, Cambridge and Harvard Business School have played decisive roles in shaping the destiny of civilizations. These institutions have not only provided leadership in times of uncertainties but also provided inspiration for production, management and organization of knowledge and lifestyle in normal times.

Recently S.L. Sharma and T.K. Oommen have edited a book, *Coceptualizing Nation and National Identity in South Asia*, which has emerged as a civilizational region out of the old Akhand Bharat or "undivided India." This book seeks to conceptualize the experiences of nation formation and deformation in South Asia. It helps us to understand the difference between nation, state and nation-state in India, Pakistan, Bangladesh and Sri Lanka. It also explores the relationship between state and society in sociological literature in general and the literature on South Asia in particular. The eleven essays of this volume were originally published in *The Sociological Bulletin* (Journal of the Indian Sociological Society), 48 (1 & 2) 1999.

In the introductory essay "The Discourse on the National Question in South Asia," S.L. Sharma has presented a critical review of the eleven essays by T.K. Oommen, J.P.S. Uberoi, K.T. Silva, Tanveer Fazal, Vikash Pandey, Dipankar Gupta, M.N. Kama, and P. Nandi among others. The issues of nation and nation-state have hitherto been dealt with mainly by political scientists. This volume breaks new ground by bringing a sociological perspective on South Asia.

Oommen (*Conceptualizing Nation and National Identity in South Asia*) has identified and interrogated seven ways in which the nation has been defined in the Indian subcontinent. These include nation as ancient civilizational entity, as composite culture, as political entity, as a territorial entity and as a unity of great and little nations. Oommen thinks that nation as a collection of linguistic entities is the most appropriate use of the term in the South Asian context. After critically reviewing the diverse interpretations, he settles for a definition of nation as a "fusion between territory and culture," since he views nation as a territorial cultural entity. Therefore, for him India of today is not a nation — rather it is a multinational state. He claims that there existed (before 1947) and there continues to exist an Indian or South Asian civilization, which is divided into several states. Oommen argues that Independent India constitutes only a part of this civilizational region.

Oommen shares with Uberoi, Dharampal and A.K. Saran the viewpoint that India is not a nation in the European sense of the term. The European sense of nation is equal to our territorial cultural groups. It is another matter that S.L. Sharma, P.N. Mukherji and many others call these territorial cultural groups ethnic groups and not nations. Oommen deconstructs the colonial legacy in Indian sociology and asserts that "South Asia is home to a long and enduring civilization, which was earlier referred to as the Indian civilization" (p. 15). S.L. Sharma agrees with Oommen when he says that "there is ample evidence to suggest that India was envisaged as a nation in terms of its civilizational thrust by seers and intellectuals long before the colonial encounter" (pp. xiv–xv).

Oommen argues that the characterization of Indian culture as a composite culture is only partially correct. Those who characterize the fundamental unity of the Indian nation in terms of a composite culture recall the examples of emperors like Candragupta Maurya (a Hindu), Aśoka (a Buddhist) and Akbar (a Muslim) as shining examples of statesmen who nurtured this idea. But it is often forgotten, Oommen claims, that in empires there are elites, subjects and slaves and therefore the adjective "composite" connotes different layers of a hierarchy. In retrospect, Oommen says, the idea of composite culture was a political project intended to mollify both Hindus and Muslims and to avert the Partition. Despite the nobility of intention, the project failed. Compositeness implies assimilation and fusion whereas pluralism is the celebration of diversity in order to facilitate the coexistence of cultures, in spite of their distinctiveness. Oommen claims that Indian civilization respected diversity and plurality from the very beginning. Oommen can be criticized, however, for not giving his concept of civilization and for not explaining the factors which sustained diversity and pluralism in Indian civilization before 1947.

This is where J.P.S. Uberoi's contribution to the debate about Indian civilization is significant. In his paper, "On Civil Society," Uberoi argues that the nature and pursuit of the national civil society in power and culture can be put in the form of four propositions in the Indian context: (a) Civil society is truly the locus of God-realization or self-realization as well as of the common usage or custom of the people; (b) It is the sovereign arbiter of custom as against the priest, custodian of tradition, and the prince, maker and executor of the state and its law; (c) Civil society alone has inherent power to find a people's principle of history and so to change the common usage, the custom of the country, as well as itself, as in the Gandhian view of self-rule and self-reform; and (d) Whenever the prince and the priest rule together, either through a state-established religion or a religion-established.

Unity and Diversity in Indian Civilization

One of the most striking features of India is its "unity in diversity." In fact, this overworked or overused cliché has become a part of India's self-identity. India is a country of subcontinental proportions. From north to south, east to west, people from diverse backgrounds have mixed and cultures have intermingled over the centuries. Nevertheless, there has been an underlying continuity in identity. There are very few countries on earth which have such an enormous cultural diversity that India has to offer.

Beneath the bewildering diversity of religion, language and customs of this vast country, the underlying unity is striking. The idea of unity is traced back by scholars to ancient times. The underlying cultural unity was strengthened further with the administrative unity brought about during the British rule and with the construction of India as a modern independent nation-state after Independence. The enduring nature of Indian unity has always been fascinating. Indian unity is the product of certain historical factors that are present in the various fields of Indian social life. It appears as if the inhabitants from the Himalayas in the north to Kanyakumari in the south and Kutch in the west to Arunachal in the east are woven together into a beautiful tapestry. In the process of its evolution, Indian society has acquired a culture characterized by stable patterns of pluralism. But the acceptance of cultural pluralism does not detract from the idea of promoting economic, political and social integration.

European sociology conceptualizes unity in a society in terms of linguistic nationality or in terms of political sovereignty. Thus the primary basis of unity is belonging to a nation-state. According to many Indian sociologists, however, unity in India and the whole of South Asia, in fact, has been civilizational, going back to ancient times and continuing to the present day. Thus at the civilizational level there is unity in South Asia, but this South Asian civilization is divided today into many nation-states like India, Pakistan, Bangladesh, Sri Lanka and Nepal. In terms of social institutions like the family, caste, customs and lifestyles there is fundamental unity in the different societies and nation-states of South Asia.

An important source of unity in traditional India was rooted in the processes of cultural communication and interaction. Sociologists have identified the role of travelling mendicants, traders, story-tellers, craftsmen and artists, for example potters, musicians, and dancers in traditional India in building common cultural traditions. The institutions of pilgrimage, fairs and festival provided yet another link for cultural unity. In addition to these agencies the social structure and economy forged linkages of reciprocity and interaction between regions, groups and cultural traditions.

Accommodation without assimilation has been the characteristic of Indian civilization. Accommodation is a social process by which different elements of a society are integrated without losing their separate identity. Assimilation on the other hand is a type of integration where the earlier identity of the elements is dissolved. In Indian history and culture the addition of new components has not meant the discarding of old ones. The accommodation of diversity has been the underlying ideology and numerous social and cultural factors have contributed to the enduring nature of Indian unity. Order and stability were maintained not primarily by the state but through social, cultural, moral and technological values and institutions of Indian civilization. The Indian civilization gave enough freedom to practise any way of life although different customary ways were ranked hierarchically. This creates inequality as well as integration.

The Factors of Unity and Diversity

Geographical and Physical Factor

The first striking feature about India is its diversity because of India's geographical environment and enormous population. It is difficult to imagine the vast territory that stretches from north to south and east to west as one continuous territory. It is nearly fourteen times as large as Great Britain and over ten times the size of the entire British Isles. The temperature varies from extremely hot to extremely cold. The temperate, tropical and the polar climates are found in India. The flora and fauna is varied and rich. In terms of physical features of the population one can notice diversity in appearance, skin colour, eye colour, height and figure. There is also cultural diversity, which India presents through her large population with the diversity of languages, manners, customs, cults and cultures. The distribution of material traits (such as dress, habitation, material arts and crafts, endless variety of food eaten and their preparation, variation in the food under different geographical conditions) makes India a living example of regional diversity. Within regions there are further variations of customs, rituals and social policies, which can often not be linked to the geographical conditions.

However, geography seems to have played an important role in engendering Indian unity and the sense of Indianness. Shut off from the rest of Asia by the inaccessible barriers of the mighty Himalayas and the seas and the ocean on all other sides, India is clearly marked out to be a geographical entity. Not only are her territories thus sharply demarcated from the rest of the world, but also its nature is generously placed within her boundaries that humans need for developing a rich and creative life. Thus, Indian geography has facilitated unity and continuity of her history as a country. Attempts either to divide the country or to expand it beyond its natural frontiers have mostly failed.

The vastness of the land influenced the mind of Indians in two ways. The great variety in landscape, climate and conditions of life prepared in the mind a readiness to accept difference. Besides, the vast spaces offered room for slow infiltration by newcomers and allowed each locality unhampered scope of development along its own lines.

The geographic unity of the country has had its effects on the economic life of the people. The size of the country and quality of the land permitted gradual increase in the population and expansion of cultivation. The fact that India has continually developed and maintained an agricultural economy for almost 4000 or 5000 thousand years explains in part the depth and tenacity of her culture and traditions. The primarily agricultural economy led to the development of common characteristics and a common outlook.

The geographical unity of India is easily missed in her vastness and variety. A permanent and characteristically Indian expression of unity is found in the networks of shrines and sacred places spread throughout the country. The visit to holy places as an imperative religious duty has made travelling a habit for Indians. Similarly the multitude of monuments associated with Buddhism and Jainism which have adorned the land influence the geographical consciousness of large numbers of people.

Religious Factors

India is a multi-religious country. According to the 1991 census there are seven major religions in India. The Hindus constitute the majority of the Indian population (about 82 per cent). The Muslims constitute the second largest religious group (about 12.12 per cent). The Christians (about 2.34 per cent), the Sikhs (1.94 percent), the Buddhists (0.76 per cent), the Jains (0.40 per cent) and others (the Jews, the Zoroastrians or Parsis and the animists — about 0.44 per cent) may not be numerically big, but their contribution to India is as significant as the bigger groups.

The scheduled tribes constitute 6.9 per cent; many of the tribes have a close affinity with Hindus. Many have been assimilated into Hindu society while a sizeable number have been converted to Christianity. Each major religion is sub-divided along the lines of religious doctrines, sects and cults. The Hindus are now broadly divided into Śaivite (those who worship Śiva and his Śakti), Vaiṣṇavite (worshippers of Viṣṇu), and Smārta (those who worship all these). Even among them are sub-divisions based on doctrinal differences and ritual details. The Muslims are divided broadly into the sects of Sunnī and Śiā. Christians are divided into Roman Catholics, Protestants, and Eastern Orthodox Church and into many denominational groups. Sikhism is a synthesizing religion that emphasizes egalitarianism.

Buddhism is traditionally divided into three important sects, Theravāda, Mahāyāna and Vajrayāna. In contemporary India Theravāda is the dominant sect of Buddhism. Jainism is divided into two main sects — Digambera (unclothed) and Śvetāmbera (white robed). The Jewish people, the Pārsīs and the animist tribes are smaller communities and these are relatively homogenous.

Religion is both a factor of unity and diversity in Indian society. All religions are differentiated internally. Caste or caste-like status groups are found in Hinduism, Islam, Christianity and Sikhism. Within a homogeneous religious group religion plays a highly integrative role but by the same token in a multi-religious society religion can become an issue of contention and lead to conflicts. Traditionally different religious groups have coexisted in India in a more or less peaceful manner. In recent years, however, the religious harmony, which in India is referred to as communal harmony, has been put under strain.

There are two major aspects of any religion, the spiritual and the temporal. The spiritual aspect is quite similar in all religions. In every religion an emphasis is placed on the moral conduct and transcendence of the selfish ego. While this aspect of religion is a matter of personal devotion, the temporal aspect of religion is always related with the group identity, and solidarity is maintained by religious rituals and community's beliefs. At the temporal level, different religious groups differ from each other.

In India, there has not only been a great degree of religious tolerance among the different religious communities, some religious places have acquired a character and popularity that goes beyond a single religious community. Similarly, some religious festivals are celebrated, at least in a limited way, by many religious communities. Places like Varanasi, Ujjain and Ajmer Sharif are some such religious centres. For instance, a large number of Hindus also visit Ajmer Sharif, a Muslim pilgrimage centre. Also, the economy of these religious centres often involves shopkeepers and service providers from other religions.

In the field of *bhakti* and devotion the Hindu saints and Muslim Sūfī saints had many similarities and commonalities. Some religious festivals like Diwālī, Dussehra and Holī have two aspects, ritualistic and cultural. The ritualistic aspect is restricted to Hindus but the cultural aspect is more or less celebrated by all communities. In the same way, Christmas and Id-ul-fitr are also celebrated at many places by different religious communities. Kabīr, Akbar, Dara Shikoh and Mahatma Gandhi have been instrumental in developing a common ethos among the different religious communities in India.

Persian Sūfism took a new shade of colour in India. Poets and religious teachers — Ramanand and Kabir — tried to combine the best and condemn the worst in Hinduism and Islam alike. At the courts of Awadh and Hyderabad there grew aesthetic standards in painting, in poetry, in love and in food, which drew on the courtly traditions of Rajasthan and Persia. Muslims borrowed caste from Hindus, Hindus took *purdāh* from Muslims.

Religion, however, is also a factor of diversity and animosity. The country was partitioned into India and Pakistan primarily on religious-communal lines. Even after Partition the communal problem raises its head from time to time. Communalism, which breeds hatred and violence against other religions, is the result of fundamentalism. Fundamentalism is an attitude of some religious people who emphasize the letter of religious dogmas over the underlying sprit. It is a product of ignorance as well as deliberate mischief by vested interests to gain political power and economic benefits by exploiting religious sentiments of the faithful, and dividing people along communal lines.

Cultural Factors

The story of Indian culture is one of continuity, synthesis and enrichment. Culture is also a source of unity as well as diversity, like religion. Powerful kingdoms and empires such as the Mauryas and the Guptas did not aggressively intervene in social and cultural matters; leaving much diversity intact. Although Islam was the politically dominant religion in large parts of the country for several centuries, it did not absorb Hinduism, or offend the Hindu social structure. Nor did Hinduism, which was demographically and otherwise dominant, question or attempt to eliminate the beliefs and practices other religions. Various beliefs and practices are pursued and maintained by Hindus, Muslims and Christians alike. Over time Indian society has come to be divided into innumerable tribes, castes, sub-castes, clans, sects and communities, each of which seek to maintain their own style of life and their own code of conduct.

Many sociologists have recorded in detail the immense variety in the habits, practices and customs of the people in different geographical regions. The distribution of material traits such as dress, habitation, arts and crafts, endless variety of foods eaten and their preparation makes India a living example of regional diversity.

The role played by Indian religion, philosophy, art and literature in bringing about unity is conspicuous. Social institutions like the caste system and the joint family, which are found throughout the length and breadth of the country, are typically Indian. The celebration of festivals is observed all over India in much the same fashion. Likewise, similarities in art and culture engraved on the temple and palace walls all over India have generated the feeling of oneness. In spite of their distinctiveness co-existence of cultures is celebrated.

Political Factors

It is generally believed that India's continuity as a civilization was social and cultural rather than political. Order and stability were maintained not by means of the state but through culture and society. The vastness of the country's extreme diversity of physical features, endless variety of races, castes, creeds and languages and dialects have made it difficult to establish an all Indian empire. This also accounts for the fact that political unity is not the normal characteristic of ancient and medieval Indian history.

However, the idea of bringing the whole country under one central authority has always been on the minds of great kings and statesmen of India. It was with this purpose that the kings of ancient India proclaimed the idea of *cakravartī*.

Kings like Candragupta Maurya, Aśoka, Samudragupta and Harṣavardhana had put this idea into practice. The socio-political contributions of some Muslim rulers such as Akbar and Jehangir were also highly commendable. Akbar's *Dīn-e-elāhī* and Jehangir's emphasis on justice deserve special mention in this regard.

In a sense, India has never been a well-organized political unit under the government of a single state. Even British India was a part of India and did not comprehend the whole of it, which was split up into about 600 states, large and small but separate and independent as autonomous entities. The British, however, tried to establish political unification under a paramount power in regard to the defence, external relations, foreign policy and certain economic matters within the whole of India.

After Independence India was united politically and administratively, but it got divided between India and Pakistan. After Independence the unity of India is expressed through the institution of the nation-state. It is the product of the freedom movements as well as the constitutional legacy of the British rule. There is political and administrative unity today but there are different political parties and diverse political ideologies. Therefore, politics is both a factor of unity and diversity.

Linguistic Factors

India is a multilingual nation-state. Language is another source of cultural diversity as well as unity. It contributes to collective identities and even to conflicts. The Indian Constitution lists eighteen languages. All major languages have regional and dialectical variations, for example, Hindi has Awadhi, Brij, Bhojpuri, Magadhi, Bundeli, Pahari, Nimari, Malwi and several other dialects. The situation is further complicated since 179 languages and 544 dialects are recognized in India. These languages and dialects are divided into three linguistic families — Indo-Aryan, Draviḍian and Mundari. Indo-Aryan family of languages includes Sanskrit and other north Indian languages such as Hindi, Bengali, Oriya, Marathi, Gujarati, Punjabi, etc. and their dialects. The Draviḍian family of languages includes Tamil, Telugu, Kannada and Malayalam. The Mundari group of languages and dialects are found among the tribal communities of India.

During the medieval period Persian, Arabic and Urdu became popular languages. Urdu developed in India with Hindi around the same period as Hindustani language. During Medieval Era Arabic and Persian languages replaced Sanskrit and Pāli languages as the official or court languages.

In the modern period, English replaced Arabic and Persian as the official and court language. After Independence, Hindi was made the national language but English remained the language of the central government and of the courts. English has also remained the language of higher education and research in India after 1835.

The importance given to English in independent India has also had an impact on Indian languages and literature, as well as on social structure and divisions in Indian society. The social and economic distinction between an English-speaking, prosperous elite and the masses who speak the Indian vernacular languages or dialects is quite pronounced.

Linguistic diversity has posed administrative and political problems. But language too has an underlying role in the unity and continuity of Indian culture. Although there is bewildering diversity in the languages and dialects of India, fundamental unity is found in the ideas and themes expressed in these languages. There is unity also at the level of grammatical structures. Sanskrit has deeply influenced most languages of India with the vocabulary of the Draviḍian languages also containing a number of Sanskrit words today. Persian, Arabic and English words too have become part of the Indian languages and dialects today. The spirit of accommodation, which united the different ethnic groups into one social system, also expresses itself in the literatures of India.

Language is also a factor of diversity and separatism. Linguistic separatism has a strong emotional appeal. Political mobilizations and conflicts have arisen from time to time between different linguistic groups. However, it is important to note that neither political mobilization, nor linguistic antagonisms flow naturally out of linguistic diversities. These political mobilizations and antagonisms are the products of modern historical circumstances.

After Independence the linguistic problem of India was centred on three issues:

- The official languages issue;
- The demands for the linguistic reorganization of the provinces of India whose boundaries during the British rule did not conform to linguistic division; and
- The status of minority languages within reorganised states.

After much deliberation, Hindi was made the official language of India but English was retained at least for a transition period. Earlier, this transition period was supposed to last for fifteen years. In 1965, English was given the status of an "associate additional official language" of the union and of inter-provincial communication. The major regional languages are used in their own provinces and recognized as "national" languages through their incorporation into the Eighth Schedule of the Constitution. Hindi is the official language of the country but the "associate additional official language" (English) has retained its power, status and glamour.

Elements of Unity in Traditional India

Due to culture and economic interaction and geographical mobility there has emerged an all-India style: a series of interlinkages and much commonality between different regions of India. The elements of all-India structure include the following:

1. The concept of "Mārgī" in Indian tradition and its relationship with the "Deśī." The Mārgī or the Indian equivalent of "Great" or "classical" is commonly accepted in different regions, whereas the "deśī" or regional cultures are unique to different regions. The "Mārgī" or the great tradition of India is expressed in Sanskrit, Prākr̥t, Pāli and Tamil languages of India.
2. The Sanskrit Brāhmī Script for Indian and other sub-continental languages and literature.

Common to each linguistic region are specific agriculture castes which form the core of rural communities, along with their complementary artisan and service castes. These were involved in a *yajamān-kāmin* relationship. In the urban areas these were predominantly castes of *baniās* (traders), crafts-persons and castes such as brāhmaṇas and kāyasths.

In the institutions of administration and defence both social and physical mobility existed. Cosmopolitan recruitment also took place due to traditional cultural institutions such as *gharānās* of music and dancing. There were also "schools" of medicine, śāstric schools of learning, *pīṭhas*, and *akhāṛās* of devotional sects.

Pilgrimage centres have also led to a type of unity at the all-India level. Barriers of caste-class and other social taboos were almost absent at pilgrimage centres during several cultural occasions. People from different regions were able to interact at the pilgrim centres with each other leading to the establishment of cultural bonds. Trans-sectarian pilgrim sites include Kāśī, Hardwar, Rāmeśvaram, Dwārkā, Badrīnāth, Ajmer Sharif, etc.

Cultural identity is maintained by a common metaphysical base, such as the idea of ethical compensation (*karmaphala*) and the idea of transcendence.

Variants of all-India epics and mythology, which emphasize certain values and goals, are found in all regions. Examples are *puruṣārtha* (achievement ideals), *r̥ṇas* (obligations), *dāna* (sharing), *saṁskāra* (sacraments) at birth, death and marriage, *vrata* (the ritual to earn merit) and *prāyaścitta* (penance or expiation). Traditional personal laws and social customs of the Hindus were applicable in different regions. The Dayābhāga system of inheritance was popular in Bengal whereas the Mitākṣarā prevailed over the rest of the country, except in Kerala. Most Indians believe in the ideas of heaven and hell and cherish the idea of salvation, *mokṣa, nirvāṇa* or liberation from the cycle of life and death. This concept of *mokṣa* or *nirvāṇa* is linked with the perception of the one ultimate *Brahman*.

Elements of Unity during the Medieval Period

In the Middle Ages when the world witnessed the most intensely fought religious wars in Europe and the Middle East, India stood out as a country where a multiplicity of religions co-existed in relative social harmony. Akbar tried to bring the best thinkers from all religions together to evolve a common faith — *Dīn-e-elāhī*, while his council of scholars prepared the basis for such a world religion. This new faith did not gather any following and was formally abandoned by Akbar's successors.

Islam seems to have strengthened the de-ritualizing and egalitarian trends in Medieval Hinduism, while Hindu philosophy seems to have strengthened the mystical spiritual strain in Muslim religious thought. For example, the *bhakti* movement initiated by the Āḻwār and Nāyanār saints of south India found strength in the context of Islam and Muslim dominance in north India. In the same way, the mystic and devotional aspect of Islam was strengthened in the philosophical milieu of Hinduism. Ramanand, Kabīr, Nanak and Dara Shikoh played a significant role in the spread of mutual understanding among the Hindu and the Muslim masses.

A unified culture in language, music and the arts developed during the medieval period. Hindi and Urdu are the products of this unified Hindustānī culture of medieval

India. Both languages have common roots, common vocabulary but these are written in different scripts (Devanāgarī and Persian respectively). In music and the arts, the Hindus and the Muslims had come together. North Indian (Hindustānī) music was nurtured at the Muslim courts, in the Hindu temples and in the *koṭhās*. Hindus sang at the Muslim courts and Muslims have sung *bhajanas* at Hindu temples. Kṛṣṇa, Rādhā and the *gopīs* have provided the staple theme for many of the compositions sung by Hindu and Muslim masters alike.

In architecture the process of blending Hindu and Muslim elements was perfected during the medieval period. During the rule of Akbar, a synthesis of the Turko-Persian conceptions with Hindu-Indian style was attempted. In Jehangir's time the Hindu influence seems to have increased. The tomb of Akbar at Sikandra shows, in spite of its Muslim arches and domes, the general pattern of Buddhist *vihāras* or of the *rathas* of Mahābalipuram. Jain influence is found on the mosques of Fatehpur Sīkrī and Mount Abu. The Mogul architecture acquired new qualities which neither the Persian nor the old Indian styles had ever possessed.

Painting also developed a new style during this period through the blending of the Turko-Iranian with the old Indian style. Akbar founded an academy of painting at his court where Indian and Persian artists worked together. Jehangir was not only a patron of art but was himself an artist and during his time Mogul painting reached its zenith.

Elements of Unity in the Modern Period

During the colonial rule different factors led to significant changes in the structure of Indian society. The traditional framework of unity in Indian civilization came under tremendous stress. Modern education introduced by the colonial rulers initiated a process of cultural Westernization.

The freedom movement (1857-1947) created new sources of unity in Indian society now, nationalism replaced religion and culture as the cementing force within Indian society. Despite Partition in 1947 the experience of freedom movement is still the foundation of Indian unity in modern India.

After Independence the nation-state and its different organs have become the pillars of unity in India. The Constitution built on the pre-existing unity of India by emphasizing the values of equality, fraternity, secularism and justice.

The Indian Constitution is the most fundamental source of unity in India today. Indians believe in the basic framework of the Constitution.

Indian Parliament is the national legislative organ of the Indian state. Representatives are elected by the people and every adult citizen of India has a right to vote. This represents the people's will in general.

The Government of India is formally headed by the president who rules on the advice of a council of ministers headed by the prime minister.

The Judiciary is the legal guardian of Indian people. The judiciary is an autonomous body at the local, regional and central levels. It works as the custodian of the Indian Constitution.

The bureaucracy, the police and other educated professionals such as engineers, scientists, doctors, academics and journalists have played an important role in governing the country, maintaining law and order and in carrying out the various development projects and schemes of the government. The military services deserve special mention in view of the wars, insurgency and the inter-border tensions experienced after Independence (1947-2010), as also during national calamities like floods, earthquake, cyclones, etc.

Modern means of communication — the networks of railways, surface transport, civil aviation, post offices, telegraph, telephones, the print media, and radio and television have played important roles in maintaining and strengthening the national ethos and creating "we" feeling among Indians.

Industrialization, urbanization and other economic factors have led to the creation of the capitalist and the middle classes and have also created mobility of labour and services throughout the country.

Problems of Nation-Building and National Integration

The formation of consciousness of identity in terms of culture, custom, way of life and language, etc. gives rise to ethnicity and ethnic groups. Ethnic conflicts and ethnic self-consciousness result invariably from perceived or real experiences of domination or subordination of one group by another, i.e. politically, economically, culturally or socially. A caste group, tribe, linguistic, religious or cultural group may also act as an ethnic group in its competitive quest for access to resources.

A large part of ethnic demands can be resolved following a strategy of constructive reconciliation. There were and there are many ethnic demands in post-Independence India. Attempts have been made to reconcile some of the ethnic demands of minority religious groups, scheduled castes, scheduled tribes and other backward classes in the Indian Constitution itself. There was also a demand for linguistic reorganization of regional states. There has been the Ḍraviḍian movement, ethnic assertions in Kashmir, the North-East, Gorkhaland, Punjab and other places.

The Constitution offers two types of policies for nation-building in India: (a) Positive discrimination in favour of the traditionally deprived and exploited sections of society; and (b) A broad national policy of social, economic and political development based on principles of civic culture and judicial, administrative and institutional modernization.

The biggest challenge to effective nation-building and national integration comes from continuing poverty, economic polarization and regional imbalances in development. On the one hand, globalization is opening up new opportunities for the educated and the well-off who have the education, skills and financial resources to compete in the national and global marketplace. On the other hand, a large number of rural and urban youth and families continue to languish in poverty, unemployment and underemployment. Socially, the divide between the metropolitan, Westernized, prosperous "India" and the semi-literate, poor, rural-based and culturally rooted "Bhārat" persists and may even be widening.

On the cultural front, however, films and television channels and programmes have created and strengthened a national "collective consciousness" that emphasizes traditional and religious themes like spirituality and the epics, on the one hand, and the various issues of governance and democratic politics on the other. Another major concern in the media, particularly the audio-visual media, is sports like cricket and "modern" and Western forms of entertainment.

Conclusion

Thus India has been helped both by her nature and her long and rich historic experience, by her religious co-existence and political ideas, to realize her unity amidst great geographical and cultural diversity. Traditional India was, and even modern India continues to be, remarkable for its spirit of synthesis and reconciliation. The modern world is faced with the challenge to see that old and new values must not clash with each other. The task is to achieve a new synthesis in which the heritage of the ancient, the medieval and the modern world will be reconciled and enriched.

References

Ahmad, Imtiaz, P.S. Ghosh, H. Reifeld, 2000, *Pluralism and Equality: Values in Indian society and Politics*, New Delhi: Sage.

Béteille, Andre, 1997, *Society and Politics in India: Essays in a Comparative Perspective*, New Delhi: Oxford University Press.

Borden, C.M. (ed.), 1989, *Contemporary India: Essays on the Uses of Tradition*, New Delhi: Oxford University Press.

Bose, N.K., 1975, *Culture and Society in India*, Bombay: Asia Publishing House.

———, 1977, *The Structure of Hindu Society*, New Delhi: Orient Longman.

Bottomore, Tom, et al. (eds.), 1983/2000, *A Dictionary of Marxist Thought*, New Delhi: Worldview Publications.

Bulmer, Martin, 1987, *The Chicago School of Sociology*, Chicago: Chicago University Press.

Cohn, B.S., 2000, *India: The Social Anthropology of A Civilization*, Delhi: Oxford University Press.

Coomaraswamy, Ananda K., 1972, *History of Indian and Indonesian Art*, New Delhi: Munshiram Manoharlal.

———, 1989, *What is Civilization?*, Delhi: Indira Gandhi National Centre for the Arts; New Delhi: Oxford University Press.

Durkheim, Emile, 1915, *The Elementary forms of Religious Life*, London: Allen & Unwin.

Elias, Norbest, 1994, *The Civilising Process*, Oxford: Blackwell.

———, 1996, *The Germans: Power Struggles and the Development of Habitus in the Nineteenth and the Twentieth Centuries*, Oxford: Polity Press.

Fekete, John (ed.), 1984, *The Structural Allegory: Reconstructive Encounters with the New French Thought*, Minneapolis: Minnesota University Press.

Frawley, David, 1993, *Gods, Sages and Kings: Vedic Secrets of Ancient Civilizations*, Delhi: Motilal Banarsidass.

Gandhi, M.K., 1938, *Hind Swarāj or Indian Home Rule*, Ahmedabad: Navajivan Publishing House.

Ghurye, G.S., 1962, *Cities and Civilization*, Bombay: Popular Prakashan.

———, 1963, *Style and Civilization in Anthropo Sociological Papers*, Bombay: Popular Prakashan.

———, 1965, *Religious Consciousness*, Bombay: Popular Prakashan.

Gore, M.S., 2002, *Unity in Diversity: The Indian Experience in Nation-Building*, Jaipur: Rawat.

———, 2000, *Introduction to the Study of Hindu Doctrines*, New Delhi: Munshiram Manoharlal.

Guenon, Rene, 1999, *The Crisis of the Modern World*, Varanasi: Indica Books.

Horkheimer, M. and T.W. Adorno, 1979, *Dialectic of Enlightenment*, London: Verso.

Inden, Ronald, 1990, *Imagining India*, Oxford: Basil Blackwell.

International Sociology, 2001, 13(3) Special issue on Rethinking Civilizational Analysis.

J.G. Herder on Social and Political Culture, 1969 (ed. F.M. Barnard), Cambridge: Cambridge University Press.

Lévi-Strauss, 1987, *Introduction to the Work of Marcel Mauss*, London: Routledge.

Madan, T.N., 1995, *Pathways: Approches to the Study of Society in India*, Delhi: Oxford University Press.

Malik, S.C., 1975, *Understanding Indian Civilization: A Framework of Enquiry*, Simla: Indian Institute of Advanced Study.

Marriott, Mckim, 1963, *In Old Societies and New States*, ed. Clifford Geestz, Glencoe: The Free Press.

Mauss, M., 1954, *The Gift*, London, Cohen & West.

Mukerji, D.P., 1979, *Sociology of Indian Culture*, Jaipur: Rawat.

Mukerjee, Radhakamal, 1964, *The Destiny of Civilization*, Bombay: Asia Publishing House.

———, 1964a, *The Flowering of Indian Art: The Growth and Spread of a Civilization*, Bombay: Asia Publishing House.

———, 1964b, *The Sickness of Civilization*, Bombay: Allied Publishers.

———, 1965, *The Cosmic Art of India*, Bombay: Allied Publishers.

Mukherjee, Ramkrishna, 1979, *Sociology of Indian Sociology*, New Delhi: Allied.

Pallis, Marco, 1994, *The Way and The Mountain*, Bombay: Rupa & Co.

Ramanujan, A.K., 1994, *Folktales from India*, New Delhi: Penguin Books.

Redfield, Robert, 1956, *Peasant Society and Culture*, Chicago: Chicago University Press.

Renou, Louis, 1987, *The Civilization of Ancient India*, Delhi: Indological Book House.

Rundell, John and Stephen Mennell, 1998 (eds.), *Classical Readings in Culture and Civilization*, London: Routledge.

Saran, A.K., 1998, *Traditional Vision of Man*, Sarnath: Central Institute of Higher Tibetan Studies.

Saraswati, B.N., 1970, *Contributions to an Understanding of Indian Civilization*, Dharwar: Karnatak University Lectures.

Sharma, S.L. and T.K. Oommen, 2000 (eds.), *Nation and National Identity in South Asia*, New Delhi: Orient Longman.

Singh, Yogendra, 2000, *Culture Change in India: Identity and Globalisation*, Jaipur:

Rawat.

———, 1993, *Social Change in India*, New Delhi: Har-Anand Publications.

Skinner, Quentin (ed.), 1985, *The Return of Grand Theory in the Human Sciences*, Cambridge: Cambridge University Press.

Spengler, 1959, *The Decline of the West*, London: George Allen and Unwin.

Stoianouich, T., 1976, *French Historical Method: The Annales Paradigm*, Ithaca: Cornell University Press.

Swaroop, Ram, 2000, *On Hinduism: Reviews and Reflections*, New Delhi: Voice of India.

Tarlekar, G.H., 1975/1991, *Studies in the Natya Sastra*, Delhi: Motilal Banarsidass.

Toynbee, Arnold, 1947, *A Study of History*, London: Oxford University Press.

Tripathi, G.C. and Herman Kulke (ed.), 1994, *Religion and Society in Eastern India*, New Delhi: Manohar.

Uberoi, J.P.S., 1999, *Religion, Civil Society and the State*, Delhi: Oxford University Press.

———, 2002, *The European Modernity: Science, Truth and Method*, Delhi: Oxford University Press.

Unnithan, T.K.N., Indra Deva and Yogendra Singh, 1965, *Towards a Sociology of Culture in India*, New Delhi: Prentice Hall of India.

Vatsyayan, Kapila, 1994, "Sastra and Prayoga: Marga and Desi, On Conceptual Frameworks of Indian Culture" in G.C. Tripathi and H. Kulke (ed.), *Religion and Society in Eastern India*, New Delhi: Manohar.

Venugopal, C.N., 1990, "Reformist Sects and the Sociology of Religion in India", *Sociological Analysis*, vol. 51, no. 8, Supplement.

———, 1998, *Religion and Indian Society: A Sociological Perspective*, New Delhi: Gyan.

Vijay Lakshmi, M., 1996, *A Critical Study of Sangita Makaranda of Sage Narada*, New Delhi: Gyan.

Weber, Alfred, 1921/1998, "Civilization and Culture a Synthesis: Fundamentals of Culture Sociology: Social Process, Civilizational Process and Culture Movement", in Rundell and Mennell (eds.), 1998, *Classical Readings in Culture and Civilization*, London: Routledge.

2

The Study of Religion
Some Conceptual Problems

Wagish Shukla

THE origin of the word "religion" is debated since antiquity. It is supposed to have been derived from Latin *religio* which means, what attaches or retains, moral bond, anxiety of self-consciousness and scruples. The Romans, before Jesus Christ, to indicate the worship of the "demons," used the term religion in this sense. Cicero said it comes from "relegere" which means to read again, to re-examine carefully, to gather in the meaning and to carefully consider the things related to the worship of gods. Later, Lucretius, Lactancius and Tertullianus see its origin in "religare" which means to connect to "the bond of piety that binds man to God." Initially used exclusively to mean Christianity, religion gradually extended to all the forms of social demonstration in connection with the sacred.

Thus, earlier it had "to carefully consider the things related to the worship of gods" and later "the bond of piety that binds to God" comes in the picture. Basically, the difference between "gods" and "God" is a point of conceptual differentiation. But more than numerical accuracy is at stake here; it is the open-ended architecture of "reading again, to re-examine carefully" against the closed architecture of "the bond of piety that binds to God." Incidentally, a website on comparative religion lists religions as only those that are monotheists, like Judaism, Christianity and Islam.

Interestingly, the website also lists Sikhism, like Bahá'í as a sect of Islam. This attempt to include "Sikhism" in the list of "Abrahamic faiths" is not new; Frederick Pincott wrote an article on Sikhism for the "Dictionary of Islam" edited by Thomas Patrick Hughes in which Sikhism appears as a "sect of Islam."

The word "interfaith dialogue" is generally taken to be a byproduct of what is known as "Post-Conciliar Catholicism." "Post-Conciliar" refers to the developments in Catholicism after the Second Vatican Council, or Vatican II, a congress convened in the autumns of the four years from 1962 through 1965. Pope John XXIII presided over the Council on 11 October 1962, with bishops from all over the world where they discussed the nature, scope, and mission of the Church. Of the 2,908 clergy entitled to attend the Council, 2,450 did so. The Council closed on 8 December 1965. These developments are summarized by the famous words of Pope John XXIII, "I want to throw open the windows of the Church so that we can see out and the people can see in."

Apparently as a consequence of that, an interfaith conference called "The Present of Man, the Future of God: The Place of Sanctuary in Relation to the Sacred" was organized in Portugal by Father Guerra, Rector of the Catholic Shrine of Fatima in October 2003. One of the catholic speakers, Father Jacques Dupuis, said that conversion is an option and not an obligation. He also said that the dogma that there is no salvation outside religions of what is better called "The Fourth World" was indefensible. In this Fourth World I include all the Amerindian systems, the indigenous African systems, the Wicca, and so on.

The term "Pagan" is a cover-name for all of those beliefs and practices that the Judaic religions defied, decimated and destroyed in the course of history. However, I will mainly talk about the only pagan system with which I have some familiarity; the *dharma* as it is known to outsiders. It happens to be the only surviving functional paganistic system that has refused to be integrated into the genealogy of faith. And despite the most vigorous onslaughts, it has retained an unbroken continuity.

There is thus an inherent contradiction between the concepts of a global religion, the name I have preferred over "world religion," and "codwelling" which is the name I have preferred over "harmony." It follows that it is impossible for me to technically reconcile the two loaded terms. So it is time to think that perhaps the idea is to shift to another set of terms that one can use more fruitfully.

Pagan and Anti-pagan

In spite of the bitter histories associated with the words, I think the oppositional term-pair "pagan–anti-pagan" bears the required load of the problem that we should address. Both the terms are defined contrastively with each other. "Pagan" derives from "Paganus," meaning "rustic," and thus essentially stands for the "jaahiliyyaa" or "ignorance." The advent of the anti-pagan systems then stands for "knowledge." The normative use is because of a power equation, which derives from a long history of political domination of the pagan systems by anti-pagan systems. Some terms are used interchangeably; for example, "local" and "open-ended" for "pagan." The opposed word "global," however, does not cover all anti-pagan systems since not all anti-pagan systems seek to convert and do not claim to be universal. Some indeed emphasize the exclusivity of the favour of God to a particular set of people. However, all anti-pagan systems seek to impose a tyranny of Truth. This I think is a defining characteristic of anti-paganism. Thus it is not correct, in my opinion, to define pagan in terms of merely the terminology employed by mainstream Christianity or Islam. In particular, the multiplicity or unicity of God, the image-worship or its denial, are not deep differentials. In this article, I discuss some syncretic Armenian and African belief systems that qualify as pagan cults but behave like the Judaistic anti-pagan religions.

Most of the Amerindian and African syncretism is an assertion of the protest against the persecution and the betrayal by the white races against the black populations while pretending to bring them into a Kingdom of God, which is meant for all believers. This has led many of these people to believe that this power that has accrued to the white races originates from a part of the Bible, which the latter have deliberately concealed from the black populations. Sir Walter Raleigh says about Guiana:

> Guiana is a country that hath yet her Maydenhead [sic], never sackt, turned, nor wrought, the face of the earth hath not been torne, nor the vertue [sic] and salt of the soyl [sic] spent by manurance, the graves have not been opened for gold, the mines not broken with sledges, nor their images puld [sic] down out of their temples. It hath never been entered by any armies or strength, and never conquered or possessed by any Christian prince. . . .

This obviously called for remedial measures, which were duly taken. As a later tangential development, a Makusi native of Guyana whose name was Bichiwung, met an English parson and was taken to England. He heard the parson saying that the Makusi would not be given the full Bible. Queen Victoria's spirit then took Bichiwung to God in a dream where God gave him a piece of paper known as The Indian Bible and told him to guard it carefully because the English were going to steal it just as they had earlier stolen the English Language. On returning home, The Hallelujah Church was founded by Bichiwung.

In the same way, Rastafarianism, a Jamaican phenomenon, has many components from Christianity, Judaism, and African Traditions. Marcus Mosiah Garvey (1897-1940) who promoted the Universal Negro Improvement Association in the 1920s and spearheaded the Back to Africa movement during the 1930s founded this sect. It is also inspired by the accession to the throne of Haile Selassie I as the Emperor of Ethiopia. The term Rastafari dates from the coronation of Haile Selassie in 1930.

In this religion, Africa is regarded as a spiritual focus, a true home, heaven on earth, and Rastafarians regard black people as the true Jews and chosen people of God. Haile Selassie, as Ras Tafari, is the true and living God (Jah), and salvation for black people is only through return to Africa. Rastafarians emphasize the ethos of peace and love, truth and right action. They recognize all 87 books of the Bible, including the Apochrypha and the Book of Enoch, as opposed to the 66 books of the Authorized Version used by many Christian churches. The case of Dawkins vs. Crown Suppliers (1989) held that a Rastafarian couldn't be refused employment because of his refusal to cut his hair (dreadlocks). Attorney General of the United States Janet Reno (1993-2001) during the Presidency of Bill Clinton ruled that Rastafarians do not have the religious right to smoke *gāñjā* in violation of drug laws. There is no centralized, hierarchical structure of a Rastafarian church and no specifically designated places of worship and people normally meet in their homes. Singing and drumming, especially reggae music, are important ways of communicating the ethos of the movement. Following the Rastafarian interpretation of the Bible (St Mark, chapter 12, verses 19-25), the adherents do not perform any formal marriage ceremony, but a man and a woman who cohabit are automatically treated as husband and wife by the community, and fidelity is highly valued. Since there is no belief in death as such, and Rastafarians view life as eternal, moving from one generation to the next through spiritual and genealogical inheritance, there are no special ceremonies on death, or following death. Many Rastafarians follow the customs of the communities in which they reside. In 1954, Jamaican authorities destroyed the Rastafarian Pinnacle commune and Rastafarians were humiliated by having their sacred dreadlocks cut-off. This makes it amply clear that many religious sects that may appear to be paganistic are actually quite contrarily similar to the anti-pagan, Judaic religions, especially, Christianity.

DHARMA

One can start by noting that none of the pagan systems has a self-given name; they have to be described by something like "local tradition" when outsiders need to talk about them. This is exactly the reason behind the coinage of the word Hindu, a pejorative Persian word meaning "the contemptible Indian" distinguishing such a contemptible Indian from "Hindi" who is just a resident of India. In the Maithilī play *Pārijātaharaṇa* by Umapati Upadhyaya, King Hariharadeva, a chieftain in Mithilā who reigned in the first quarter of the fourteenth century CE (common era, normally four centuries after the crucifixion of Christ, or since the Council of Constantine at Myciea), is repeatedly called *pati* or, the protector of the Hindus. This was done in full knowledge of the pejorative semantics of the word; the Maithila poet Vidyāpati, 75 years later, in his *Kīrtilatā*, records in graphic detail, the insults associated with the label when deployed by the Turk.

In the medieval literature, "Hindu" and "Turk" are two distinctive socio-religious units and by the time the British Crown came to establish a government after 1857, "Hindu" and "Muslim" had become fully established markers of religious differentials and negotiated in the co-operative–competitive games of political and social engineering. The question of harmony was founded in the differentials in the practice of the religion and the secular socio-economic attributes that religious affiliation brought along with it and not at the level of the theoretical. While a superficial and elusive "unity of thought" was never pushed out of picture, there was an agreement on economic and humanitarian ground realities and a kind of working consensus that barely tolerated co-existence. This is well summarized in the words of Pratap Narayan Mishra, a staunch nationalist in the eyes of contemporary historians of nineteenth-century Hindi literature, as follows:

> Hindu and Muslim are two arms of the Mother India. One arm can never be happy by trying to chop off the other.

This is perhaps not "harmony" since there is no insistence on a fundamentally orchestrated music. But it is a happy metaphor for the logic of "co-dwelling" on the principle of mere friendliness.

Conclusion

In the above light it can be said that there is hope in the study of religion if the Tyranny of Truth can be discarded. At present the harmony *mantra*s seem to emphasize that all religions are positively willed by God and the purpose of ecumenical dialogues is to make a Christian a better Christian, a Hindu a better Hindu and so on. This smacks of religious indifferentism to many and certainly leaves no room for those who do not believe in a Creator and Controller. This is no place to detail out an account of philosophies; suffice it to say that the majorities of Indian philosophical systems do not postulate a God and as such, will always be unreachable by religions willed by God. If no deep transformation of data is attempted, if no re-semanticization is imposed, if people are left to their spiritual demonstrations, social or individual, without interference from a holding company of Merchants of Truth, in short, if de-paganization drives cease and desist, then there is hope. Otherwise, an interfaith co-operative is likely to turn into a corporation-merger game seeking to globalize in order to wipe out localities.

3

Culture, Institutions and the Contemporary Ecological Crisis

Satish K. Jain

PASSENGER pigeon used to be one of the most numerous of birds in the north American continent.[1] The European colonizers describing the abundance of passenger pigeons used expressions like "beyond number or imagination."[2] John Audubon encountered an immensely large flock of passenger pigeons on a journey in 1813.[3] The European settlers slaughtered passenger pigeons in large numbers for meat and

---

1. According to Schorger (1955) as quoted by Catling (2001): "Passenger pigeons occurred throughout much of eastern North America. Only a few centuries ago their population density was 5-6 birds/acre and the total population was 3 to 5 billion. It comprised 25-40 % of the total bird population in the U.S. at the time."

   "One of the larger breeding colonies in Wisconsin in 1871 was 125 miles long and 6-8 miles wide, and was estimated to include well over 100 million adults. Yes, truly, 'the Passenger Pigeon (Ectopistes migratorius) moved around and nested in such enormous numbers as to confound the senses.'" [Schorger (1955)].

2. See "Extinction of the American Passenger Pigeon: The True Story", http://www.wildbirds.org/apidesay.htm, based on Forbush (1917).

3. "In the autumn of 1813, I left my house at Henderson, on the banks of the Ohio, on my way to Louisville. In passing over the Barrens a few miles beyond Hardensburgh, I observed the

→

fat. The most destructive of the devices which were used was that of the net. Large numbers were trapped under them and killed. The extension of railroads and telegraph lines enabled the netters to follow the birds wherever they went. Pigeons were pursued from one nesting place to another, netters sometimes following the birds a thousand miles at one move. The passenger pigeon became extinct in 1914 when the last of them died. A concatenation of factors doomed the bird. While deforestation reduced their numbers greatly, market forces reinforced by the newly discovered technology brought the bird to the brink of extinction. Even then the bird might have been saved from extinction if the appropriate legislative measures had been enacted.[4]

Today the situation is much grimmer. Many species have already become extinct. Thousands of species are on endangered lists. The concatenation of factors which brought about the extinction of the passenger pigeon is not only very much there, but many times more powerful.

→ Pigeons flying from north-east to south-west, in greater numbers than I thought I had ever seen them before, . . . Before sunset I reached Louisville, distant from Hardensburgh fifty-five miles. The Pigeons were still passing in undiminished numbers, and continued to do so for three days in succession."

According to Wenninger (1910), "This bird was once exceedingly common, so common that reports on the number of this pigeon contained in some of the treatises on Ornithology of the last century, are little short of fabulous. In 1813, the celebrated Audubon observed a flock of passenger pigeons numbering at least 1,115,000,000 individuals."

4. Wenninger (1910) writes: "This author also concludes with a reference to the growing scarcity of the bird. 'The vast numbers of this pigeon' he writes, 'have greatly diminished during recent years and now the bird is on the verge of extinction. It is certain that unless laws are made for its protection, its extermination is only a matter of time.' "

On passenger pigeon generally see Audubon (1831), Forbush (1917), Kalm (1911), McGee (1910), Schorger (1955) and Wenninger (1910) among others.

There can be little doubt that millions of individuals are deeply concerned about the contemporary environmental and ecological crisis; and have been so for several decades now. The concern and disquiet that large numbers of people have been feeling do not, however, seem to have made any dent in the situation. In fact, in all its facets the crisis seems to be becoming more severe, and at an accelerating pace. The main purpose of this article is to analyse the reasons because of which concerns about the ecological and environmental crisis are unable to bring about any meaningful change in the situation. It would be argued in the article that the main causes of the contemporary crisis are to be sought in the culture underlying the conception of modernity; and that although not a cause of the crisis, market, as it has emerged in the contemporary times, is the chief factor propelling the crisis.

As in social contexts, concerns of individuals are invariably mediated through institutions, first one must enquire whether there is something in the very nature of modern institutions which makes articulation of environmental and ecological concerns ineffective. A careful consideration of the nature of modern institutions, in relation to the environmental and ecological crisis, shows that such indeed is the case. Thus at one level one can treat the crisis as a case of institutional failure. In this article it would be argued that causes of this institutional failure are in their essence mainly cultural.

The article is organized in two sections. Section 1 looks at institutions from the perspective of individual preferences and values. The term "culture" in this article is used in a specific and somewhat technical sense. Section 2 is concerned with spelling out its relationship with the environmental and ecological crisis.

Preferences, Values and Institutions

One of the most natural ways of looking at institutions is to regard them as ensembles of rules within which the individuals in the society must act. While individuals are motivated to act in accordance with their values and preferences; their actual actions to a certain extent depend on the institutions which define the framework of rules. The actions of individuals determine the social outcomes that result. The social outcomes that result as a consequence of individual actions can be analysed from various perspectives. One perspective is that of values; one could ask which social values are satisfied by the outcomes and which are not. One could also look at the outcomes from the perspective of their responsiveness to individual values and preferences.

An institution could give rise to outcomes which are responsive without necessarily doing so invariably. That is to say, for some configurations of individual values and preferences and under certain conditions the institution in question could give rise to responsive outcomes; while for some other configurations or for the same configurations but under different conditions, could give rise to non-responsive outcomes. The institution of market is highly responsive to individual values and preferences provided the preferences and values are backed by money. If a set of preferences and values are not backed by money they would have no impact whatsoever on the market outcome. Market, like any other institution, filters in only some kinds of preferences and values under certain circumstances and filters out the remainder. If left to market, few individuals bent upon destroying biodiversity, for whatever reasons, would have greater decisiveness on the eventual outcome than a large number of people interested in ensuring survival of species if resources at the command of the former are greater than those at the command of the latter. The number of individuals who were netters and who so relentlessly pursued passenger pigeons to extinction was surprisingly small. According to one estimate, in 1860 there were between 400 and 1000 netters. The number of people who were concerned about dwindling numbers of passenger pigeons in 1860 is highly unlikely to have been as small as a thousand. According to a BBC report, in a single year 26,000 sq. km. of Amazonia had been cleared.[5] It is obvious that the numbers involved in the deforestation are much smaller compared to those who feel strongly about the preservation of Amazon rainforests.

In the context of the institution of the market not everyone counts equally. The importance that one has in the market is proportional to the amount of money that one has at one's command. Market is a peculiar kind of democracy where the number of votes one is allowed to cast is equal to the number of dollars that one has. When the domain of market expands, the importance of those with poor command over resources, no matter how numerous, declines. The victims of ecological and environmental devastation are not confined to non-human species only. Poor people the world over suffer the harmful effects of the environmental degradation. Expansion of the domain of market is thus resulting in the shrinking of the domain of ecological justice.

As mentioned earlier, although individuals motivated by their values and preferences can be expected to act in accordance with them, their actual actions would depend on the institutional framework within which they are constrained to act. If individuals are deciding on their actions within the framework of responsive institutions then they can be expected to act in accordance with their values and preferences. On the other hand, if the institutions are non-responsive it makes little difference as to what individuals do. In the context of non-responsive institutions it would not be a particularly good idea to make inferences from the observed choices of individuals regarding the individuals' values and preferences. If the institutions in question are

---

5. According to the figures released by the Brazilian government, 26,000 sq km of forest were chopped down in the 12 months prior to August 2004, which means almost a fifth of the entire Amazon has now been cut down. See "Amazon Destruction Accelerating" by Steve Kingstone, *BBC News*, Brazil, dated 19 May 2005.

perverse, one could even expect behaviour contrary to the actual preferences and values.

From the above, two points seem clear. In general, different institutions are required for proper articulation of different values and preferences. One institution might do an excellent job of articulating one kind of preferences and values; a second institution for another kind of preferences and values. Even for the same preferences and values different institutions might be optimal under different circumstances. Secondly, individual actions can differ widely depending on the institutional framework, even though the underlying motivational preferences and values remain constant. Market may or may not be the most appropriate institution for articulation of preferences and values of economic kind; but there can be no doubt that it is completely inappropriate for articulation of values and preferences relating to environment. An institutional framework which has been responsible for ecological and environmental degradation in the first place cannot be expected to articulate concerns relating to preservation of species. If an activity, destructive of habitat of a species, is more profitable than alternative avenues for investment, then the profit motive would result in the undertaking of the activity and the consequent destruction of the habitat of the species. The only way to stop the activity within the institutional framework of market is to persuade the person contemplating undertaking of the activity not to undertake it by compensating him for the profits forgone. But, given the fact that it is a fundamental characteristic of the modern economic system that almost all activities which are economic value-creating are also at the same time destructive of the environment, it follows that persuasion by compensation is a non-starter. The question of finding solutions to ecological and environmental problems within the institutional framework of the market does not arise. The possibilities for finding solutions can emerge only if the domain of the market is made to shrink.

So far we have been discussing institutions as sets of rules.

The institutions can also be viewed as embodiments of values. After all institutions are created for some definite purposes. To identify the embodied values with the purposive considerations would, however, in general, be not correct. There could be many reasons for the divergence between the objectives for the fulfilment of which the institution in question is supposed to exist and the embodied values. From our point of view, the most important reason has to do with possibly the most profound characteristic of institutions that the realized values under them can never be invariant with respect to the values and preferences of individuals who interact within their framework. For instance, when individuals act according to their assigned roles the results are quite different from when they act solely in their self-interest. The values which would materialize if all judges gave judgements solely on the basis of law and evidence are bound to be different from those which would if they gave judgements to further their own self-interests. In this connection an interesting question arises, namely: On what basis does an individual decide whether she or he would act in accordance with the assigned role or act in accordance with her or his self-regarding preferences and interests?

So far we have been taking individual preferences and values as given; and have only considered how they are mediated through the societal institutions. Needless to say, this is only an analytical simplification. Social institutions have a profound influence on individuals in relation to the formation of preferences and values. If a social institution is of great importance in the social order, the values that the institution embodies are bound to have significance for individual values and preferences. The institution of market puts completely selfish behaviour on a high pedestal. In the marketplace only those who have imbibed the spirit of competitiveness and are capable of ruthlessness and predation of a high order are likely to succeed; not those with full of sympathy and compassion for their fellow human beings or for living things in general. It is of course perfectly possible for a person to be selfish in one domain; and altruistic in another. But if the society is so structured that its pre-eminent institutions encourage completely selfish behaviour, then it is quite likely that many individuals, if not all, would internalize the motto of completely selfish behaviour to such an extent that even in the context of institutions where they are supposed to act in accordance with their assigned roles, they may not be able to do so. Thus one possible answer to the question which was posed at the end of the last paragraph is that whether individuals by and large would act in accordance with their assigned roles or in accordance with their self-regarding preferences to a large extent depends on the nature of the dominant institutions of the society. If the dominant institutions of the society are such that they encourage self-regarding behaviour, then one can expect that individuals on the whole would not act according to the assigned roles. The dominance of the market in the contemporary context then has the implication that in the context of non-market institutions as well we should expect from most individuals self-regarding behaviour even though the design of these institutions might be such that their successful functioning depended on individuals performing their assigned roles, and not acting in their narrow self-interests.

Thus we see that there is a symbiotic relationship between institutions on the one hand and individual values and preferences on the other. The nature of an institution is partly determined by individual preferences and values. The most important determinant of the character of an institution is whether individuals act in accordance with their assigned roles or whether they act in accordance with their self-interests. Institutions on the other hand impact individual preferences and values in two different ways. Institutions, by filtering in some preferences and values and filtering out the others, determine which preferences and values would be articulated and which would not be. The preferences and values which are filtered out and consequently do not find articulation are bound to become insignificant sooner or later, if not disappear altogether. Secondly, the formation of individual values and preferences themselves is profoundly affected by the values embodied in the institutions, particularly those which are dominant.

In the light of this way of looking at institutions we can see the several distinct ways in which the institution of market is contributing to the environmental and ecological crisis. These are: (i) market filters in values and preferences which are environmentally and ecologically destructive and filters out those conducive for preserving the environment and the ecological balance; (ii) the dominance of market tends to weaken the pro-environment values and preferences; and (iii) the dominance of the market paradigm is also resulting in more and more individuals acting, in the context of non-market institutions, including those having relevance from the perspective of preservation of species and their habitats, in accordance with their narrow self-interests rather than in accordance with their assigned roles, even though acting in accordance with the assigned roles might be crucial for the proper functioning of these institutions.

What has been said here about the institution of the market holds also for those institutions which have been designed to facilitate the working of the market and for those which have been transformed because of the ascendancy of the market paradigm so as to mimic the market.

Culture and Values

The two-way relationship between individual values and preferences on the one hand and institutions on the other, consisting of institutions playing a significant role in the formation of individual values and preferences and individual values and preferences partly determining the character of institutions, does not mean that the equilibrium of individual and social values which would obtain under a particular set of institutions would necessarily be unique. A particular set of institutions in general can co-exist with quite different equilibria of individual and social values. This naturally raises very important questions: What determines as to which equilibrium of individual and social values would materialize? Is it a matter of chance as to which equilibrium is arrived at; or is there something which systematically determines as to which equilibrium would be realized? The position that is taken in this article is that the equilibrium of social and individual values in its ultimate analysis is culturally determined.

The expression "culture" is used in many different and divergent senses. The usages of the expression vary widely in scope as well. Some uses of the word are so wide in scope as to be almost synonymous with civilization; and some are so narrow that they mean nothing more than some aspect or the other of aesthetics. In this article the expression "culture" is used in a specific and precise sense. The meaning which would be attributed to the expression is elaborated in what follows. It is possible to argue that the meaning which is attributed to the expression here captures our intuitive understanding of the social category of culture better than other ways of defining the expression.

A profound fact about values is that the acceptance of a value does not determine its domain of application. Most values can be applied with widely differing domains. The importance of determining the domains of values arises from the fact that whether one considers a single individual or the society as a whole, there are competing values. A value may be able to co-exist with some values but not with some others. Some values can coexist with each other in some circumstances but not under some other circumstances.

For determining the domains of various values a meta-principle is required. The viewpoint which is taken in this article is that the social category of culture performs this role of a meta-principle. Thus, "culture" can be defined as that social category which determines the domains of different values, the expression "value" being defined sufficiently broadly to encompass all criteria for making judgemental and evaluative statements. To put it somewhat differently, it is the culture which is the ultimate determinant of what is considered as appropriate and what as inappropriate.

Take for instance the right of an individual to act in her or his self-interest or the right of a collective or a society to take measures for enhancing its material prosperity. Few would deny such a right. But it is not so much the question of asserting or denying the right which is important. Rather, the really crucial question concerns the scope of this right. Is one's right to act in one's own interests so wide that one can treat non-human living creatures in any manner whatsoever without any moral compunction? Are all non-human creatures to be treated as mere resources? Does the objective of finding a cure for some human ailment justify the most gruesome and devilish experiments on animals including primates? Does an increase in GDP justify measures which would lead to extinction of many species?

Although anthropocentric thinking, viewing of all non-human creatures as mere resources being an integral part of it, is nowadays very widespread, if not universal, it would be a serious error to think that it is either natural or common to all cultures. In fact the culture underlying the modernity is unique from this perspective. While non-modern cultures differed widely in their attitudes towards non-human living beings, there was none which reduced all non-human life forms to mere resources to be used by humanity in any manner whatsoever as does the culture underlying the modernity. No non-modern culture ever assigned such a wide domain to self-interest as is taken for granted by most nowadays.

Although American Indians also used passenger pigeons for meat and fat as did the European settlers, the Indians of Canada did not molest the pigeons in their breeding places until the young were able to fly. They did everything in their power to prevent the whites from disturbing them, even using threats, where pleading proved to be of no avail. It is highly probable that if the European settlers had exploited the passenger pigeon within the bounds set by the American

Indians, the extinction of the species might not have taken place.

The culture underlying the modernity is unique not only from the perspective of regarding all non-human life forms as mere resources but also for not putting any value to ecological integrity over and above its usefulness to humankind. One of the clearest statements of this viewpoint is to be found in Coase's paper "The problem of social cost":[6]

> To give another example, Professor George J. Stigler instances the contamination of a stream. If we assume that the harmful effect of the pollution is that it kills the fish, the question to be decided is: is the value of the fish lost greater or less than the value of the product which the contamination of the stream makes possible.

Although the non-modern cultures differed widely in the extent they accorded intrinsic value to the idea of ecological integrity, as they did with respect to the stringency of norms that they developed for the treatment of animals, none regarded the concept of ecological integrity to be as devoid of intrinsic significance as does the culture underlying modernity. In fact, in some ancient texts the notion of ecological integrity has been put on such a high pedestal that all acts of contamination of waters, whether of seas, rivers, lakes or springs, have been uniformly declared as ignoble. In almost all non-modern cultures one can find an unbroken thread of imputing intrinsic value to the idea of ecological integrity, even if such imputation did not hold sway at all times of these cultures' periods of significant influence.

It is remarkable that some ancient Indian texts of Āyurveda where the curative properties of many animal products are discussed, not to speak of regarding animals as mere resources, are quite emphatic in proclaiming the essential unity and similarity of all life. Vāgbhaṭṭa, the author

---

6. This enormously influential paper by Coase is one of the most cited papers in economics as well as in law; and is an important building block of the market ideology.

of the great Āyurvedic classic *Aṣṭāṅga Hṛdayam*, says that one should not consider even insects as insignificant; all life forms should be treated on an equal footing.

Two different, although interrelated, aspects of actions for furthering material prosperity need to be distinguished: How high one evaluates such actions morally; and whether undertaking of them has the implication of abandonment of values in conflict with them. It is possible that the actions for furthering material prosperity are not at the expense of any important value; in which case viewing of these actions favourably does not pose any difficulty. The actions for furthering material prosperity could also be at the expense of some important value; in which case while one can understand the rationale of the actions one does not have to view them approvingly. For instance, the development of a particular way of life might have made consumption of animal products an integral part of human diet; but this does not alter the moral considerations. Necessity or inevitability of something does not necessarily render it moral or praiseworthy. The moral clarity, in this context, in Yudhiṣṭhira's reflections in *Mahābhārata* on the treatment of animals is extraordinary.

The most remarkable aspect of the modern value system is twofold: Not only are there no limits as to what one can do to animals for the sake of material prosperity, but all such acts are praiseworthy. Activities which result in material prosperity belong to the highest pedestal; individuals undertaking such activities being worthy of the highest approbation.

If one reflects on the question why the modernity considers even the most abominable treatment of animals as morally permissible, it seems probable that the anthropocentric morality in its ultimate analysis might be found to be based on power. Because man has ascendancy over animals, has power over them of life and death; no matter what he does to them it can never be immoral. Because animals are inferior in power, they are also morally inferior. It is inconceivable that a being inferior in power could be morally superior. It was possible for Yudhiṣṭhira to reflect on moral wrongs committed by man on animals; but such a possibility does not exist within the cultural framework of modernity.

The logic underlying the culture of modernity is of course bound to find expression in the context of intra-humanity interactions as well. One who has truly imbibed the culture of modernity is unlikely to be squeamish about treating fellow human beings that one considers to be inferior to oneself in repugnant ways. The same considerations which make any treatment whatsoever of animals morally justified could make any treatment whatsoever of certain sections of humanity morally justified. As one does not have any sense of guilt when one commits an act of abuse against an animal; one does not feel guilty at mistreating a *homo sapiens* of an inferior kind. It is the animals who are morally inferior; and those of *homo sapiens* of inferior kind. Jeffrey Amherst, the commanding general of British forces in North America during the final battles of the French & Indian war (1754-63), is infamous for deliberately planning genocide of Indians by getting blankets meant for Indians infected with smallpox. An application of the contemporary international law would find him beyond any doubt guilty of acts of genocide. The letters written by him are highly revealing. Not only does he not exhibit any sense of guilt but his belief in his own moral superiority notwithstanding the utterly contemptible actions that he was planning and in the moral inferiority of his unsuspecting victims seems to be rock solid. In his letter to Colonel Henry Bouquet, dated 16 July 1763, he approves the plan of infecting blankets in a postscript and also suggests "to try Every other method that can serve to Extirpate this Execrable Race."[7]

7. In the letter to Sir William Johnson, Superintendent of the Northern Indian Department dated 9 July 1763, Amherst talks of ". . . Measures to be taken as would Bring about the Total Extirpation of those Indian Nations," and in the letter to George →

Jeffrey Amherst's case might be an extreme one. But, it would be a mistake to treat him as an aberration. In some ways his actions and attitudes are more representative of the culture underlying modernity than may seem to be the case at first glance. The genocidal character of modernity, in all its aspects, is an integral part of the culture which underlies it; although the character of the contemporary discourse is such that it is almost impossible to bring it into sharp focus. The nature of the contemporary discourse is so much constrained that even those who are concerned about the devastations brought about by the enormously powerful processes currently transforming the world are forced to invoke the very values of the modernity for expressing their

---

→ Croghan, Deputy Agent for Indian Affairs dated 7 August 1763, he says that ". . . their Total Extirpation is scarce sufficient Attonement. . . ." On Jeffrey Amherst's genocidal intents and acts see Dowd (2002), Fenn (2000, 2001), Nester (2000), Parkman (1886), Stannard (1993) and Thornton (1987) among others.

In her major study Fenn (2000) has argued that in eighteenth-century America biological warfare was far more widespread than has been believed hitherto. She says: "Our preoccupation with Amherst has kept us from recognizing that accusations of what we now call biological warfare — the military use of smallpox in particular — arose frequently in eighteenth-century America. Native Americans, moreover, were not the only accusers. By the second half of the century, many of the combatants in America's wars of empire had the knowledge and technology to attempt biological warfare with the smallpox virus. Many also adhered to a code of ethics that did not constrain them from doing so. Seen in this light, the Amherst affair becomes not so much an aberration as part of a larger continuum in which accusations and discussions of biological warfare were common, and actual incidents may have occurred more frequently than scholars have previously acknowledged."

According to historian David Stannard "The destruction of the Indians of the Americas was, far and away, the most massive act of genocide in the history of the world." Stannard's estimate of native Americans who were killed is about 100 million.

concerns which in the first place are responsible for these devastations.

A perusal of the literature dealing with the issues relating to extinction of species currently going on with alarming rapidity shows that the most important and frequently made argument for the need to take urgent steps to halt this process of extinction consists of contending that the humanity would lose out much in terms of possibilities forgone of industrial and medical uses which could be made of the extant but endangered species. It is the anthropocentric values which in the first place have resulted in the grave ecological crisis. Then how can one expect the invocation of the very same values to rectify the situation? The current ecological crisis is of extreme gravity and requires urgent and concerted actions. But they can be forthcoming only if the cultural paradigm underlying the modernity is rejected first. Mahatma Gandhi in his *Hind Swaraj* was quite categorical that nothing less than a complete rejection of modernity would do. The complete rejection of modernity today appears to be even more necessary and pressing than it was almost a century ago when *Hind Swaraj* was written.

References

Audubon, J.J., *Ornithological Biography*, vol. 1, Philadelphia: J. Dobson, 1831.

Catling, Paul M., "Extinction and the Importance of History and Dependence in Conservation", *Biodiversity*, 2(3), 2001.

Coase, R.H., "The Problem of Social Cost", *Journal of Law and Economics*, 3, 1-44, 1960.

Dowd, Gregory Evans, *War Under Heaven: Pontiac, the Indian Nations, & the British Empire*, Baltimore: Johns Hopkins, 2002.

Ellsworth, Joshua W. and Brenda C. McComb, "Potential Effects of Passenger Pigeon Flocks on the Structure and Composition of Presettlement Forests of Eastern North America", *Conservation Biology*, vol. 17, no. 6, 1548-58, December 2003.

Farrow, Scott, "Extinction and Market Forces: Two Case Studies", *Ecological Economics*, 13, 115-23, 1995.

Fenn, Elizabeth Anne, "Biological Warfare in Eighteenth-Century North

America: Beyond Jeffery Amherst", *Journal of American History*, 86, 1552-80, March 2000.

———, *Pox Americana: The Great Smallpox Epidemic of 1775-82*, New York: Hill and Wang, 2001.

Forbush, Edward Howe, "Passenger Pigeon: Ectopistses Migratorius (Linnaeus)" in *Game Birds, Wild-Fowl and Shore Birds*, Massachusetts Board of Agriculture, reprinted in *Birds of America*, T. Gilbert Pearson, Editor-in-chief, The University Society Inc., 39-46, 1917.

Kalm, P., "A Description of the Wild Pigeons Which Visit the Southern English Colonies in North America, during Certain Years, in Incredible Multitudes", Auk, 28, 53-66, 1911.

McDaniel, C.N. and J.M. Gowdy, "Markets and Biodiversity Loss: Some Case Studies and Policy Considerations", *The International Journal of Social Economics*, 25, 1454-65, 1998.

McGee, W.J., "Notes on the Passenger Pigeon", *Science*, New Series, vol. 32, no. 835, 958-64, 1910.

Nester, William R., *Haughty Conquerors: Amherst and the Great Indian Uprising of 1763*, Westport: Praeger Publishers, 2000.

Parkman, Francis, *The Conspiracy of Pontiac and the Indian War after the Conquest of Canada*, Boston: Little Brown, 1886.

Schorger, A.W., *The Passenger Pigeon: Its Natural History and Extinction*, Madison: University of Wisconsin Press, 1955.

Stannard, David E., *American Holocaust: The Conquest of the New World*, New York: Oxford University Press, 1993.

Thornton, Russell, *American Indian Holocaust and Survival: A Population History since 1492*, Norman: University of Oklahoma Press, 1987.

Wenninger, F.J., "The Passenger Pigeon", *American Midland Naturalist*, vol. 1, no. 8, 227-28, 1910.

4

Power, Culture and Civil Society
The Context of India

Anand Kumar

THE concept of civil society has become academically active since the economic liberalization and the consequent globalization in 1991. It has found a respectful location in the context of the debates about modernization of Indian society, the nature of Indian state, liberalization, social movements, political culture, globalization, rise of market forces in mediating social changes, and the quest for justice among women, the dalits, and the other marginal groups. While the concept of civil society has its origins in the philosophy of Hegel, yet it is used in India for quite the opposite political purpose. While Hegel imagined that the civil society would be a space where the individuals would emanate out of their particular contexts into universal beings in the public space, in India, we use civil society more as something that helps guard particular identities against the sweeping universalization of the modern State. Historically, the *bhakti* movement where individuals rose above caste and language differences and mingled into the sect was essentially a Hegelian movement. Even in the Freedom Struggle, Gandhi inspired Indians to emerge from the socio-economic particularities and participate in the vast public space of anti-colonial struggle. Civil society, as a means to protect particular identities from being submerged into the universalism of undifferentiated citizenship, is a recent feature in Indian politics.

The idea of "civil society" is a good conceptual catalyst in the present Indian context partly because it has generated an interesting debate that looks beyond the usual dichotomies of tradition and modernity, class and caste, interest and identity, and nation building and globalizations. Besides, the concept has also created a new capacity of expression for those who are disenchanted by the "brutality" of the post colonial state, "consumerism and co-modification" due to market forces, "loss of identity" due to modernization, "failures" of representative democracy, and "homogenizing" pressures of the nation-state. Discussions around civil society have provided anchorage to the critiques of post colonial state and proponents of "identity politics," and it has also created space for the radical social activists who were looking towards something to take over the role of the State after the end of Soviet socialism, shift in the Chinese regime towards marketization, and loss of legitimacy of Nehru-Indira Gandhi approach of putting state in charge of ensuring economic equality and development.

The paper suggests that the idea of civil society in India became very powerful during the Independence Movement. It was also during this time that civil society had, for the time being, lost much of its discursive charm in Europe. Let us look at *Hind Swarāj* (1998) by Mohandas Karamchand Gandhi, which is an authentic text for the proponents of the Indian version of the idea of "civil society." It is rooted in the idea of "civilization" which is defined as moral order for the elevation of moral being in everyone everywhere through "good conduct" based upon self-control, and not the fear of any external agency, particularly state or faith order.

It is also suggested that the Indian version of the concept of civil society continued to play a vital role after Independence as "Lok Swarāj," an antinomy of the state-centric projects of modernization and "development." It was employed to stress decentralization and communitarian democracy. But it had limited appeal due to the overwhelming legitimacy and infatuation that the Indians had with the idea of a nation based upon a strong State where the State would lead an urban-centric, factory oriented and high technology dependent industrialization. Such an idea of the nation required the convergence of the visions of the capitalists and communists, upper caste and lower castes, urban elite and rural poor all of whom wanted to grow economically prosperous and be modernized too.

The Indian version of the concept of civil society had its own distinct features in terms of its own definitions of —

(a) human beings as essentially equipped with capacity of moral evolution and goodness,

(b) society as a system in existence due to love force and not fear of the king or God,

(c) religions as a code of good conduct rather than a body of rigid rituals and identity patterns, and

(d) Western civilization as a non-sustainable godless way of life that revolved around greed and possessions of material things. It aimed at "de-colonization" of the Indian society so that the path towards real freedom gets unfolded, and demystification of the old state-centric models of "good governance" and market and machine-oriented approaches of "progress." In that sense, it had limited "genetic" affinity with the Hegelian orientation about the concept of civil society. But it shared the historical context and intellectual agenda of the European thinkers associated with it as it was an engagement to find the possibility of a social order beyond the family and the state but also without princes and priests.

Let us take the path of "culture" to make sense of the relevance and necessity of developing intermediate institutions between the priest and the prince in the Indian context as articulated in *Hind Swarāj*.

To begin with, Gandhi saw historical continuity between divine kingship (chief priest of the state) and its secular version of totalitarian states of the twentieth century. He saw them as two faces of the same culture engaged in a journey from unity of God and king to nation and ruler. Secondly, Gandhi recognized the delinking between God (and His way — religion) and the king (an alien who got implanted through ungodly ways) in the colonial order of things; thus, here was a separation between the ruler and the nation as the two belonged to two separate civilizations and streams of culture. He offers an explanation in *Hind Swarāj* in three parts; first, there is the definition of civilization. Then there is explanation of the differences between the civilizations of India and Britain, the latter of which represents the West as a whole. Finally, there is a suggestion of unity between the East and the West.

What is civilization? To quote Gandhi, "civilization is that mode of conduct which points out to man the path of duty. Performance of duty and observance of morality are convertible terms. To observe morality is to attain mastery over mind and our passions." The Gujarati equivalent for civilization means "good conduct."

If so, then what is the difference between the king's/ state's civilizational orientation and that of the nation and its people in a colonial setting? Gandhi says, "In no part of the world, and under no civilization, have all men attained perfection. The tendency of Indian civilization is to elevate the moral being, and that of the Western civilization (read "modern industrial") is to promote immorality. The latter is godless; the former is based on belief in God."

Furthermore, he makes a significant clarification about his concept of "the Western civilization" and its "specimens" ruling over India. This clarification has been missed by a variety of scholars and activists while analysing Gandhi on the issue of "Western civilization." He wrote,

> You English who have come to India are not good specimens of the English nation, nor can we, almost half Anglicized Indians, be considered good specimens of the real Indian nation. If the

> English nation were to know all you have done, it would oppose many of your actions. The masses of Indians have had few dealings with you. If you will abandon your so-called civilization and search into your own scriptures, you will find that our demands are just. Only on condition of our demands being fully satisfied may you remain in India; and if you remain under those conditions, we shall have learnt several things from you and you will learn many from us; so doing we shall benefit each other and the world. But this will happen only when the root of our relationship is sunk in a religious soil.

This distancing from the colonial state and its civilizational (cultural) project was not a call for return to the religious dogmas of "Hindutva." It was a rejection of the total range of modern state patterns, including the mode of governance adopted by the Indian princes. Thus Gandhi actuated the Indian perspective about the need of universalistic civilizational endeavour for evolution of a moral way of dealing with each other as human beings and nations on the basis of "good conduct" and "human duty." It was synonymous with *dharma* but too wise to be confined to any particular faith-community and its sectarian beliefs, institutions, and practice (including Hindu, Muslim, Christian and Parsees). Therefore, it may be termed as the recognition of universality of a religious soil or moral universal space that existed between or beyond state and family or prince and priests for a joyful togetherness of all human beings in society.

The Indian discourse on power and authority, as evolved in the colonial era mainly through the debate on Gandhian propositions and mobilizations, was not in convergence with the Hobbesean view of the modern state. According to Hobbes, the possibility of good governance and progress is contingent upon the surrender of liberty by all members of society to the law and the sovereign state and their instruments. But it was contradicted by the colonial state as well as the anti-colonial national movements in India. It demonstrated that there is always a threat to the human freedoms from the modern state as well. The modern state has the capacity and tendency to get engaged in partisan, alienating and brutish ways. Therefore a better form of governance has to be evolved through cultivation of the art and science of truth and non-violence. Here the citizens would have to be always vigilant about both the self and the state.

Gandhi mistrusted the monopoly of brute force and exclusive command over the means of violence enjoyed by the modern state in the name of maintaining and promoting "common good" and "national interest." He recognized the perpetual conflict between the state and the community of citizens when the homogenized laws hegemonized and objectified the diverse reality in which citizens lived. He argued for the critical significance of the need to learn to "rule ourselves" and not be ruled by the state, whether brute or benign. He argued for the need to have space for civil disobedience in a sharp contrast to the Hobbesean advocacy of "surrender of liberty to state and its law." He was not alone in his apprehensions as Tolstoy and Thoreau preceded him in doubting the capacity of the modern state in creating a humane social order on its own. For Gandhi and his fellow thinkers, *Swarāj* or freedom was a state of benign fearlessness on the basis of good conduct through truth and non-violence. He wanted human societies to be free of all forms of brute force, from lawless kings to the modern democratic states.

Gandhi has stated "it is *Swarāj*, when we learn to rule ourselves." Otherwise a set of new fear-generating instruments and persons, including natives, will replace the prevailing set of foreign bodies. He found an echo of his concerns in the position of Mazzini and a contradiction in the approach of Garibaldi — the two outstanding symbols of nationalism from Italy at the end of the nineteenth-century world system. Both were committed to the Italian quest of freedom from the Austrian yoke. The Austrian troops had to withdraw because of the resistance by the nationalist forces of Italy. But afterwards the gain for the ordinary citizens was only nominal because the reins of government went into the hands of the King of Italy and his henchmen. Gandhi stressed that

> My patriotism does not teach me that I am allowed to let people be crushed under the heels of Indian princes if only the English retire. If I have the power, I should resist the tyranny of Indian princes just as much as those of the English. We have to learn and to teach others, that we do not want the tyranny of either English or Indian rule.

He used the metaphor of "servants" to contrast with the prevalent notion of "rulers" to underline his concept of the role of the state and its functionaries in the affairs of society.

How can this be carried out on a large scale when it may have never occurred before in history? The Gandhian response is in two parts. First of all he wants the human mind to transcend the limits of historical experiences in its quest for a sane society. He states that "To believe that what has not occurred in history will not occur at all is to argue disbelief in the dignity of man. At any rate it behoves us to try what appeals to our reason."[8] Secondly, the idea of human freedom or *Swarāj* (a concept which is equidistant from the tyranny of the state as well as false religious forces at one level and from brute force-based rule of alien and indigenous rulers) is achievable through a fourfold path:

(i) Real Home Rule is self-rule or self-control.

(ii) The way to it is passive resistance; that is soul force or love force.

(iii) In order to assert this force, *svadeśī* in every sense is necessary.

(iv) What we want to do should be done, not because we object to the English or because we want to retaliate but because it is our duty to do so.

Let me summarize the discussion about the emergence of an Indian contribution in recognizing the critical value of the idea of "civil society" as the basis of creating and sustaining a universalistic civilization based upon freedom and rooted in the faith in the capacity of "good conduct" by human beings in togetherness across nationalities and religious and linguistic communities. Here the "culture route" to "civil society" recognizes the particularistic role of faith system, language and territorial specificities in terms of presence of "nation" as the genuine basis of group identity. At the same time it argues for the inevitability of universalistic normative togetherness despite diversities as the basis of survival of a nation and its civilization. It rejected the idea of kings and/or priests as the guards of social order and its members. Similarly, it considered the power factors and associated inequalities, disparities, and discriminations in the context of the social spheres and their arrangements. But it urged to go beyond blind belief in the capacity of the modern state to act as the guardian of citizens and nations with brute force at its command. Instead, it suggested evolution of a way of life beyond the centrality of state. Self-control, soul force, *svadeśī* and dutifulness would be the four pillars of a free and good society.

References

Chandhoke, Neera, 1995, *State and Civil Society*, New Delhi: Sage.

Civil Society: Europe Facing Other Civilizations (outline note for the thematic part of the CiSoNet Meeting), 12-14 June 2003, MSH, and Paris.

Gandhi, M.K., 2001/1908, *Hind Swarāj* (Ahmedabad, Navjeevan Trust, 1938 edition/14th rpt.), pp. 52-55, see chapter VI, also p. 87, chapter XV and chapter XX, pp. 57, 90.

Pandey, Vikash N., 2000, "State and Civil Society: Reframing the Question in the Indian Context", in S.L. Sharma & T.K. Oommen (eds.), *Nation and National Identity in South Asia*, New Delhi: Orient Longman.

Uberoi, J.P.S., 1999, "On Civil Society", *Sociological Bulletin*, vol. 48, nos. 1-2.

Part II
Religion in India

5

Dialogical Relationship between Tribal and Non-Tribal Religion*

C.N. Venugopal

ROBERT Bellah[1] has analysed the different religions of the world from an evolutionary standpoint. Primitive religions are those in which myths provided a totalistic framework for the society: all human activities were guided by them. A unique aspect of primitive religion is that the men and women of the tribe identify themselves with their deceased ancestors during ceremonies. The primitive society is unstratified and there is an absence of a priestly class. The archaic religions such as Hinduism, Taoism and Shintoism are pantheistic. There is a difference between the priests or ritual specialists on the one hand and the common people who come to the temples for prayers. The relationship between human beings and divinity is marked by closeness. In the past, the Babylonian, Assyrian, Greek and Roman religions also had an archaic character. They share a common ground with the primitive religions by worshipping rocks, trees, water and other natural phenomena. They differ from the former because usually the priestly class is literate and there is a sacred literature.

---

* This paper was earlier published under the same title in M.C. Behera (ed.), *Tribal Religion: Change and Continuity*, New Delhi: Commonwealth, 2000.

1. Vide Roy Willis, "Evolutionary Theories of Religion" in Michael Mann (ed.), 1983, *Student Encyclopaedia of Sociology*, London: Macmillan, p. 118.

The historic religions which originated in West Asia — Judaism, Christianity and Islam — share a common ground. They all believe in monotheism and transcendentalism of the divinity. In the evolution of these "Abrahamic" religions, historical covenants have played an important role. The Prophets from Moses to Mohammed entered into communion with the transcendent god under specific historical situations. In contrast, the archaic religions do not have a specific history.

The historic religions gained ascendency in West Asia and Europe by marginalizing the older, existing religions. The Pagan cults of Assyria, Babylonia were centred around the worship of a mother goddess who was propitiated through the observance of fertility rites. The religions of Greece and Rome included planetary worship, oracle consultation and animal sacrifices in fulfilment of vows. These practices were replaced by a patriarchal social order geared to the monotheistic belief system. In contrast, the archaic religions have been more accommodative. For example, Hinduism, Taoism and Shintoism have co-existed with other religions.

Tribal Interaction with Other Groups

At the outset, it may be stated that tribal religion cannot be studied in isolation from the other religions of India. Cultural contacts, socio-economic factors and the zeal of charisma have brought them together. Hinduism, Buddhism and Christianity have influenced the tribes of India on a large scale: therefore, the focus in this article is not on tribal religion *per se* but on the composite religious culture which has emerged through a dialogical process. In the interactions between tribals and non-tribals in the sphere of beliefs and practices, some common elements have emerged. There have been tensions and rivalries in the exchange; nevertheless an integrative framework has resulted from the interaction. The dialogical process may be viewed in terms of existential, ideological and normative dimensions. The term "existential" would include historical-cultural factors such as migration, physical proximity, diffusion or other forms of contact. The term "ideological" would imply cognitive content or world view. The term "normative" would include ethical perceptions which provided the values for religion. These elements are separable only in an analytical sense and in reality they are often found together.

A number of studies done from an ethnographic or anthropological perspective have highlighted the dialogical process. T.C. Hodson's work on Meiteis of Manipur,[2] N.K. Bose's depiction of Tana Bhagat movement in tribal Bihar,[3] Surajit Sinha's study of Bhūmij kṣatriyas — a Hinduized tribal group — in West Bengal,[4] G.S. Ghurye's study of Mahadev Kolis in Maharashtra,[5] and Haimendorf's study of Gonds in Andhra Pradesh[6] have provided an understanding. A reference to the Meiteis will be in order: some time in the eighteenth century, the Rājā of Manipur got converted to Bengal Vaiṣṇavism, which centred around Sanskritic culture, bhaktism and normative prescriptions for daily living. In turn he converted his Meitei subjects to the Vaiṣṇavite path. The caste system with its hierarchic notions, purity-pollution norms was incorporated into the Meitei society. However, the Shamanistic practices of the pre-conversion phase were retained under the rubric of the Sanamahi cult. The Meiba and Meibi are the Shamans who tend sick people or foretell the future. Thus, the tribal heritage was not completely given up but modified to suit the requirements of a literate sacred culture from the plains. Till recently, Manipur Hinduism flourished and also made a notable contribution in evolving the Manipur classical dance which draws from the *bhakti* tradition of

2. T.C. Hodson, *Meiteis of Manipur*.
3. N.K. Bose, (1975), *The Structure of Hindu Society*, Delhi: Orient Longman.
4. Vide D.G. Mandelbaum, 1984, *Society in India*, Bombay: Popular Prakashan, pp. 603-10.
5. G.S. Ghurye, (1957), *Mahadev Kolis*, Bombay: Popular Prakashan.
6. C.V.F. Haimendorf, *Tribes of India*, New Delhi: Oxford University Press, pp. 175-84.

Hinduism. At present, there are dissenting voices heard in Manipur: the youth are moving away from Hinduism as many of them are keen on reviving the pre-conversion tribal past.

Christianity has made a powerful impact on the tribes of north-east, south-west and south-central India. There has been a shift from the animistic tribal past to a monotheistic, church-based religion. Although Christianity ended the tribal isolation and welded them into a universalistic group, inter-ethnic clashes among converts — for example Nāgās and Kukis — have caused political instability and economic hardship in the north-east. The adoption of patriarchy by the matrilineal Khāsīs and Gāros who converted to Christianity has also brought in tensions on different levels. Remarkable strides in education were made by tribal converts to Christianity in the north-east. Yet Church sectarianism and ethnic tensions have often come to the surface.

Islam in India did not extend its influence to tribes on a large scale. But there are folk-tribal communities such as the Meos of Rajasthan and Western U.P. (Meerut), the Gujjars of Jammu & Kashmir state and small sections of north-eastern tribes which have been converted to the Islamic way of life. Elsewhere, Islam has had a bigger impact. In North and Central Africa, Islam has had many adherents among the tribals. Usually, these Muslims are under the control of Sūfīs or Marabouts. In India most of the Muslims have been drawn from former caste groups. Even after conversion many of them have retained features such as endogamy, concern about social status, etc.

Popular Hinduism has absorbed a number of tribal elements such as animistic deities, totemic symbols, magical formulae and exorcist rites. In many caste groups across the country these elements are noticeable. The Vedic *gotra*s are few in number but there are a number of *gotra*s of tribal origin in India. Many castes in India have also a tribal origin. Manu listed only 36 castes as having been the product of *varṇa saṁkarī* (miscegenation). In fact, some of these castes were occupational in origin. How do we account for the 3,000 castes of India? The explanation lies in the tribal background of the caste system.

Among the Sherpas, Lamaist Buddhism with its high tradition of reincarnation, pursuit of the middle path and cessation of birth through the liberation from worldly bonds has co-existed with the popular magical cults, beliefs in sorcery and spirit worship. The Sherpas have also drawn from Hindu religion and caste system. There are many tribal groups in the Indian subcontinent such as Bhoṭiyā (who are allied to Sherpas) and Chakmās of East Bengal which have come under the fold of Mahāyānist Buddhism. Many of these tribes are nomadic and live in sub-montane regions.

Caste-Tribe Interactions on the Religious Plane: A Psychoanalytic Perspective

The caste-tribe interactions have varied from region to region. In the coastal part of Karnataka, there is an important Vaiṣṇavite centre called Udupi. Madhvācārya (thirteenth century) established his Vedāntic school (called "Dvaita Maṭha") here. Later in the sixteenth century Caitanya Mahāprabhu of Bengal visited the place and his own teachings were considerably influenced by this tradition. Since then this form of Vaiṣṇavism has flourished here in the midst of popular animistic cults whose focal point is the worship of spirits (called *bhūtas*). Likewise, the Śaivite centre in coastal Karnataka called Dharmasthala is also in the midst of Shamanistic cults. In fact, in this region there is a complementary relationship between the two. The *bhūtas* are believed to be appointed by high gods for the defence and safety of the area. Hence, people propitiate them through rites.

One artistic variant of this complementary relationship in coastal Karnataka is *yakṣagāna*, a folk drama. Its themes are drawn from the epics and the Purāṇas. The costumes, weapons and other paraphernalia are influenced by tribal motifs. The *yakṣagāna* is similar to *kathakalī* which is popular in adjacent Kerala and *chau* dance performed in Orissa and Bihar.

All these forms are infused with an elemental vitality or a burst of energy. Their spontaneity and originality are noteworthy. Buddhism in Sikkim, Bhutan and Ladakh also has masked dances performed by the Lamas to propitiate good spirits and ward off evil. All the above forms are outdoor displays, which are witnessed by common people. A common theme which runs through these artistic displays is that it is beneficial to the hosts who sponsor them and to those who witness them. In this sense performing art in India is attuned to religious meanings.

Sigmund Freud[7] held the view that religion was a kind of neurosis. It represented an infantile regression into the primitive past; guilt lay behind totem and taboo. For him religious behaviour was guided by feelings of emotional insecurity, fear of punishment, etc. In contrast, Carl von Jung[8] regarded religion as the main inspiration for mankind. For him mental illness was not always traceable to sexual repressions. Ethical dilemmas and religious enigmas could also lead to mental stress. Jung proposed the theory of collective unconscious. All humanity shared the same unconscious mental structure. While analysing the dreams of his patients he came across recurrent motifs which he termed the "universal archetypes." These included the symbols like cross, snake, phallus, crescent moon, etc. In the major religions of the world they were sacred symbols.

Analysing Christianity in Europe Jung noted that it retained creativity and vigour so long as it was in contact with the unconscious. By twelfth century CE the church which had grown into a powerful organization "closed its doors to the unconscious." In other words, it came to be guided by theology and dogma which valued ratiocination in the pursuit of religious truth. Two kinds of reactions followed as a result

---

7. Sigmund Freud, (1927), *The Future of an Illusion*, London: Hogarth Press.

8. Carl von Jung, (1969), *Psychology and Religion : West and East*, London: Routledge.

of this stringent approach. Satanic cults — including sorcery, witchcraft, demonology — flourished in secrecy inside the church as well as outside of it. Besides, alchemy — which aimed to create gold out of baser metals — began to thrive, as a way out of religious myopia. Usually, alchemy was described as an unscientific, misguided venture. It was no doubt dubious but Jung discovered a hidden purpose in it: it metaphorically sought to sublimate human beings to higher levels of consciousness. As the organized religion was stifling the human spirit, alchemy became an outlet. Jung suggested that religion can renew itself by keeping in contact with the unconscious. Eastern religions such as Buddhism used the *maṇḍala* — the circular image — as the focus on the self.

Following Jung it is possible to hold that the mystical or divine experiences attributed to prophets, saints and others all over the world can be described as acts of delving into the unconscious: These chosen few have changed society or attracted followers after such experience. The journey into the collective unconscious is a prelude to the valourization of an existing religion, i.e. making it more dynamic and forward-looking. The masked dances or costume dramas of popular Hinduism and Buddhism are a kind of attempt to reach into the unconscious. In the case of prophets, it is an individualistic journey; here it is an attempt through collective participation. Just as classical psychoanalysis took much time to solve individual cases, here also it is a long-drawn process. The periodic celebrations underline the need for repeated performance by the role players or participation by the folk.

In many parts of India, these above artistic displays are regarded as a kind of therapy. It is now empirically confirmed that stress-induced ailments (for example, chronic pains, breathing disorders, etc.) are cured through "faith-healing" sessions. If constructively interpreted these experiences are aimed at the renewal of ties with the unconscious. The Hindu-tribal or Buddhist-tribal interactions have discernible psychoanalytic implications. The numerous icons in wood, stone, metal and the paintings which are produced under the aegis of religion have revealed the burst of psychic energy. In particular, what is described as tāntric in design or motif is reminiscent of the stream of unconsciousness.

Dialogical Tensions

The dialogical process not only includes areas of agreement but also disagreement. The legendary Padmasambhava established Buddhism in Tibet amidst strife and tension created by the tribal Bon religion. At present, Manipur Hinduism is passing through a crisis, as the youth are keen on restoring their pre-Vaiṣṇavite identity. Hindu norms are regarded as an imposition on tribal mores. Therefore, protest against the Hindu hegemony — real or perceived — is expressed through discarding the Hindu heritage. Likewise, Haimendorf's study of Gonds of Andhra Pradesh[9] has shown that Hindu reformism has given rise to resentment among some sections of the tribe. In the north-east tribal identities are not completely dissolved through conversion to Christianity.

The dialogical process within Hinduism also has shown a disjunctive side. In north Karnataka a place called Saundatti has been a cult centre for the last few centuries. Here the patron goddess is Yellammā (a form of Durgā). Every year till recently thousands of young women from lower castes would take to the *devadāsī* path. This was preceded by a ceremony in which the women were given in "wedding" to the goddess. Although the purpose of this ceremony was sacral, the *devadāsī*s (or *basavī*s in local parlance) were sexually exploited by temple priests, rich landowners or businessmen. During the last two decades, Karnataka state has enforced several stringent measures. The Hindu reformers have been agitating for an end to the *devadāsī* system. But the reforms are not very effective. Yellammā cult has many adherents even now, not only in Karnataka but also in Andhra Pradesh and Maharashtra. Till the time when the *devadāsī*s themselves decide to reform, the problem would remain unsolved.

9. Haimendorf, op. cit.

In the non-brāhmaṇa movement of Tamil Nadu and Maharashtra there was a widespread protest against the brāhmaṇa's priestcraft. Jyotirao Phule in Maharashtra established Sathyashodhak Samaj in the early part of the twentieth century whose aim was to curtail the ritual hegemony of brāhmaṇa. Similarly, in the first quarter of that century, Ramasami Naicker who launched the Dravida Kazhagam mobilized the Tamilians for a "self-respect" movement. The brāhmaṇas' authority over the people was challenged. Thus, in both Maharashtra and Tamil Nadu rituals related to life crises ceremonies were modified.

Long before these events, the Liṅgāyats of Karnataka questioned the Brāhmanical authority. They developed a distinctive set of rituals for holding ceremonies. The various *bhakti* movements also presented an alternative to the Brāhmanical paradigm. The nineteenth-century reforms by Arya Samaj, Brahmo Samaj and other similar organizations were striving to give a new interpretation of Hinduism. The latest to join the issue is the Dalit movement. Thus, both in the interactions between caste and tribe and between different sections of Hinduism there has been a ferment.

Sacred Geography

In India it is common to come across holy places located in remote or inaccessible areas. The cave of Amarnath in Jammu & Kashmir state, Śabarī Malāī in Kerala on top of which the Ayyappā temple is built, Sri Sailam in Andhra Pradesh are just a few examples. Besides, in the hill districts of U.P. there are many temples dedicated to the goddess. These places — till the arrival of modern transport — were difficult to reach. The security of pilgrims was often in danger due to wild animals and lack of medical help in case of sickness. The journey to a holy place usually took months for to and fro travel. The classic example is Badrinath in the U.P. Himalayan region. Situated at an altitude of more than 10,000 ft above sea level, it is on the bank of the fast flowing Alakanandā River. Till recently, it was a dangerous and arduous journey for pilgrims from all over

India. A number of them simply did not return home since they fell prey to accidents, sickness, etc. Yet for centuries the pilgrims' trek to this place has continued.

Examining the pilgrimage in a comparative perspective Victor Turner[10] has suggested that it entailed suffering but it also stimulated sharing with others. It resulted in the formation of an "anti-structure" wherein there was no hierarchy, no ethnic separateness and no nationality. Turner's approach is, of course, an ideal-typical construction.

In Indian society many important shrines are located in the areas where there is a tribal culture. The above-mentioned temples provide a few examples. Millions of pilgrims visit Vaishno Devi, Śabarī Malāī and Sri Sailam sharing food and water with co-travellers who come from the most diverse backgrounds. In this fast movement there is very little scope for maintaining a separate caste identity or observe the norms of purity-pollution. Even if some of them make their cooking arrangements, there are no caste barriers in bathing at holy rivers or entering the public temples. It is only in private temples that restrictions on entry are imposed on visitors.

However, there is a spectrum in pilgrimage, which accommodates a variety of religious practices. In Bodh Gayā — where a shrine of Viṣṇu is located — pilgrims throng to conduct libational rites for their deceased ancestors. Here, rituals are performed mainly under the guidance of brāhmaṇa specialists. In contrast Sri Sailam temple — where a Jyotirliṅga of Śiva is installed — allows any pilgrim to touch the *liṅga* and perform rites without priestly mediation. Those who desire priestly help can get it here but it is not binding. There are also many purely tribal religious centres in India, which attract cross-country pilgrims. The main difference between Hindu and a tribal centre is that the former usually follow a literate tradition based on Sanskrit texts. (The liturgy is drawn upon the Vedic or Purāṇic heritage.) In the latter a

10. Victor Turner, (1974), *Fields, Metaphors and Dramas*, London: Cornell University Press.

Shamanistic or animistic element and a non-Sanskritic liturgy are the usual features. Thus, Hinduism and tribal religions have enriched each other. Indian religious culture has survived in spite of caste barriers and parochial restrictions.

Institutional-Ritualistic and Charismatic Modes of Religious Behaviour among Castes and Tribes

There are two patterns of religious behaviour in the dialogical process, especially on the individual level: (a) the institutional in which solidarity is established through the observance of prescribed rituals; and (b) the charismatic in which a person invested with a magical or spiritual authority guides the individuals in a crisis. Nearly all the groups in India — castes and tribes — have a priestly section. If we look at the caste system in India there are two types of hierarchies. Firstly, the all-India scheme in which the *varṇa*s (brāhmaṇa, kṣatriya, vaiśya and śūdra) provided a broad framework for the integration of numerous castes. This may be called the macro-level hierarchy. Secondly, each caste has its own internal divisions based on kinship and lineage distinctions, totemic identities, norms of purity and pollution, etc. There is a priestly section in each caste which is entrusted with the task of guiding others in the performance of rituals. This may be called micro-level hierarchy. Both of these hierarchies are simultaneously present in India.

The reason for such complexity lies in the fact that the rituals in India have sprung up from diverse sources: Vedic, Purāṇic, regional or local mythical events. The priests at different levels are thus engaged in the institutional-ritualistic work. It is incorrect to hold that only the brāhmaṇas are priests in India. Even within the temples of the Great Tradition, non-brāhmaṇa priests have been employed. Chitralekha Gupta has noted that Brāhmanical authority could not replace the previous networks. Thus, in the Liṅgarāja temple at Bhubaneswar several non-brāhmaṇa priests are operating.[11]

11. Chitralekha Gupta (1983), *Brahmanas of India*, Delhi: Sundeep Prakashan, p. 137.

Likewise in Tamil Nadu the priests are drawn from both the brāhmaṇa and non-brāhmaṇa groups.[12] Similarly whether such priestly groups are within the castes or not the temples have become an integral part of India's institutional-ritualistic complex.

The tribes of India are in some respects similar to castes. Thus, there are Bhagats, Ojhās, Meibas and Meibis. The tribes outside the Hindu fold such as (non-Christian) Nāgās, Mizos, etc. have also magicians or medicine men. In the caste order the priests have derived their authority from texts, whereas the religious authority in tribes is derived from a "Supernatural" source.

What is described as Shamanism in anthropological literature is none other than charisma. In Hinduism, priests can be contrasted with the *guru*s. The priests are mainly ritualistic, while the *guru*s are charismatic. In fact, a number of *guru*s during the *bhakti* resurgence came from a non-Brāhmanical background. Many of them also did not belong to the literati trained in Sanskrit. In spite of this they were esteemed because of their spirituality. An outstanding example in modern times is Ramakrishna Paramahamsa. He was born in a village in Bengal and acquired only a rudimentary education in Sanskrit and vernacular. But he absorbed much religious knowledge from listening to the stories of epics and Purāṇas narrated in Bengali by itinerant *sādhu*s, *guru*s and pilgrims. As he grew up people recognized his intense spirituality which was based on his personal experience of divinity.

What is stated above can be discussed in the light of the dialogical process in India. The presence of charisma in both Hinduism and Tribal religion attests to a common element. It is the same spirituality, which is at the basis of both orders, although it may assume diverse forms. The many interactions between the two have modified each other. Also, the problems

12. Vide G.S. Ghurye, 1963, *Caste and Race in India*, Bombay: Popular Prakashan, pp. 369-73.

of individual members — men, women and children — are more effectively handled through the charismatic authority of the tribal guide or the Hindu *guru*. The tribal or Hindu social structures are thus considerably modified by the agency of the charismatic figure. In this process, a dynamic element is imparted to the religious behaviour. In the institutional patterns an individual's lapses and transgressions are dealt with in terms of stringent methods. The expiatory rites are enforced upon the deviants, in order to uphold the authority of the social system. In the charismatic mode, there is a greater attentiveness to the individual's specific problems. If the expiatory acts are enforced the individual's dispositions are recognized; in other words there is no fiat issued in the name of collective authority. Many *guru*s (past and present) have exercised a benign influence on their followers; they have reformed them through a dyadic (person to person) interaction rather than stern command.

In Hindu society the decline set in when the *guru*s were deified and turned into godheads (*Bhagavān*s) especially after their demise. This led to a ritualization and formalization. The living *guru* is a warm, affable person; the *Bhagavān* is a revered personage who is worshipped by his followers. It is for this reason that although there were many *guru*s in the past, even now new *guru*s are emerging in India. The present time has thrown up new crises in the lives of individuals: the *guru*'s presence amidst them provides an opportunity for resolving existential problems. Thus, the renewal of faith is mediated by charisma.

Maintaining a balance between the two modes of religious behaviour seems to be a difficult task. In a religious system, one or the other becomes assertive: there is either an excessive ritualization or a charismatic impulse which is antinomic. The absence of a central Church in Hinduism has in a sense contributed to this tension. The heterogeneous groups — castes and sects — have multiple ritual centres, which are autonomous. Not all the *guru*s are genuine and so the charisma can be put to wrong ends or used for manipulative purposes.

Thus, both the institutional and the charismatic modes can be problematic. Both curtailment of the ritual and the containment of the charisma claim the attention of society at one point of time or the other.

Among the tribes in India and elsewhere oracles, shamans, witch doctors, and magicians have provided a measure of social control. They have exercised a normative control in the individualistic sense. Evans-Pritchard's study of the Azande society[13] in Africa has revealed the constructive part played by oracles in diagnosing the witchcraft and also providing guidance to remove it from the individual's life. Elsewhere, curing sickness, controlling epidemic, appeasing the angry spirits, etc. are taken up by magicians, medicine men or shamans. At the same time, the deleterious activities of these charismatics cannot be overlooked. The magician may indulge in sorcery or the witch may be pressurized by a resourceful section in the society to punish an innocent individual. Outsiders to the tribe tend to view oracular or shamanistic activities as undesirable. What has caused these problems is the misapplication of charisma. Malinowski showed that magic had a benevolent effect on Trobriand society; it stimulated them to cultivate the garden, build the canoe and carry on Kula trade. Magic or witchcraft still remains the key idea to understand a pre-literate society.

In the dialogical relationship, the interplay between objective and subjective elements can also be discerned. In the priest-client relationship, the emphasis is on the transmission of ritualistic conduct, which is based on the objectively oriented social structure. In contrast, in the *guru-śiṣya* interaction, there is a subjective understanding which often results in the reduction of individual conflicts, etc. In fact, in Indian society the *guru* often acts as a psychoanalyst[14] who delves into the

---

13. E.E. Evans-Pritchard (1937), *Witchcraft, Oracles, and Magic among the Azande*, London: Oxford University Press.
14. Sudhir Kakar, 1991, *The Analyst and the Mystic*, New Delhi: Viking, pp. 45-49.

sub-conscious layer of his mind and locates the source of the *śiṣya*'s problem. The healing is likely to take place with the *guru*'s gentle guidance. The healing touch is also strengthened by the individual's participation in the *satsaṅga* where there are others in search of inner peace and harmony. Indeed, the *satsaṅga* may be compared to a hermeneutic circle in which the *guru*'s aura is experienced by all the members.

The subjective interpretation of the signs or certain activities also provides a key to the religious behaviour of individuals in tribes. When a magician "studies" the stomach or intestine of a sacrificed goat or sheep, he not only derives meanings subjectively but also conveys them to the client through signs. The "outsider" is unable to understand the cryptic act; he is likely to conclude that it is an instance of irrationality. The fact, however, is that there are definite meanings[15] derived from witnessing the divinatory ritual. Garfinkel has shown in an experiment that "yes/no" answers mechanically given by councillors to a group of clients led to a surprising result: the members derived meanings and resolved some problems in their lives.

Summing Up

The Indian religious scene is characterized by heterogeneity and interaction. There are societies in which plural groups may exist together but they may not interact with each other. These are the cultural enclaves whose focus is on the maintenance of separate boundaries and preservation of separate self-identity for their members. By contrast, Indian religious pluralism is based on interactions among different groups, Tribal, Hindu, Buddhist, etc. The intercaste interdependence is seen in such activities as village festivals wherein the different sections participate actively. The caste-tribe interdependence is noticeable in several sacred centres of India.

---

15. H. Garfinkel (1967), *Studies in Ethnomethodology*, Englewood Cliffs, N.J.: Prentice-Hall.

India's culture — art, music and literature — is essentially a product of interactive religions. In the temple sculptures, murals, etc. the different ethnic elements are blended into an artistic mosaic or turned into contrastive motifs: whether it is Ajanta art, medieval sculptures or modern icon we see the same process at work. Both in religion and culture there is an underlying current which has sustained India's compositeness.

6

Christian Influences on the Hindu View and Way of Life

Rabindra Ray

DESPITE Buddhism, Islam, Christianity and latterly, the Sikhs vigorously proselytizing religious movements and its own indigenous heterodoxies such as the Brahmo Samaj and the Liṅgāyats that have, at one time or another, wished to shed the appellation, Hindu, India still remains predominantly Hindu. It is hardly to be expected that these other religions, which have co-existed with Hinduism in the subcontinent for such a long period of time, would have not affected the Hindus, positively or negatively, over and above, or under and beneath such individuals and groups as have abandoned the Hinduism of their birth for another faith. Each case is a special one with peculiarities of its own. The Christian impact has been inextricably intertwined with the response to Europe, the British and the West, even though it is claimed Christianity came to Kerala earlier, and the current attempt of the Christian churches to indigenize their rituals and practices. In what follows, I will be concerned with certain broad sociological ways in which, it seems to me, Christianity has affected Hindus, without persuading them to change their religion.

There is consistent and recurrent difficulty in separating the Christian from the Western, both in the way they present themselves and the way the Hindu population perceives them, though this may well be in a process of change. The presence of Christian Anglo-Indians for a long period, with their distinctive subculture and latterly the peculiarly Westernized Christian hill people is an added complication. To illustrate what I mean, I will cite only an incident from the late 1960s. My parents then were staying in Rishra, near Calcutta, and two cousins of mine had come to spend the day with us from Calcutta. They were extremely "forward" girls and had come dressed in the mini-skirts that had so taken the Western world by storm then. As I accompanied them to the Rishra railway station and was waiting for the suburban train to take them back to Howrah, an anonymous local boy spat out loudly the epithet "Christian." If the ordinary Hindu population finds difficulty in distinguishing things Western and things Christian, the more knowledgeable sections, extremely attracted to the Western way of life, cannot escape the deep impress of Christianity on things Western. I will not try to disentangle this complexity here or indeed, dwell on it, but treat the less controversial Christian elements in what follows, though it is, to my mind, impossible to escape this difficulty in what may seem even the most straightforward cases.

The most striking and comprehensive way, in which the West and the Christians have influenced the Hindus, has been in the matter of caste. Caste practices have changed considerably over the years and are still in a process of change, not only through the efforts of reformers after their exposure to Western and Christian ideas, or the vicissitudes of the Pandora's box opened with the ideas of equality and democracy, but the schooling of what may be called the conscience of the population at large in its exposures to Western and Christian ideas, so that the alien ideas of these modes of thought have been internalized and responses, pro and con, to the preservation of the caste system have begun to be perceived and put forward as nothing other than common sense. Equally, the leading sections of the intelligentsia, brought up to ignore and avoid caste considerations, have become sensitive to the "essentializing" of India and Indians as caste ridden by Westerners and

Christians. It bears mention here, as noticed by Dr Rowena Robinson in her doctoral dissertation, that the older Christian communities of India, particularly in and around Goa, have themselves been Indianized to the extent that they are riddled with caste considerations in matters of prestige, ritual, status, and family honour. The influence has perhaps been mutual. But it is more marked, overt and perhaps even important on the Hindu side — important, because as the majority and as constituting the larger part of the intelligentsia, the Hindus are perhaps more influential in formulating the laws of the land and changes in it. The very Constitution of the Republic, indeed, shows a different attitude to caste than was customary in the earlier years or even centuries immediately preceding it. Part of this is the outcome of leaders of the scheduled and depressed castes themselves, but perhaps even this has been a result of exposure to Western and Christian ideas. Part has been the accommodation of upper castes and the efforts of so-called reformers, idolized currently in children's books, and it is almost certain that this crisis of conscience has been precipitated in no small measure by the exposure to an alien Westernism and Christianity. I am not saying that the source of such reform cannot be found in Hindu traditions themselves, but that, historically, the prizing of individual conscience as against tradition and the appearance of aspects of tradition as against conscience (of which I shall say a little more, shortly) — leading to reform and in the reformist impulse itself, was provoked to some extent at least by interaction with Europeans and the British, and Christian missionaries particularly. If we, for instance, take the case of Mahatma Gandhi, who thought *varṇāśrama vyavasthā* as good and desirable but untouchability a crime, it is an arguable question whether his reforming ideas of caste stemmed from his contact with Westerners and Christian missionaries and his study of the Christian religion or from his contact/interaction with the Jains as a child. Mahatma Gandhi is on record as having said — and the quotation graces the front of the National Library in Calcutta — that he would remain open to all ideas and influences while exercising his own discrimination and belief in what he thought was right. In any case, caste practices in India have been changing over the years and the period of intimate contact with the Europeans and the British, to my mind, is the most significant period when the Western world and Christianity influenced Hindu customs and practices.

Almost equally important is the issue of conscience in the appropriation of tradition (that I mentioned earlier) in case of the intelligentsia exposed to the European, the British and Christian thought. Halbfass shows how almost all the thinkers of the so-called Bengal Renaissance, so influential in the future course of India, who took to Western ways and instituted reforms for which they are remembered in children's books while maintaining the superiority of the Hindu spiritual tradition and its ability to teach even the West, did not approach this tradition in the same respectful ways as had been customary, but only in the light of what they themselves understood, exercising discrimination as to what to retain and what to dispense with. In the case of these heterodox sects like the Brahmo Samaj, the whole of the appropriation of the given tradition was so to say that which the conscience itself took for commonplace what it saw with its new, changed outlook. Thus in the Bengal Renaissance the Vedas and a peculiar reading of the Vedas was prioritized, dispensing with a great deal of the other written tradition. Swami Dayanand Saraswati, the founder of the Arya Samaj, in this very spirit excluded a large part of the written tradition from the canon as superstitious and dross, choosing to retain only so much as was compatible with the demands of the Reason of the European Enlightenment, and introduced a peculiar and new reading and translation of the Vedas, for which he offers an extended justification in the opening sections of *Satyārtha Prakāśa*. The Bengal Renaissance and to a lesser extent Swami Dayanand Saraswati have been greatly influential in moulding the accepted orthodoxies of subsequently educated Indians, creating a schism between the canon of discrimination of educated opinion and the customs and practices of popular belief. If I am not wrong, one will find running through this the same shame as provoked by the Christian and Western encounter with/ influence on the indigenous belief and customs that has led to the transformation of the caste system in our own times. True enough, those inclined to orthodoxy continue to try and abide by traditional attitudes and readings and their number is simultaneously dwindling and expanding; dwindling because of the proliferation of the established educational system instituted by and encoding this transformation, and expanding — albeit in a transformed way — with the inability of the educational system to address those aspects of knowledge, faith and worship addressed by the excluded texts.

These transformations and influences have become institutionalized and ongoing processes. The chief vehicle and manifestation of this institutionalization is the modern, modernist and modernizing educational system. In the modern educational system in India these influences and changes are commonplace in the curricula and the syllabi, and may well be the kind of spirit and temper that the educationists who formulated these wish to inculcate. Certainly, a caste-free India or at least an India free of dead/ venomous/redundant customs and practices not compatible with "enlightened" Western and Christian opinion is part of the inspiration for the concerted push to educate and perhaps has always been. The situation has created anomalies and may well be at the point of a crisis. Hindu thought and way of life find no place in the educational system underwritten by the secular government which excludes orthodox Hindu opinion from serious intellectual debate in the institutions of learning and higher learning, when other informed religious opinion is not so excluded. Especially the university system seems to have grown completely out of touch with the surrounding population, with no regard for the sentiment, opinion and orientation of the public at large — being so much at odds with the development of the university systems of Europe that it seeks to emulate. Christian opinion and Western ideas, on the other hand, are especially well represented in the curricula, syllabi, the temper and spirit of formal teaching and learning in India. However, this has proceeded without any self-consciousness of the Christianity or Westernness of ideas, sentiments and opinions propagated, and no awareness at all or only a very little awareness of the Western way of life or Christianity (Christ-centredness) or of the Christian teaching, or the permeation of Western ways of life, pro and contra by the Christian teaching and the long triumphant history of European and Western Christianity. The paradox may well be that Christianization and Westernization have proceeded apace while losing sight of the Christian and Western source and inspiration of these beliefs and ideas, and complete forgetfulness of the distinguishing distinctiveness of Christianity and the West that make them alien. This alienness, however, has been singularly and unequivocally adopted right into the native mainstream in the same way in which Indian nationalism perceives the nature of doctrine and dogma and the way in which, in this light, it has formulated its own doctrines and dogmas. I shall say more about this presently. Nevertheless, complicating even this complication, the whole is caught up with the peculiar and unique situation of Indians in the contemporary world. It will help here, I think, if I offer an example from my own experience. I spent some time in England and noticed that while Indians there always seemed to presume they were no different from the British — and I, particularly, among them — and struck up conversations with the natives in that spirit, the English in their responses seemed far more interested in the peculiar distinguishing customs and practices of Indians. On my return from England, I went directly to Bhutan. Bhutan is being aided in its efforts to develop by India, and there is a sizeable expatriate Indian community there. While there I noticed that whereas the educated Bhutanese approached Indians in a spirit of being no different from them, the Indians were usually far more interested in the peculiar distinguishing customs and practices of the Bhutanese. Response to the West and Christianity seem to be inextricably intertwined with the process of industrial development, and India has come to occupy a unique and contradictory place in the overall picture of development.

I would now like to briefly dwell upon the transformation in the understanding of dogma and doctrine involved in the ideology of Indian nationalism. This element requires more attention, even though it is concerned with more vexatious and controversial ground. Customary Western scholarship sees individualism and individualistic ideas as somehow characteristic and distinctive of the modern West, but ascribes a more communitarian ethic and attitude to life and its issues to non-Western people where society and social mores are relatively more important than the free individual and his or her personal values. To me this partial truth actually reverses the comprehensive state of affairs, for even if the West prizes individual and personal judgement and discrimination, it is thoroughly conformist with only slight variations in degree of personal prediction and sometimes-prized personal idiosyncrasy and eccentricity. On the other hand, non-Western people and especially Indians tend to prize radicalism, revolutionism/revolution and outstanding individuals to a greater degree where, it is true, for the main part, they seem to have lower levels of tolerance in respectable society for deviants and outcastes (outcastes in the modern sense rather than the Hindu). The situation to me, in historical perspective, seems precisely the reverse of the case argued by customary Western scholarship, at least with respect to Hindu India and Christian Europe. Hinduism is an individualistic, rather fiercely individualistic, religion in comparison to Christianity, which seems to emphasize, like Islam, a community of believers — the church. The arrival of Christianity and Europeans in India has led to the growth of communitarian sentiments to such an extent that religious pursuit of personal and individual salvation has begun to take on a communitarian cast(e). Even *sādhus* — the itinerant individuals without home or name in search of a personal salvation — have begun to be organized in institutions like the "Sādhu Samāj." This shift of perspective is intimately involved in the appreciation and understanding of the nature of dogma and doctrine. In fact, communitarian values of Indian nationalism argue for a changed understanding of the nature of dogma and doctrine in which ideology can replace the discrimination to *sva-dharma* as the "true" *dharma*. There is, however, yet another controversy caught up with this issue of community and the individual. I argue here that this communitarian shift from the original and relatively greater individualism is the Christian and Western influence on Hinduism. However, there are others, like Prof. Uberoi in the Department of Sociology and Mr Dwivedi who taught Ancient Indian History in St Stephen's College, who argue that this issue of the community and the individual is as old as Buddhism. With the *śramaṇa* — Buddhist point of view emphasizing the collective *saṁgha* and an anti-*Brahman* casteless thrust, and the traditional Hindu Brāhmanism emphasizing individual *sva-dharma* and the ritual sacrifices of *varṇāśrama dharma* to which the *Brahman* is essential, both Prof. Uberoi and Mr Dwivedi argue that these are recurrent and perpetual structures of the life cycle enacted in India. Against them I would argue that the collective organization of Hindu Dharma is a relatively recent phenomenon, immediately following the Christian and the Western impact and certainly Indian nationalism, as propagated today, is a peculiar hybrid of traditional and modern ideas of Christian and Western influence on and transformation of the whole world of ideas.

All of these influences are of the most general kind, of the widest possible effectivity — ways in which so to say the very atmosphere of the practice of Hinduism has changed. Indeed, it could well be argued, and if I am not mistaken, has already been argued, that the very term "Hindu" and the notion of a distinctive Hindu religion alongside other religions, in the very subcontinent of India, owes much, if not all, to its encounter with other religions and particularly Christianity. The idea of Hinduism, particularly, has grown and been elaborated in the years since the first contact with Europeans and Christians and developed in contradiction with and assimilation of Western and Christian points of view, chiefly the discipline of Indology, whether religious or secular. This is much more true of the hetorodox reforming sects which have been so influential in forming and transforming the modernity of India but it is doubtful whether or not Sanātana Dharma needs to take cognizance of these and associated changes. The degree of self-consciousness of these influences tends to vary. Assertive Hinduism is in fact the most affected or the most strictly orthodox. Usually the reverse blindness and insensitivity, particularly among the so-called "believers," is altogether too usual even though a consciousness of the distinctiveness of Christianity seems common enough and a special attitude towards it not infrequent, though again there is considerable variation in the degree of credence accorded to its dogmas and doctrines and wide difference in the attitudes of acceptability or tolerance of its message and teachings. From Hindus who are willing to accept the whole of the Christian teaching as one manifestation of the divine mystery alongside their own inherited traditions to others who accept its moral teaching but reject the contention of the divinity of Jesus, to those who find its moral teaching lacking in ascetic observances that seem to them a necessary part of religious practice, to others who resent their superior attitudes and proselytization claiming base motives and motivations in these conversions and attempts at conversion, to a whole host of other and diverse response, the focus and the understanding of Christianity among Hindus differs over a wide range, but almost all acknowledge its distinctiveness and accord it special status and consideration, even though negative.

To explore the variety and range of attitudes to Christianity among Hindus in India, would require a different kind of sociological research than this exercise in phenomenology, philosophy, and anthropology. Not to anticipate such research and its findings, but in the spirit of illuminating some of the issues we may well consider here the general features of the way in which Christians are portrayed in commercial Hindi cinema. I choose for attention only five of the most general features of such depiction. The first point worth noticing and emphasizing is the fact that Christians do share the screen space. It seems to indicate that Christians are regarded as significant alters, in fact, highly significant ones, by the makers of Hindi cinema and the Hindi population at large. The second point worth mentioning is that whenever they are being presented, their religion is specifically drawn attention to. It is not, so to say, a matter of indifference of the secular civilized society, rather an attitude quite different from that depicted in the anecdote dealing with the Indians' approach towards the English in England and Bhutanese towards the Indians in Bhutan. The fact of religious difference is considered significant and highly significant. The third point I want to put forward is that when the Christian in a film invokes God, he or she invokes Jesus (*hamāra*) God. Two things are of significance here. First and more important, the Christian sense of the distinctiveness of the Judeo-Christian tradition and its verity seem to be preserved against the welter of the polytheism of Hinduism that that tradition except for St. Paul has fulminated against. The second only slightly less important, by highlighting the purely personal relation to the creator and not for instance drawing attention to Universality, Omnipresence or Omnipotence the Christian religion seems to me to be rendered intelligible in a Hindu lexicon with Jesus Christ as a desired deity (*iṣṭa devatā*), i.e. the personal choice of the Deity at whose altar one sacrifices and worships. Coming back to the five features, the fourth point I find interesting and important is that when Christians are portrayed they are almost invariably good Christians in the sense of the first two of the Ten Commandments — the injunctions to love

God and to love one's neighbour. This seems, to my mind, significant in two ways. One that there is admiration for Christianity and the Christian as a wise superior moral teacher. However, there is also a second side to it, which I might well be mistaken in seeing that such an overly done correctness in showing appreciation of and justice to the religion and its practitioners, might well indicate a discomfort with difference, in which the depiction of ordinariness or sinfulness (the great Christian teaching of the fallen nature of man) is actively guarded against through a sense of distance and propriety. The final general feature I wish to mention here is that the Christian in Hindi cinema is usually a subsidiary character yet of great importance in the unfolding of the destiny of one of the more important central Hindu characters — a fact which seems to my mind to require no further comment. Christians, it seems, come in for special treatment as and when they appear in Hindi cinema.

Before moving on to some of the more peculiar features of the Christian influence on the Hindu view and way of life, another important aspect of the general impact of religion needs to be emphasized. As a general rule and especially in intellectual matters the influence of Christianity seems to be more marked amongst educated rather than uneducated Hindus and most marked among the so-called leftists, atheists and atheist Marxists particularly, the whole of the latter atheists' approach to and understanding of religion being usually derived from European atheist analysis and condemnation of the nature of Christianity. My contention that Christian influence marks atheism in India may seem paradoxical — I shall dwell upon it a little more but before that the question of the so-called leftists.

The left is a distinctly imposing and influential presence in the Indian letters, academics, and the media. It is even represented in the Constitution of the Republic in its secular and socialist aspiration. Quick to pick-up Western inventions in the notions, sentiments and morality of justice the left is the champion of "forward" causes animated simultaneously by a partisanship with the masses and the inability to live with them, except on its own terms. The leftist mentality is an ideological one dedicated to the realization of rationalist utopias and the extirpation of what it feels are superstition and backwardness. The relationship of leftists to the Hinduism of their birth is almost always entirely negative. But apart from the self-conscious leftists, there is a large penumbra of those unconsciously and unselfconsciously under the influence of leftist ideas, who, while claiming to be Hindu and having familiarity with Hindu doctrines and practices, indulge in the same wilful interpretation of Hindu practices and customs, themselves being usually unfamiliar with Sanskrit or the authoritative texts characteristic of the "conscientization" of the tradition among the early heterodox reformers noticed by Halbfass. This is not the place to enter into a glossary of leftist terms and attitudes to indicate its vast and pervasive influence. With the exclusion of the orthodox tradition from established academics and intellectual debate and the strong emphasis on Western rationalist values in the educational system, the leftist tendency has acquired prevalence in the intellectualist ambience of the country greatly out of proportion to its democratic or even social or effective weight. A great deal of such opinion is not infrequently just idle or "mere" opinion about which intellectual contestants are passionate enough, but often at odds with opinions closer to the personal lives of intellectual contestants — sometimes even aspects of a Hinduism. Yet, often enough to be thoroughly significant and important, leftist ideas of one or another kind, are a driving force in the lives certainly of those who *claim* to be leftists as also among those who are not so conscious or self-conscious about it and may even oppose aspects of leftism or even the left generally which they see as distinguished from themselves. However, even a cursory acquaintance with the history of ideas (in India) will be sufficient to indicate the leftist character of the thought of these latter.

The self-conscious sections of the left are usually agnostic or atheist, or as they themselves tend to put it when they write, materialist. But the nomenclature of materialism creates more confusion than it clarifies whereas "agnostic or atheist" provides a clearer access to the polemic of their so-called materialism. They are careful to distinguish their esoteric materialism from the crass pursuits of hedonism or cupidity that they claim to be opposed to and despise. Even when it is a hedonism that they defend, it is usually in the light of some high-sounding and high-minded principle or ideology such as liberty or equality or fraternity or sorority. Leftists in India tend to be much more sympathetic to Christians and Christianity than they are to the Hindus and usually the Hinduism of their birth. Radical Christians or perhaps even the Christians in general, return the compliment and tend to find leftist and "leftized" Hindus far more acceptable than the general run of Hindus. The tie-up of the left and Christianity is more widespread than this purely local Indian affinity, though at this point it would lead us too far afield to go into the nature of this widespread and general rapprochement in the West which involves reverse influences of atheist revolutionism upon Christianity in addition to the issue of Christian influence on the left and agnostic and atheist revolutionism that I am concerned with here. The fact of affinity, sympathy, and association can hardly be referred to as "influence." How can I maintain that Christianity and Christians have influenced the development of the agnostic and atheist left in India?

The question of Christian influence on the emergence of the left is a deep and complicated issue. Here I shall touch upon only four aspects that seem to demonstrate quite clearly the Christian origin and character of leftist ideas — Christian rather than affiliated to any other doctrinal system. I have already mentioned the word "origin"; Christian influence and inclination is demonstrably manifest in both the historical origins of the ideas of socialism and those associated with the left. However, it is not so obviously though undeniably present in the ontological nature of Christianity and leftism that pervade the existential choice that leads to a leftist commitment in each particular, personal, and individual case. Indeed, it is the close affinity of leftist ethics with arguably consistent and coherent interpretations of sections of the New Testament, claiming to represent its essential spirit, which has made possible the reverse influences of agnostic and atheist leftism on Christianity. Without establishing the case for these contentions, I shall merely point out that the whole partisanship with deprivation characteristic of the left and its orientation to an earthly realization, draws deeply on the New Testament and even its orthodox interpretations. The issue of earthly realization indicates the second aspect of Christian influence on leftist sensibility. At the core of the leftist criticism and its utopias is an awareness of community and an orientation to the communitarian sentiment that is in its very nature deeply influenced and permeated by the teachings of the New Testament and the practices of the Christian Church. The very aspiration to a communitarian *telos* and form of fulfilment seems to my mind Christian in character and orientation. The third aspect in which contemporary leftism seems to draw on Christian sources is the notion and practice of asceticism, characteristic of the left. This asceticism is broadly Christian-Western in character and distinguished from the asceticism of the great religions of the East, particularly Hinduism. The last aspect of leftism that shows its rootedness in Christianity, though it is characteristic of the secular Enlightenment generally, is its opposition to what it believes myth and superstition. True, there are equal grounds for a leftist criticism of Christianity as well, but the sources from which such criticisms spring are arguably the same as those which lead Christians to maintain theirs as the true, historical religion. One could well elaborate each of these aspects into a separate study itself, indicating the Christian filiations of leftism in India and its distance from and opposition to the Hinduism of its birth.

However, currently the leftists seem terrorized by the prospect of a resurgent Hinduism that they claim to hold in contempt.

These general, interpretive observations lead to considerations of the more specific influences of Christianity on Hindus in India. I have repeatedly emphasized the Christian impact on the ideational and intellectual system and made mention of the Christian influences on the educational system as a whole. Though part of this is inextricably intertwined with Western influence in its most general aspect, a difficulty I mentioned at the outset, there are features of the current empirical situation that illustrate this condition. Christian and Christian missionary institutions of education enjoy great prestige among the Hindus. They are much sought after as educational avenues. It is perhaps debatable whether a public school education or training in a missionary school is considered most desirable for boys, but certainly, for girls a convent education claims perhaps the highest prestige amongst the educated middle class Hindus. In higher education, Christian institutions enjoy great eminence and popularity. I will not go into the issues of the nature and content of such education, a worthwhile study in itself, but merely mention a fundamental dislocation between the Christian purveyors of such education and its Hindu purchasers. For the Christians, their institutions are charitable organizations oriented to introduce the spiritual light into a benighted India, whereas for the Hindus, the Christians just seem to be offering among the best available options as regards the education of their children, whereas the Christians are guided by, so to say, missionary criteria in their offer of education to Hindus, the Hindus and secular India generally seek to regulate these available services as among the best on offer, with an eye to a sense of secular justice, rights and fair play. If an oversimplification were ventured here, it might clarify what is at stake. While the Christians offer a secular package for what they hope is their essentially Christian message, the Hindus hanker for the available service as the most acceptable form of the agnostic and atheist West in India. However, the picture is far more complicated than that. On the one hand, there is the Christian querulousness in the face of secular values, in the very light of the teachings of the Gospels, and Christian desires of late to push the sectarian communitarian Christian interest of a growing body of converts, whereas on the other hand, there is the Hindu preference for the Christian, rather than, atheist face of the West and the Hindu inclination to the Christian reappropriation and redefinition of its "own" traditions. To mention only the most obvious ways in which the oversimplification I have offered needs to be qualified. The Hindu inclination towards Christian institutions of learning, however, seems indubitable, as also the tension between such institutions and their Hindu clientele.

In a similar vein, the Christian teachings of these institutions and the various aspects of the Christian teachings, that their continued presence has rendered popularly accessible, are not viewed with a lack of sympathy, even though the surrounding Hindu population might resist them. Hindus may not venerate stories from the Bible and the story of Jesus Christ, but they are usually willing to grant them credence on par with the moral stories of their own tradition, even though occasionally animated with a spirit of criticism in their very acceptance of these stories. The accommodation to Christianity has been, in the main, extremely large-hearted and not a series of grudging admissions, so to say, coerced from an unwilling public, though with respect to this there seems to be considerable regional variation, with Bengal being the most enthusiastic and peculiarly, Bihar, just alongside the least. As I have continually indicated, the instances of a reverse extremism, a partisanship with Christianity in the very evaluation and appropriation of the traditional Hindu wisdom, seems to be much more common within the educated class. However, among the educated and the uneducated, a native orthodoxy and a return to native orthodoxy, after the Christian and agnostic and atheist exposure, is alive, well and flourishing, with a significant qualification. Sanskrit learning — proficiency in *devabhāṣā*

Sanskrit — and the authentic rendering of the Sanskrit texts in their bearing on the present, has become highly uncommon, and most educated Hindus are content to adopt *laukika* renditions of Sanskrit texts, as also the common shorthand sloganeering, rather than the return to a reading and an examination of the texts themselves. This de-brāhmanization of the brāhmaṇas, if one may so call it, is *not* an influence of Christianity. It is part of a much longer ranging historical tendency, of which the growth of vernacular *bhakti* cults in the Muslim period and the decay of the *tols* remarked on, well before the advent of English education, are indications and symptoms. What is, however, of Christian influence, is the assault on the Hindu tradition and Hindu traditions of learning, both in public life and in academics, not infrequently from people who are themselves born Hindus. The academic assault on Hindu learning is best exemplified by the debate between D.P. Mukherjee and Andre Béteille in Indian sociology. Where Mukherjee contends that a reading of Sanskrit texts is essential to an understanding of Hinduism and thus of the sociology of India, Béteille strikes this down as Brāhmanism, content to take Dumont's superficial rendering of Hinduism more seriously than the rich corpus of the traditional literature. That popular sociological opinion seems to stand behind Béteille, certainly in the practice of sociology, has as much to do with a lazy inertia and the de-Brāhmanization I have mentioned, but it is equally evident of the deep Christian influence on the mentality of Hindu India. Despite this, the Hindu practitioners of sociology do remain Hindu and tend to see such accommodation to anti-Sanskrit views, as an accommodation to the interest of truth, knowledge and science, when in fact, truth, knowledge, and science are seriously compromised by such procedures. Nevertheless, granting even the tenability of the lazy viewpoint, yet such Hindus who adopt a stricter viewpoint [and equally non-Hindus (like the German and Korean governments who have begun to insist on Hindi if not quite yet some native classical exposure for Indian scholars)] tend to be open, in a host of ways, to the Christian teachings. Many Hindus are willing to acknowledge the moral teachings of Christianity valid at par with their own, whereas, if I am not wrong, such admission tends to be more grudging for the Muslims and even if Hindus find difficulty with the fundamental Christian mysteries of divinity, some Hindus are even willing to accept these as adequate to the Christian path.

What I have described so far, are the elements of an ambivalence — an ambivalence of Hinduism — to what it has experienced as the ambiguousness of Christianity, both with regard to what it has to say in and for itself and to itself, as also with regard to what the understanding of that tradition has provoked in the perception of Hinduism itself and its attitude to itself. This is partly a result of the ambivalence and ambiguousness of Hinduism to Christianity and the Christian attempts at conversion. However, here I will not go into the Christian side of the matter. As for the Hindu side, what I have described are the elements of an ambivalence, such ambivalence that has long passed the threshold of querulousness and ambiguity and been assimilated into the lives and views of both the folk and the intelligentsia, in a segmentalized, compartmentalized way avoiding the tensions of self-contradictions. This may well begin to appear to the non-Hindu (or perhaps the non-Indian) and to the deraciné Hindu (and perhaps colonial) intelligentsia, as the characteristic form of contemporary Hindu or Indian syncretism. However, that does not mean that these issues have been settled and resolved. The contemporary accommodations are open for re-evaluation as what the distant prospect holds, is far from certain. Nevertheless, the element of ambivalence and ambiguity, contemporarily held in abeyance with respect to the features I have described is far from being outdated, though resolved for the present in these accommodations. The undertow of anxiety, still present and potentially conflict-ridden, manifests itself in the Hindu view to Christian charity. By Christian charity, I do not mean the moral values of Christianity that have led to the evolution of the phrase, though that too is certainly involved in the ambivalence, but principally, the institutional forms of Christian charity disbursal, linked always strongly with missionary urges and activity. The Christian ambivalence, on its part, is overtly manifest in the missionary impulse itself. Heterodox sects like the Arya Samaj and the Rashtriya Swayamsevak Sangh, not to forget the Ramakrishna Mission or ISKCON, have responded with social work programmes of their own, equally linked with missionary urges and zeal and invented rituals of conversion and reconversion. This whole area of ambiguity and ambivalence is especially sensitive currently and threatening to get out of hand.

Christianity has had, at the same time, a very limited success in India and an impact on a scale beyond what it could have imagined for itself. The number of converts it has won is still very small, but its influence, in changing the very native ways of life and thought, has been immense. It is paradoxical, that Christianity, beleaguered in its home of European Christendom, as believed by the German theologian Rahner, has achieved vitality and resilience in alien Indian surrounding, quite unlike the hopes of the missionaries who had come to India. Hindus, transformed by their encounter with Christianity, have begun to take stock of this interaction, though they are yet hesitant to read the Vedas that they claim to revere, in the *devabhāṣā* in which they are written.

7

Religion and Environment
Some Insights from the Case of the Bishnois

Vinay Kumar Srivastava

FOR survival, each society derives its resources from the environment. At one time it was thought that the dependence of human beings on their habitat is far greater in simple societies, the so-called tribal and peasant, than in complex urban and industrial societies. Perhaps, we were wrong. The direct dependence of human beings on their environment is easily visible among tribals and peasants. One may see hunters traversing long distances in search of game, or people with baskets tied to their backs gathering leaves and fruits. One may come across rainmaking ritual performances in Indian villages, or those explicitly concerned with warding off the fear of venomous snakes.

This is exactly what we do not see in modern society and hurriedly infer that it is liberated from the shackles of environment. However, a sensitive look at things around us, the food we eat, the water we drink, the habitations we build, the clothes we wear, and from where they and their appurtenances actually come, will lead us to the womb of nature. The mere fact that a large number of contemporary movements for preserving environmental resources and endowments have surfaced in urban-industrial society, amply indicates that modern man is devoutly concerned about the state of his depleting habitat, and before it is rendered uninhabitable, thus jeopardizing his survival, he would like to save it from further degradation.

In other words, all human beings know, consciously or sub-consciously, that whatever they need for their existence comes from their environment. They also know that if they fail to protect it adequately, they will be doomed in reality. They know full well the savage fury of nature and also its unbounded love. Nature has the strength to annihilate the human species; at the same time, none can provide the nurturance that nature does. The dual role of nature — of creating and destroying — is well known to humans. What they have always tried to find out is how nature can be protected, how its forces can be put to benefit, thus securing human existence, and how it should be worshipped for its blessings on all forms of life. Human societies have always desired to know how and in which ways they should establish a relationship with nature and its multiple forms.

Today, the movements to conserve environment have gained momentum throughout the world. There are peoples' organizations — in fact, small neighbourhood associations — that are making micro-level attempts to save their habitats as well as protesting against the plundering of ecological resources. Felling down of trees — even trimmings or converting them into pollards — ignites strong sentiments. A nuclear experiment or emission of industrial effluents into rivers precedes protest marches and strong letters to editors. In each one of them, the issue is the deleterious effect of technology on habitat. The question that occupies our attention is how we should save our habitat. We are told about the techniques of using and re-using the resources — renewable, not-so-easily-renewable, and non-renewable. We also come to know about the technology — quite expensive for the developing world — which checks eco-despoliation. But confining to techniques will not really solve the problem, unless a phenomenal change occurs in man's attitudes to his environment.

Many environmentalists and social thinkers submit that primary importance should be given to attitudinal changes. Once people have respectful attitudes towards their habitat and unswervingly follow the prescriptions (and also, the proscriptions) towards it, they will definitely succeed in conserving their resources, making certain their growth and safety for future generations.

In this context, one appreciates the views of local environmentalists, many of whom follow the Gandhian ideology of frugality. They think that many communities, especially of the industrial West, have viewed nature as a foe, one that should be domesticated in a never-ending relation of war. By submitting to it, or pleading with it, we cannot overcome the nature's ruthlessness. We can do so by resisting its forces, bringing them under definite control. Man can occupy the summit of the hierarchy of animals when it succeeds in "controlling" nature. The terminology used to indicate a relationship with nature is from the analogy of conflict and attrition. Man tames, enslaves, or humbles nature; he conquers its forces; he emerges victorious in this war — or deal — with nature. By extending this analogy, we find that nature is usually seen as "female," whereas the conquerors of nature are "male." The social order where females are subjugated to males is extended to the relationship of human beings with nature. Nature is female, and as females are subordinated to males in patriarchal as also in matrilineal societies, in a similar way, nature is subordinated to the designs of its exploiters, the human beings, who carry out their exploitation of nature with the help of culture. Incidentally, an American anthropologist, Sherry Ortner (1974), says that what nature is to culture, female is to male.

This attitude has been handed down to us from the last century and a half, the history of our colonization. However, Indian philosophy and religion is far away from the materialistic conception of nature. For Indians, nature is far more than a repository of resources, exploited and invariably overexploited, for the survival and unlimited comforts of humans and their burgeoning population. Nature is symbolized as female, but not just as a female to be mastered by her male counterpart, symbolized in the form of culture. She is the mother — the bountiful mother goddess — who feeds the inhabitants of earth as her own children. In the event of a shortage of resources, a flood or drought, the people beseech nature for compassion rather than confronting it. In the traditional religion, nature is worshipped in a variety of forms: the rivers are goddesses, the trees are the abodes of supernatural forces, some of them being deities themselves, gods send rains, the natural entities are divine things. According to the traditional thought, nature gives all means and wherewithal — and has the infinite ability to give more and more — because it is an embodiment of divinity. In case it is annoyed, it can unleash unimaginable terror to remind its exploiters of its immeasurable strength.

Against this background, one may easily contrast the Eastern and the Western perspectives on nature. In simple terms, materialism reigns the West whereas spiritualism is the core value of the East. These perspectives are respectively extended to nature, as they envelop the other spheres of social living. If for the West, nature is a soulless mine of assets, for the East, it is a living deity whose ability to generate resources of all types is beyond our imagination. Nature's secrets are fully knowable, so believe the Western scientists. By contrast, the Eastern philosophers submit that nature reveals what she wants to and she herself decides which secrets of hers are to be exposed and in what measure, and which should remain concealed for the time being.

Our predictions of natural phenomena and their behaviour often fail because we cannot fully grasp the designs of nature. Howsoever optimistic we may be in scientific terms, perhaps we shall never succeed in mastering nature, such is the belief of the people from the East. Moreover, whenever we boast of our knowledge of nature and mastery over her, we encounter her almost unsurpassable wrath.

Notwithstanding our claim of our knowledge of natural phenomena, our people and the life on the planet have perished in earthquakes, floods, droughts, landslides, cyclones, and tornadoes. The Eastern philosophy exposes the lacunae of the Western view of controlling nature, suggesting that our chief good lies in cultivating a reverential attitude towards her. Therefore, in the Eastern thought one finds an intimate relationship between religion and environment. Religion safeguards the environment, and in so doing guarantees its salubrious perpetuation. In fact, the Eastern view has gained ascendancy in several environmental movements that have taken off in the last two decades or so in Western soil. Not only that, other religious movements have also adopted a more spiritualistic view towards nature; for instance, the White Witchcraft movement in West regards the earth as the "mother" (Gaia, the term it adopts for the earth), who should be protected against its unabated exploitation (Srivastava, 1990).

One of the greatest achievements of Emile Durkheim, the French sociologist, was that he made a distinction between "what people do," of which they are aware, and "what emerges from their collective acts," of which they are unaware. The first acts are intentional: people know what they are doing and why. What they do not know — and perhaps cannot anticipate — is the unanticipated consequence of their actions, and it is for the observers of their actions to envisage the outcome. Durkheim (1976) showed in his work on Australian totemism, which since then has become a classic in the sociology of religion, that the periodic totemic rituals create a sense of solidarity among the clanspersons. People certainly do not assemble for a ritual with an explicit aim to generate cohesiveness among them; they come together to venerate their totems that are their ancestors; they perform rituals for the multiplication of their totems. From all this would follow a sense of well-being, which is essential for their continued existence. But these rituals would create and rejuvenate ties between people within the clan as well as of different clans. Because of these rituals, the individuals are integrated in a whole. No more are they isolated and lonely. It is the sense of adhesion that gives them a meaning for life.

Durkheim's ideas, later substantially developed by many anthropologists and sociologists, can be usefully applied to the religious practices of people to understand their unanticipated consequences (Merton, 1957). An example will make this proposition clear. Some religions instruct their members to dispose of their dead by the method of burial, rather than by cremation. An unanticipated outcome of this practice is environmental conservation: the woods are saved, pollution caused by the burning of wood and corpse does not occur, the rivers are spared from being polluted by ash and charred bones. Communities may legitimize the practice of burial on religious grounds — an idea that we emerge from the earth and return to it, or in graves the dead would lead their own existence with the other dead. These are the anticipated goals, but an unanticipated consequence of this practice is environmental conservation. It is also possible that a religious ideology may issue overt instructions about protecting the environment. People may desperately desire the health of their eco-systems but lack the requisite sanctions. The directions their political bodies (such as village and caste councils) issue may stand ill-respected and flouted. Against this background, religion performs a miracle, by providing an ideology that directly saves the environment.

Against this background, let us have a look at the religion (*dharma*) of the Bishnois, a community of north India, which is described by Bishnoi and Bishnoi (2000: 247) as a "religion born out of environmental compulsions and convictions." The basic philosophy of the Bishnois, enunciated in twenty-nine principles — is that all living entities (plants and animals) of different types have a right to survive and share in the available resources. Founded by Guru Jambheshwar-ji Maharaj, fondly known as Jambho-ji, Bishnoi *dharma* has solely contributed to much of the greenery in arid Rajasthan. Wild life has been able to sustain itself because of the attitudes of Bishnois towards it.

It is well known that the twenty-eighth principle (*niyama*) of Bishnois prohibits its followers from eating non-vegetarian food (*māṁsa nahīṁ khānā*). Bishnois know that armed with lethal technology and weaponry, human beings can unleash terror in the world. They can kill animals not only with the intent to eat them but also for sport, as enjoyment, to prove their supremacy over the world and its beings. The example of Salman's chinkara case could be mentioned here. They can uproot trees not only to meet their needs of fuel and house-building material, but also to prove to themselves that they can transform the environment in the way they want. If this attitude continues unchecked, both animal and plant life will be imperilled. Keeping this in view, the Bishnoi *dharma* contains maxims that promote the sentiments of compassion and sympathy. The tenth principle (*chamā sahanaśīlatā rakhanā*) submits that human beings should pardon others. They should also develop in themselves the capacity to tolerate and bear. According to the eleventh principle (*dayā namra-bhāva se rahanā*), Bishnois should be kind and approach all around them — the floral and faunal world — softly, patiently, and compassionately. When strong sentiments for living and non-living beings have developed, then only would one have feelings for them and serve as their guardian and vanguard. In principle number eighteen, it is clearly stated that one must shower compassion on animal life (*prāṇī mātra par dayā rakhanā*). It is closely connected to the twenty-third principle (*baila ko badhiyā nā karanā*) that forbids Bishnois to castrate the bull as it causes pain and injury to the animal. With this, another principle of Bishnois (i.e. *ṭhāṭh amara rakhanā*) preaches that they should take care of goats, sheep, and other benevolent (*paropakārī*) animals.

The Bishnoi *dharma* knows that people need wood for their hearth. If they fall short of fuel, their survival may be endangered; hence for cooking (and keeping themselves warm) they need a minimal level of natural products. But for fuel (or any other thing), one should never cut the "live" (i.e. green) trees: this is the nineteenth principle of Bishnois (*hare vṛkṣa nahīṅ kāṭanā*). However, one is permitted to collect dried wood. While gathering, one should take care that it does not harm the colonies of termites or any other parasite; this principle is coupled with another: milk should be sieved before drinking (*īndhan bīn kar ve dūdh chān kar leṅ*). Besides cleaning, it will also be separated from any of the living objects. This idea is also contained in their eighth principle: they should sieve water before drinking (*pānī chān kar piyeṅ*). This principle also has another part, which emphasizes the purity of one's speech (*vāṇī śuddha boleṅ*). They should also control their passions (*kāma*), anger (*krodha*) and lust (*moha*) — this is Bishnoi's twentieth principle (*ajar ko jarnā*).

Bishnois are also expected to cook their own food: this is their twenty-first principle (*apne hātha se rasoī pakānā*). By doing so, they will be able to preserve the purity of their food. When others (especially those of other castes) cook for you, you cannot be sure whether they have cared for the mores of purity and cleanliness. If you wish to practise strict vegetarianism, then it is imperative that you cook your own food. This would explain why Bishnois avoid eating in non-vegetarian households even when they (the non-vegetarian) may cook vegetarian food for their guests, or in restaurants that serve both vegetarian and non-vegetarian foods. At the same time, they do not keep commensal relations with those who eat meat. I have come across Bishnois in Rajasthan who do not eat in the house of anyone except that of a member of their faith.

The environmental concerns of Bishnois are staunchly supported by their principles that insist on cleanliness. They should bathe every morning before performing any worship (*pūjā*) — this is their third principle (*prātaḥkāl snāna karanā*). Bishnoi women are advised to remain in seclusion for five days during menstruation. This means they cannot enter the kitchen; they should abstain from conducting ritual performances, and observe distance from members of their family, especially their husband. This is Bishnoi's second principle (*pāñcha din kā rajasvalā rakhanā*). Closely connected to this is their first principle: the kind of seclusion women observe during the period of their menstrual flow is also applicable to newly delivered women. They follow the period of "impurity" for thirty days, six times of what it is for menstruating women (*tīsa dina sūtaka rakhanā*). Further, Bishnois should keep themselves in a state of bodily purity, and should observe the tranquillity of mind and contentment (*śīla, santoṣa va śuddhī rakhanā*).

Then follow the Bishnoi principles that deal with the nature and style of their rituals. Every Bishnoi should conduct *pūjā*, meditation, and contemplation every morning and evening (*prātaḥ, sāṅya sandhyā karanā*). Every evening they should wave lamps around their principal deity, Bhagvān Viṣṇu, a ritual act known as *āratī* (*sāñjha āratī, Viṣṇu guṇa-gāna*). It may be noted here that Guru Jambheshwar-ji Maharaj is regarded as an incarnation of the Hindu god, Bhagvān Viṣṇu. Bishnois are also instructed to sing the praises — in the form of devotional songs — of Bhagvān Viṣṇu (*bhajana viṣṇu kā karanā*). Every morning Bishnois should make offerings to the fire altar, a religious performance termed *havan* (*prātaḥkāla havan karanā*). On moonless nights (*amāvasyā*), they are expected to keep complete fast (*amāvasyā ko vrata rakhanā*).

In their personal habits, Bishnois have been commanded to follow nine proscriptions, viz. they should not steal (*corī nahiṅ karanī*); they should not denigrate others (*nindā nahīṅ karanī*); they should not engage themselves in fruitless arguments (*vāda-vivāda nahiṅ karanā*); they should not lie to others (*jhūṭha nahīṅ bolanā*); they should abstain from opium (*amal nahīṅ khānā*), tobacco (*tambākhu nahīṅ khānā va pīnā*), cannabis and other intoxicants (*bhāṅga nahīṅ pīnā*), and liquor (*madyapāna nahīṅ karanā*); and finally, they should not wear clothes of blue colour (*nīley raṅga ke vastra dhāraṇa nahīṅ karanā*). The relevance of the last principle is that blue-coloured clothes absorb sunrays and thus are unsuitable in the dry and hot weather of Rajasthan (and also other parts of north India). Bishnoi men are generally clad in white-coloured clothes, however, the married women wear colourful dresses, like their counterparts from other castes but they also avoid blue colour.

These twenty-nine principles give an identity to Bishnois. It is because of these that Bishnois have their specific name: the followers of the *bīsa-nau* (meaning "twenty-nine") *niyama* (principles). A sociological question always asked in this context and also in the context of those societies (or social categories) where there exist explicit principles according to which their members should live is how far do people subscribe to these principles in their everyday life? How relevant are these principles in the contemporary world? (Srivastava, 2000).

There is no doubt that the Bishnoi thought has made one of the greatest contributions to eco-regeneration; and in future, it will be extremely significant for inspiring people to care for their habitat, their bio-diversity. Eco-care and eco-heal are the kernels of Bishnoi *dharma*. Even those who have cursorily looked at Bishnoi habitations have found them bubbling with vegetation and animal life. Well known to every Bishnoi is the sacrifice of 363 Bishnoi women and men in CE 1730 (Saṁvat 1787) serving the auspicious trees of Khejri (*Prosopis*) (Srivastava, 1989). Since then there have been several cases of Bishnois giving up their lives for the safety and endurance of deer, peacocks, Khejri, and other living beings, and these cases have been recorded in detail in *Jambhadeśa* and *Jambhajyoti*, the periodicals of the community of Bishnois published from Jodhpur. The impact of Bishnois is tremendous on other communities. As they happen to constitute a dominant caste in the villages they inhabit, they are always in a position to lead an ideological revolution, to spread the values of vegetarianism, ecological regeneration, benevolence, and sustainable development (Srivastava, 1997).

Gradually, the state is also recognizing the micro-level efforts of Bishnois in eco-regeneration and eco-preservation: This may be inferred from the award that has been instituted in the name of Bishnois to be given to an individual or institution that has done commendable work in the field of environmental development. The Government of India has also released stamps honouring the tree of Khejri, for which Bishnois have paramount love. Incidentally, in many parts of Rajasthan, Khejri is almost equated with the sacred plant of *tulasī* (Basil) (Srivastava, 1997).

Through their practices many religions, sects, and cults have indirectly contributed to environmental preservation. The axiom of thrifty living, utilizing only those resources and only to that extent as is imperative for bare survival is found in many religious systems and this assists in a judicious use of the habitat. But quintessential to Bishnoi thought is that it makes the practices, which would lead to eco-preservation, explicit, and attribute them with religious sanctity. People do not cut green trees because they have been advised against it by their faith. They know that flouting it will be a sacrilegious act, for which they may earn the displeasure of their fellow members, which will affect their social relations and interactions adversely. They may also be levied with fines from their community council, apart from accumulating the demerits (*pāpa*) of their acts for which they would be treated punitively in this and the subsequent births. Similarly, they completely abstain from non-vegetarian food, which is one of their principles as we saw previously. All the twenty-nine Bishnoi principles enjoy an equal measure of sacrosanctity. For being a true Bishnoi, one must adhere to them as punctiliously as possible, even when the conditions may be adverse for the actual practice of a principle.

For instance, when one is travelling long distance, it may be difficult for him to subscribe to the practice of bathing everyday, but the point is that one must endeavour one's best to follow the religious precepts as conscientiously as possible.

In normal times, one should not be lax about compliance with the twenty-nine principles. It is the positive mental attitude towards these principles that counts more than anything else. Thus, when you are in an alien land, first of all, explore the possibility of cooking your own meal; if it is not feasible, look for an eating-place run and managed by a Bishnoi. If such a place is not available, then visit a vegetarian restaurant (*śuddha śākāhārī bhojanālaya*) run by any other vegetarian caste; and if none of the above possibilities work out, subsist on raw foods, fruits and vegetables, or even remain empty-stomach. What one has to avoid is eating vegetarian food at a non-vegetarian restaurant. In my fieldwork in Rajasthan, I have met Bishnois who prefer hunger to any compromise with forbidden food, or a place where such food is prepared. If you are a Bishnoi, you cannot even look at non-vegetarian food or the shops that sell meat and fish.

None of the twenty-nine principles states that one should stop others from cutting green trees or eating non-vegetarian food. What they essentially do is to advise the individual to live truthfully according to the principles that are divinely ordained. The emphasis is on the purification of the individual. If the individual is purified, he will be in a position to purify others, his or her community. In this way would result a "community of pure people," who stick to a set of principles, correct and infallible. Bishnoi religion recognizes the value of the individual, who internalizes the twenty-nine principles and passes them on to posterity.

However, Bishnoi *dharma* does not say anything about what one should do when others fell trees or kill animals for food or fun. Bishnois are least bothered if others remain unhygienically in a sullied state or their women distance themselves from birth or menstrual pollution. The Bishnoi response to these people would be of complete avoidance. Similarly with people who tell lies or nurse addictions, Bishnoi will rarely have any dealings. They would consciously refrain from their company in order to maintain their individual purity and also of their community. But when it is a matter of trees being axed in their area or animals slaughtered and hunted, they would not leave any stone unturned in saving the lives of trees and animals, whether or not an explicit principle exists to that effect.

At this moment, we shall recall the most famous Bishnoi sacrifice of the eighteenth century, alluded to earlier. When the axe-men working for the Prince of Jodhpur arrived in Jalnadi (now known as Khejarla), a village in the district of Jodhpur, to cut trees for wood to be used in building the imperial palace, a Bishnoi woman tried her level best to stop them by submitting that for the members of her faith trees were extremely dear, almost like their children. She argued that as her faith prohibited the axing of green trees, she would save them from being chopped off even if it meant laying down her own life. Her earnest pleas fell on the deaf ears of the chief axe-man, known as Bhandari, who ordered his labour force to begin cutting trees notwithstanding the robust resistance. At that point, the Bishnoi woman hugged the Khejri, as if she was trying to protect her own children from predators, challenging the axe-men to behead her first before slashing any trees. The imperial order paid no heed to the Bishnoi faith as well as the submission of the woman. Before the trees could be razed to the ground, the axe-men mercilessly slaughtered 363 people who hugged the trees with the intent to guard them from the cutters. The human slaughter eventually halted when the news of heartless killings reached the Prince who immediately called Bhandari and his men back, forsaking the mission forever. For many environmentalists, this is the first case of "saving trees by hugging them." Many regard the Bishnoi sacrifice as a precursor to the famous Himalayan movement for saving the environment known as Chipko Andolan (Weber, 1989 for a balanced treatment of various options on it).

This famous Bishnoi sacrifice offers a paradigm for

environmental protection. First, one should cultivate in oneself affection for all living beings, religiously abstaining from cutting green trees or slaying animals for food. Second, if some miscreant attempts to harm the living objects, one should stop him from doing that. If the villain of life is powerful, one should unhesitatingly sacrifice one's life for the life of plants and animals, the mute bearers of human violence. It seems to us that while practising the twenty-nine principles, Bishnois chanced upon the idea of martyrdom (*śahīd honā*) for the well-being of others. This would also explain several cases of martyrdom that Bishnoi history has recorded since the eighteenth century. Furthermore, martyrdom reinforces the Bishnoi commitment to their principles and the conviction they arouse in people.

Thus, although sacrificing one's life for the sake of plants and animals may not be an explicitly formulated Bishnoi principle, the actual practice of the principles of non-harming, compassion for others, vegetarianism, and love for green trees, and the others that support them directly or indirectly, has inculcated in them the spirit of self-sacrifice. It is not only their duty to subscribe to the principle of non-felling of green trees and observing prohibition from meat eating, but also to save the environment and keep alive its sustainability by protecting the life of plants and animals. Bishnoi *dharma* knows that imbalance is created when floral and/or faunal life is depleted. It is, therefore, necessary that all beings have an equal chance to survive in a synergistic relationship. Sustainable development will result from a harmonious relationship between different species and it is the foremost duty of human beings to guarantee the survival of all. Why human beings are the most important partner in this relationship is because being at the apex of technological development, they can rocket a reign of dread, killing the bio-diversity, and at the same time, they can direct their technology to the healthy development of the other species.

In addition to martyrdom, Bishnois also think in terms

of political agenda for environmental conservation and development. This explains their protest against the "selling of fish openly in the market" (Ahmad, 2001). A strict compliance with the twenty-nine principles, the concept of martyrdom, the political agenda and vigils for environmental works, make Bishnois an ecologically aware and committed community of India. They constitute a community whose "value preferences," to borrow Madan's words (2001: 24), should be studied in greater detail, for their religion sets an ideal example of the ways in which the tasks of eco-protection may be carried out.

Note

Written in honour of Professor Venugopal, an attempt has been made in this article to document the case of a religious order that expects its followers to save the environmental resources. It is argued here that there are religions that save the environment indirectly, but there are others, which are very explicit about it. In their religious principles, they ask their adherents to save green trees from being felled down. In this context, this article gives a brief account of the Bishnois of north India.

References

Ahmad, Meera, "Bishnoi Religion and Nature", Unpublished Manuscript, 2001.

Bishnoi, Vandana and N.R. Bishnoi, "Bishnoism: An Eco-friendly Religion", in Kishna Ram Bishnoi and Narsi Ram Bishnoi (eds.), *Religion and Environment*, New Delhi: Commonwealth Publishers, 2000.

Durkheim, Emile, *The Elementary Forms of the Religious Life*, London: Allen and Unwin (1976; First Published 1912).

Madan, T.N., *Religion in the Modern World* (The First M.N. Srinivas Memorial Lecture), Bangalore: Indian Institute of Advanced Study, 2001.

Merton, Robert K., *Social Theory and Social Structure*, Glencoe: Free Press, 1957.

Ortner, Sherry, "Is Female to Male as Nature is to Culture?", in M. Rosaldo and L. Lamphere (eds.), *Woman, Culture and Society*, Stanford: Stanford University Press, 1974.

Srivastava, Kumkum and V.K. Srivastava, "Economy, Ecology and Chipko", *Third Concept*, 3(33): 37-40, 1989.

Srivastava, V.K., "Some Aspects of Modern Witchcraft and Occultism", *Guru Nanak Journal of Sociology*, 11(1): 51-80, 1990.

———, *Religious Renunciation of a Pastoral People*, New Delhi: Oxford University Press, 1997.

———, "Social Anthropology of Pastoral Nomads, the Raika Jati and its Dharmic Order", in M.K. Bhasin (ed.), *Studies on Man, Issues and Challenges*, Delhi: Kamla-Raj Enterprises, 2000.

Weber, Thomas, *Hugging the Trees: The Story of the Chipko Movement*, New Delhi: Penguin Books, 1989.

8

Religious Philanthropy in India

Amit Kumar Sharma

Religious Philanthropy: A Philosophical and Sociological Perspective

Whether the Western concept of religion is applicable beyond the three Semitic religions of Judaism, Christianity, and Islam is an issue that has been debated endlessly. The word "religion" is derived from "religare" which means "to bind." The three Semitic religions are based on three constituent elements — the Book (Old Testament, New Testament, Koran), the Prophet (Moses, Jesus, Mohammed), and the place of worship (Synagogue, Church, Masjid/Mosque). Therefore, for Semitic people religion binds human beings into a moral community that owes allegiance to these manifest entities. The underlying assumption is that man is inherently brutish, selfish, and uncivilized — a threat to the moral order — and is controlled, socialized, or civilized by religious training centred around the Book, the Prophet and the Temple.

In the Indian tradition, Dharma or Sanātana Dharma is central. It has been suggested that one needs to use three concepts to understand the meaning of the word "religion" in India/in the Indian context: *dharma* or religious culture/ religion, *quam* or a large community of religious identity, and *pantha* or a fellowship of believers grouped around a specific line of *guru*s and their teachings. The root of *dharma* is *dhṛ dhātu*, a term in Sanskrit, which means "to wear" or "to sustain." The best efforts to define *dharma* have been illustrative. For example, the *dharma* of the sun is to sustain the cosmos, the *dharma* of the earth is to sustain *jīva* (beings), the *dharma* of the king is to sustain moral and temporal order in his state, etc. There are no universally accepted constituent elements of *dharma* in India — no book, no prophet; no temple is required to maintain *dharma*. The inherent assumption is that man is innately divine in his nature. He is qualitatively non-dual from the divine power. There is only a difference of quantity: he is a small part whereas the divine is the whole.

The eternal dhārmic tradition or Sanātana Dhārmic *paramparā* is usually considered to include not only the so-called Hinduism (which itself includes Vaiṣṇavism, Śaivism-Śāktism, Advaita, Vedānta and many other *pantha*s or forms of worship) but also Buddhism, Jainism, and Sikhism. There are, however, some differences between these different religious streams in terms of relative emphasis on certain aspects.

A Sociological Understanding of Philanthropy

While a philosophical understanding of philanthropy may focus on its religious bearings, a sociological understanding has to go beyond this to take cognizance of both the historically evolving forms of philanthropy indifferent to socio-economic formations as well as the sociological functions — manifest and latent — that it serves.

The English word "philanthropy" means a love of humankind, practical benevolence, especially, charity on a large scale. "Charity" again is defined as giving voluntarily to those in need — the help, especially money, so given, to an institution or organization for serving those in need.

In the West, the origin of the concept of charity lies in the Christian tradition of love between man and God, and between man and his neighbours. The sense of benevolence to neighbours and specifically of gifts to the needy was at first directly related to the sense of Christian love.

Nevertheless, charity in the predominant sense of help to the needy came through steadily. As an institution, in fact, philanthropy (or charity) was established by the last period of the seventeenth century. Within a hundred years, i.e. by the last period of the eighteenth century, its current usage was recognized (Williams, 1983). Today philanthropy or charity refers to the benevolence for the welfare of the needy, but this may or may not be done as a religious act.

Philanthropy was widely used in the colonized societies for social service, the care of the poor and needy, through organized effort. This typically took the form of providing literacy and education through schools and colleges, providing health care and related social benefits through dispensaries and hospitals, often set up in remote areas where modern civilization had not reached before. Significantly, this was often a part of the "white man's burden" of "civilizing" the natives. As has been noted by many observers, these were the years of missionary zeal which aimed at the conversion of indigenous, colonized people of Asia, Africa, America, and Australia into the fold of Christianity.

Philanthropy, as it is understood in recent times, is to be found only in modern capitalist societies organized on the principle of market exchange. It did have a parallel in earlier societies, but in forms that were very different. The economic anthropologist Karl Polanyi has observed, for instance, that pre-capitalist societies were dominated by gifts or ceremonial exchanges, and their economic systems were organized around the principles of reciprocity and redistribution. In these societies, the economic or monetary dimension did not exist independently and was embedded in the contexts of religion, ceremony, kinship, and politics. Thus, the functions of "philanthropy" or aid-giving too were carried out within these social and religious contexts.

Modern capitalist societies, on the other hand, are organized on the principle of market exchange, and philanthropy, primarily of the secular kind, has an important role to play in these societies. The market economy inevitably produces the haves and the have-nots, the rich and the poor, and the institution of philanthropy plays a complementary and corrective role in mitigating the large inequalities in a society. The motives for charity/giving may be many: religious/ideological (belief), moral (choice), political (legitimacy building), social (status), individual (enlightened self-interest) or psychological (emotional satisfaction).

Thus, historically, while philanthropy has been linked primarily to religion, a substantial part of the practice of philanthropy in modern capitalist society, in the last few centuries, has become secularized. This is seen especially, for instance, in the operation of the highly institutionalized contemporary international aid system that is an important part of the global social order today.

Religious Philanthropy in India

In the Indian tradition from ancient times, philanthropy has been strongly linked to religion. The concepts of *dāna–dakṣiṇā* in Hinduism and *bhikṣā* in Buddhism were central to the practice of philanthropy. Similarly, in Islam, the philanthropic concepts of *ẓakāt* (prescribed offerings) and *sadāqat* (voluntary offerings) are religious in nature.

The term *dāna* occurs repeatedly in the *Ṛgveda*. In its broadest sense, it means unilateral gift-giving. It denotes not only monetary endowments and gifts to monks and brāhmaṇas, but also alms to beggars or needy travellers. Donations for the construction of temples, *vihāras*, *bhikṣu-gṛhas*, rest houses, wells and other works of public welfare are also called *dāna*. Though, during the Vedic period, *dāna* was more or less confined to the occasions of big sacrifices patronized by chieftains or kings, in the post-Vedic period *dāna* became a much more prevalent practice among the common people.

The Buddhist and Jain movements from the sixth century BCE onwards gave rise to a large number of renouncers and wandering mendicants who lived exclusively on alms. Such alms are called *bhikṣā* and not *dāna*. There are extensive descriptions of the typology and norms of *dāna* in early Buddhist as well as Vedic and post-Vedic literature. For example, the Buddhist literature talks of *dhammadānam* (gift of spiritual blessings) and *āmisadānam* (gift of temporal blessings).

The Vedic, post-Vedic, and later commentaries of Dharmaśāstras classify *dāna* in the following way:

(a) ***Dāna*** — the most general and broad conceptual category which includes almost every type of giving/charity that is non-reciprocal or one-sided and is not motivated by immediate self-interest.

(b) ***Dakṣiṇā*** — that form of *dāna* which is given to a priest by his *yajamāna* (whether a king or a householder) after his visit for any religious occasion. Usually, the priest officiates during the rituals and *dakṣiṇā* may be considered his service charge. However, this is not the spirit behind *dakṣiṇā*. The priest receives *dakṣiṇā* even for that occasion when he had not performed any work/service. In the classical Indian tradition, the priest gives *vidyā* or *jñāna dāna*. He may remove the evils of his clients. He usually plays the role of a *vaidya*, *jyotiṣī*, teacher and counsellor. He devotes his whole life for the welfare of the community and in return is honoured with *dakṣiṇā*.

(c) ***Bhikṣā*** — that form of *dāna*, which is given to any *saṁnyāsī*, *muni*, or monk who visits the householder. In the earlier days, *bhikṣā* consisted of food and articles for the daily survival of the *saṁnyāsī*. The Indian ethos demands that nobody should be denied food, which should be shared freely. *Dāna* of food to those who have renounced the world is regarded as inherently virtuous. Later on *bhikṣā* and *bhīkha* were also differentiated. The Sanskrit term *bhikṣā* retained its original meaning of gift to a holy man whereas the Hindi word *bhīkha* came to be understood as gift to the poor, disabled or needy. One who receives *bhīkha* is regarded as a lesser mortal because it is expected of every social person that he or she will earn his/her own living. Begging was a higher ideal for renouncers of the world, but it gave a very low status to those who were non-renouncers, and yet begged.

The Sanātana tradition forbids begging by a householder. According to the tradition, those who earn their own living represent *prakṛti*, or nature; those who eat from the earnings of others represent *vikṛti*, or deformity; and those who earn but offer their food to others before they eat themselves represent *saṁskṛti*. Thus, on the one hand begging by a worldly person is looked down upon, on the other, giving of gift, especially food, is regarded as a higher value.

The Buddhist and the Jain inscriptions describe various motives of the donor. There is emphasis on diminution of self-interest and egotism attached to gift-giving in these inscriptions. In the Śānti-Parva, a section of the *Mahābhārata*, Bhīṣma tells Yudhiṣṭhira about different motives of *dāna*, for example desire of merit, desire of profits, fear, free choice, and pity. In the same way, the *Bhagavad-Gītā* talks of three types of *dāna* based on the three inherent *guṇas* — *sattva, rajas,* and *tamas*. Sāttvic *dāna* implies selfless gift, whereas rājasic and tāmasic *dāna* imply a relatively high amount of self-interest.

Kauṭilya in his *Arthaśāstra*, however, stressed the diplomatic function of *dāna* in winning over the people of a newly occupied area. It is evident that the growth of institutions of gift-giving was derived from the socio-religious ethos and was continuously remoulded by the prevailing socio-economic and political relationships.

On the whole, the following philosophical motives of *dāna* have been recognized in the Indian tradition. The motives are of two kinds: *paraloka-hita* or for religious benefit in the other world and *loka-hita* or for the benefit of (poor and needy) people.

(i) ***Puṇya*** — the polar opposite of *pāpa* or sin. It is perhaps the most important philosophical motive of *dāna* in India. *Puṇya* is a religious virtue that helps one to get *mokṣa* or liberation from the cycle of birth and death. Traditional Indian society was institutionalized on the principles of *varṇāśrama* and *puruṣārtha*. Brāhmaṇas, kṣatriyas, vaiśyas, and śūdras are the four *varṇa*s (broad social strata of castes); *brahmacarya, gṛhastha,* *vānaprastha*, and *saṁnyāsa* are the four Ashrams (stages in life); *dharma, artha, kāma,* and *mokṣa* (religious duty, wealth, desire and freedom from rebirth, respectively) are the four *puruṣārtha*s (duties or objectives in a person's life); *dāna*, to be given to a *supātra* or suitable person, is a religious duty of every person in the *gṛhastha* Ashram.

(ii) ***Prāyaścitta*** — an act of repentance, compensation, and confession by a religious or social sinner, *prāyaścitta* is the second most important philosophical motive behind *dāna* in India. *Prāyaścitta* includes, among other things, *dāna* in proportion to the crime or sin. For an economic crime, *prāyaścitta* included economic compensation with interest. For a non-economic crime or sin, it included a very taxing physical self-torture, religious *saṁskāra*s — performance of rituals, community feast, and *dakṣiṇā* to the priests and gifts to other categories of people.

(iii) ***Aparigraha*** — non-accumulation. It has been one of the highest ideals among the Buddhists, Jains, and Hindus for the *sādhaka*s or spiritual people. Gandhiji also stressed *aparigraha* as a higher value for human beings. *Aparigraha,* or accumulation of only the bare essentials, is regarded as the most important quality of *satoguṇī* or spiritually inclined people. *Aparigraha* is a sure sign that the person is non-attached to things material and is ready for *mokṣa*.

(iv) ***Karuṇā*** — compassion for the poor and needy. This is the fourth important religious motive of *dāna* in India. Buddhists, Jains, and Hindus, like Vinoba Bhave, have stressed *karuṇā* over *puṇya, prāyaścitta* and *aparigraha*.

On the whole, *puṇya* and *prāyaścitta* imply self-interest of the other-worldly kind, whereas *aparigraha* and *karuṇā* imply collective interest in this world. The first two motives imply individual salvation and the last two imply "collective salvation" or *loka-hita* or the good of society. Whether collective salvation is possible or not has been a moot point. The Buddhist teacher Nāgarjūna is regarded as the champion of collective salvation whereas earlier sages, including Buddha and Mahāvīra, gave more importance to individual salvation as a higher possibility for common people.

Islam and Philanthropy

In the Islamic tradition, charity includes voluntary offerings (*sadāqat*), legally prescribed ones (*ẓakāt*) and good treatment of parents, orphans, and the elderly. A summary of Islam's moral code on charity is given in the Koran's seventeenth *surāh* (23-39). It says, "The Lord has decreed kindness to parents. Give the kinsman his due and the needy and the wayfarer. Come not near the wealth of the orphan." According to the Islamic tradition, God is omnipotent and human beings not only receive God's mercy but are also in danger of incurring his wrath. Hence, a believer needs to serve God regularly by means of good work and gift-giving.

The root of the Islamic as well as the Christian notion of charity is found in Hebrew thought, which itself was influenced by the Babylonian, Egyptian, and other cultures of the Near East. The Hebrew term *aheb* and the Greek term *agape* denote theologically divine love, God's love for human beings and vice versa, and love among the human beings. One's love for other people is a reflection of one's love for God. The moral obligation arising from such theological and societal relationship can be seen as one of the motivating forces behind the institutional form of gift-giving. "He who is kind to the poor lends to the Lord and he will reward him for what he has done" (Proverb 19:7 the Bible). Apart from general charity, the New Testament prescribes that all believers must offer 10 per cent of their income as a measure of gratitude to God. This spirit is also found in some of the Islamic communities like Dawoodi Boharas in Rajasthan, Gujarat, or Mumbai.

An element of social justice in the institutionalized form of gift-giving was prevalent in the Greek as well as the Hebrew tradition. In Judaism, the highest form of charity is not to give alms but to help the poor rehabilitate themselves by lending them money, taking them into partnership, or employing them. Charity or the act of giving was not to undermine the dignity and self-respect of the recipient of the gift. This element was very important in the Old Testament and early Christianity. Among the Shia sect of Islam, as well as among the Sūfī movement in India, the concept of philanthropy was institutionalized on the principles of social justice and reciprocity. It is a common proverb, "If a man shuts his ear to the cry of the poor, he too will cry and not be answered." It is also said that a gift given in secret soothes anger and when justice is done, it brings joy to the righteous but terror to the evil-doers.

II

In discussing the forms and social consequences of religious philanthropy in recent times, we need to make a few important distinctions to begin with.

The first of these is the distinction between philanthropic activity by religious institutions and philanthropy inspired by religious ideas and motivations. The former is a more specific area of study while the latter is a broader and more ambiguous phenomenon, whose boundaries may be difficult to demarcate.

The second important distinction is between collective and individual efforts. The philanthropic activity by religious institutions is, by definition, always collective. However, philanthropy inspired by religious ideas may be carried out either collectively or individually. Both, the donors and the receivers, may be either a group or only an individual.

Besides these two distinctions, there is a third distinction too, although it is more complicated. This is the distinction between the use of religious philanthropy for purposes prescribed or sanctioned by religion, and its use for purposes that are not religious in nature or not even sanctioned or permitted by religion. For instance, the use of religious philanthropy for supporting war and terrorism, or for personal aggrandizement, is all extra-religious or anti-religious. The issue of proselytization is also relevant here, although it complicates matters further because it is a part of the nature of some religions, but not of the majority.

In this article, I will primarily focus on collective philanthropic efforts through religious organizations. Most of the examples we discuss below are of this kind.

Expressions of Religious Philanthropy

Modern India is declared by our Constitution to be a "secular" society, and its economy is primarily capitalist in nature, even if characterized in part by bureaucratic socialism. However, at its core India continues to be a society permeated and influenced by religion, which plays a central role both in social organization and in the lives of individuals. Consequently, both the traditional and the modern forms of philanthropy are seen in India today.

Traditional expressions of religious philanthropy in India have been — the establishment of temples and *maṭha*s, *pāṭhaśālā*s and *madrasas*, *dharmaśālā*s (rest-houses for pilgrims and others), community halls, dispensaries and hospitals, *gauśālā*s (cowsheds), the construction of wells, ponds and roads; and feeding the poor through kitchens in temples or on special occasions. In ancient and medieval Hindu society, the temple was not only the centre of religious and welfare activities, but also had a *pāṭhaśālā* attached to it and often had guilds of artisans, which imparted vocational training to apprentices (the Kannada term for cottage industry even today is Gudi Kaigarike, or temple cottage industry). In the last few centuries, however, a disjunction of these educational and vocational activities has taken place from the temple.

The Liṅgāyats of Karnataka is one community known for its social service since the twelfth century. Their activities involved three kinds of *dāna*: *anna-dāna* (giving of food), *jñāna-dāna* (giving of knowledge) and *kriyā-dāna* (giving of physical service). Among the various philanthropic activities of the

Liṅgāyats were the running of schools and hostels where both education and food were provided free.

According to a popular story in south India, a child born in a poor brāhmaṇa family is educated with great pains by his mother. He grows up to be a good scholar and is noticed by the king, who makes him the minister of culture. The brāhmaṇa goes back to his mother to seek her blessings and asks her for her advice. The mother says: "dig wells where there are no wells, build shelters where there are no shelters, and plant trees where there are no trees." The brāhmaṇa follows her mother's advice and uses his personal earnings to carry out these activities.

The giving of *anna* has been considered the best form of "giving," by the Liṅgāyats as well as among the larger Hindu religious community, for two reasons. One, it leads to immediate and complete satiation of the receiver, unlike the giving of assets, such as land, cow or gold, which can excite the desire for more gifts. Two, *anna* can be given to everyone, without distinction, while material gifts can be given only to the brāhmaṇa.

The forms that religious philanthropy has taken in recent times in India are numerous. A large number of religious denominations, sects, and cults with sizeable following have come into existence, reflecting the need for ideological guidance among people in modern society. The religious streams, in particular, have been more responsive to the social, developmental, and psychological demands of modern society, characterized, more than anything else, by the rapid pace of socio-economic change. These new developments have been superimposed upon the diverse forms of religious philanthropy, which continue to exist since historical times.

Among the Hindu and related religious streams, the Tirupati Devasthanam, the Ramakrishna Mission, the Sathya Sai Seva Organization, the Arya Samaj, the Svādhyāya movement, the Radhasoami Satsang, the Brahmakumaris, the Aurobindo Ashram, the Swaminarayan sect, and the

Nirankari Mission are some of the prominent examples of institutions and movements that have taken up activities for social welfare and development in an organized way. The Sikhs too have carried out social welfare and development activities in a big way. Brief case studies of some of these organizations are outlined below.

Christian missionaries have been active in India for nearly two centuries and have contributed greatly in the spheres of education, health delivery, and tribal development, especially in remote areas. The work of Mother Teresa's Missionaries of Charity is very well known throughout the country. There are a large number of Muslim Wakf properties in most states of India, but there are few social welfare or development activities, other than the running of *madrasas*, which Muslim Wakfs have taken up.

In more recent times, most of these activities have continued, although the relative emphasis has changed, and some new activities have also been taken up. These include — provision of relief during the times of disaster and promotion of renewable sources of energy, done notably, by the Ramakrishna Mission and the Brahmakumaris. Sathya Sai Seva Organization and Svādhyāya have worked for the provision of providing basic amenities and in the field of rural development. Many of the religious sects and cults, in particular, have been setting up institutes of higher education (especially in the field of management studies) for example, Maharshi Mahesh Yogi's organization.

Besides the work done by these religious organizations and groups, some of the instances of the developmental contribution made by various movements and organizations, inspired by religious ideas, are also quite important. The Bhoodan movement, which used a religious idiom in the attempt to redistribute surplus land from the rich to the landless, comes under this category. The Rashtriya Swayamsevak Sangh (RSS), best described as a Hindu cultural organization, has set up Vanvasi Kalyan Kendras and

Saraswati Shishu Mandirs throughout the country in a very big way. The thrust of these has been on education, health care, and other rural development activities, especially in tribal areas where the RSS has attempted to counter the challenge of conversion by Christian missionaries.

Case Studies of Some Recent Instances

Tirumala Tirupati Devasthanam (TTD)

The temple of Lord Veṅkaṭeśvara, at Tirumala in Chittoor district of Andhra Pradesh, is one of the oldest religious institutions in the world, where unbroken religious worship has been carried on for over 1,300 years. Over 25,000 pilgrims visit the Tirumala temple everyday. The TTD administration employs over 7,500 people and administers 24 institutions that impart religious, cultural, and technical education as well as medical care to visiting pilgrims and its employees. The TTD also runs an artificial limbs centre where limbs are manufactured and supplied free of cost, to the needy and the orphans. The TTD has made substantial financial contributions to the Sri Venkateswara University, Sri Padmavati Women's University, and many colleges and schools at Tirupati including a medical college, an engineering college, and a college of veterinary and agricultural sciences. The TTD is perhaps the biggest religious charitable institution in India. Its annual income is a few hundred crores.

Ramakrishna Mission

The motto of the Ramakrishna Mission (RKM) is "For the freedom of the self and the good of the world." The Mission came into being in 1887 after the passing away, in 1886, of Sri Ramakrishna Paramhamsa, but was registered as a society only in 1909. The Ramakrishna Math had been earlier registered as a trust in 1901. The RKM now has 130 branches with its headquarters at Belur Math, Howrah district, West Bengal. Both the Ramakrishna Math and the Mission take up charitable activities; the former lays emphasis on spiritual development while the latter on welfare work. The philanthropic activities of the Math and the Mission are done in a spirit of worship of God.

The RKM provides relief during natural calamities, provides educational and medical services, including those especially for women and pays special attention to the development of tribal and rural areas. The Math and the Mission run 14 hospitals with 1,929 beds, 84 outpatient dispensaries, 22 mobile dispensaries, a TB sanatorium at Ranchi, and a TB clinic at Delhi.

Besides, the educational institutes administered by them, included five degree colleges, five teachers' training colleges, eleven higher secondary schools, 34 secondary schools, 137 other schools, seven junior technical industrial schools, two institutes of agriculture, two schools of languages, one Sanskrit college, two Sanskrit schools, four polytechnic institutes, one computer centre, and 471 non-formal education centres. Besides, there are 97 students' homes, hostels, and orphanages and a blind boys' academy. RKM institutions, being run especially for women, include an invalid women's home at Varanasi, the Sarada Vidyalaya at Chennai, and four training schools for nurses at Trivandrum, Vrindavan, Itanagar, and Kolkata.

The Svādhyāya Movement

Svādhyāya is about a five decades old socio-spiritual movement with lakhs of followers committed to its ideology and way of life. It also has a cadre of workers involved in a variety of developmental programmes and activities. Several community development and socio-economic programmes have been undertaken by it, mainly in Gujarat. It was founded by Pandurang Shastri Athavale, a scholar of philosophy and religion. The Svādhyāya followers believe in the ideology of selfless love, equality and dignity of all human beings, sharing of resources, concern for happiness and well-being of everyone in society and a constant endeavour for the growth and development of the community. Some of the activities undertaken include — collective farming, collective orchards, making available boats for fishing to the fishing communities, construction of soak pits, planting of trees on village roads and programmes of health and hygiene. *Śramaśakti*, or voluntary labour, is encouraged for community welfare.

Radhasoami Satsang, Dayalbagh

The Radhasoami Satsang began in 1860s in Agra with the teachings of Swami Shiv Dayal Singh, influenced by the Kabīrpanthīs, Sikhs, Nāth Yogīs, and Hindu Vaiṣṇavas. Today it has over a million initiates in South Asia and tens of thousands more in other parts of the world. There are at least 20 lineages in the Radhasoami family tree. The founder of Dayalbagh, Anand Swaroop, envisaged socialism of the elite and advocated "better-worldliness" — a purified spiritualized form of worldliness that is superior to the extremes of crass materialism and other worldly renunciation (Juergensmeyer, 1996).

One of the largest Radhasoami communities is at Dayalbagh, Agra. This community of 5000 people is best known for its industrial and social welfare activities. An enormous complex of industries, shops, model farms, and dairies was set up in Dayalbagh in the first few decades of the twentieth century. The factories have been run for many decades, as limited companies and co-operatives, legally owned by the Radhasoamis who work in them. The Dayalbagh Education Institute is recognized as a deemed university. Although it could not be carried out, Anand Swaroop hoped to create similar model cities all over India after completing the work of Dayalbagh.

Sathya Sai Seva Organization

Sri Sathya Sai Baba established a voluntary organization, Sathya Sai Seva Organization, 43 years ago, in 1967, to translate his teachings into meaningful work. Sathya Sai Baba's guidance to spiritual aspirants cuts across all religious denominations, for he believes that there is only the religion of love and his own mission is to construct and confirm each in his own faith. The Seva Organization has a presence in over 165 countries. At Puttaparthy in Andhra Pradesh, Sathya Sai Baba has transformed a once-barren, god-forsaken land into a hub of educational, spiritual, and social welfare activities.

The Sri Sathya Sai Institute of Higher Learning, founded in November 1981, has been recognized as a deemed university. It grew out of the colleges founded earlier by Sathya Sai Baba at Anantapur, Whitefield, and Prasanthinilayam. The curricular and extra-curricular activities combine the best of Indian traditions, like compulsory hostel living in the *gurukula* style with state-of-the-art equipment and technology.

The Sri Sathya Sai Institute of Higher Medical Sciences is a super-speciality hospital, operational since November 1991, which provides free of charge state-of-the-art diagnostic and treatment facilities to its patients. The US$ 75m project was funded by a trust made up of donations. The trust also meets the running costs of about $ 2m a year, while income from a separate fund of about $ 30m is managed by the trust to provide for other costs. Skilled professionals volunteer services for periods ranging from a few weeks to a few months. The hospital has become a leading centre for cardiac surgery and other sophisticated heart diseases. A nursing school, established in September 1992, is part of the hospital. The hospital also has the approval of the National Board of Examinations for training doctors in the fields of cardiology, cardiothoracic surgery, nephrology, and urology.

The Aum Sai Ram Blood Bank takes blood only from volunteers, not from professional donors, for use in the super-speciality hospital where patients are not asked to bring people to give blood. All the blood is meticulously tested and extra blood is supplied free of cost to other needy institutions. The bank is a member of the American Association of Blood Banks.

Sri Sathya Sai Central Trust Water Project is a large water supply project, implemented by an NGO to benefit 3.5 million people. In recognition of the humanitarian work, much of the material used was exempted from sales tax by several state governments and the Rs. 250 crore project was also exempted from paying income tax by the central government. The Sathya Sai Trust has planned water supply projects for Maharashtra, Rajasthan, and Gujarat.

The Bal Vikas Education, carried out in over 5000 centres in India, was highly appreciated by the Planning Commission Core Group Report on Value Orientation in 1992. The research for this is carried out at the International Institute of Sri Sathya Sai Education in Human Values, set up 20 years ago in 1990, in Thailand.

Brahmakumaris

The Brahmakumaris are a sect of *sādhu* and non-*sādhu* men and women which believes that Lord Śiva appeared on earth in 1937 through the corporal medium of Pita Shriji, a grain merchant of Hyderabad, Sind (Pakistan), who has since then been known as Prajapati Brahma. They believe in *sahaja rājayoga* (the *yoga* of the intellect) as the means of the realisation of God. They have over 200 centres in the world and their headquarters is at Mount Abu, Rajasthan, where they run a modern hospital and are promoting the use of solar energy in a big way. They aim to weave spiritual and ethical values into all projects of research and development, including technological research. A two-year all-India project, "Entering Golden Age through Spiritual Empowerment," launched in mid-1999 by the Brahmakumaris aims to restore values and improve life and society by holding awareness camps across the country. The mega project's message to the people is that the "golden age" is not a utopia but will be a living reality, in this century, for those who spiritually empower themselves through regular practice and promotion of human, moral, social, cultural, and spiritual values.

Nirankari Mandal/Mission

The Nirankari Mission undertakes various social welfare projects, including holding free eye operation camps, conducting vocational training programmes for women free of charge and providing *ad hoc* relief to the aged, the infirm, the handicapped and widows. It is running two hospitals in Delhi and Chennai. Another is to be set up adjacent to the Nirankari Sarovar Complex in north Delhi for which 10 acres of land has already been acquired. The Mission also runs several pathological laboratories and over 100 dispensaries across the country. All these medical outreach programmes are run on a charitable basis, open to people from all religions, particularly those from the weaker sections of society. The Mission is also one of the leading voluntary blood donation organizations, blood donation having become "a mass movement closely linked with the spirit of devotion." Since 1987, several blood donation camps are annually organized on 24 April, the day when Baba Gurbachan Singh, head of the Mission, fell to assassins' bullets in 1980.

Philanthropy among the Sikhs: the Delhi Gurdwara Prabandhak Committee

Sikhism is a monotheistic religion, which took shape in the sixteenth century through the teachings of Guru Nanak, in response to the ritualistic tendencies, idol worship, and the corruption in the priestly class of Hinduism. The notion of philanthropy is very well developed in the Sikh community. The religion emphasizes working to earn one's own bread, and prescribes that 10 per cent of one's earnings should be donated for the benefit of the community.

According to Sardar Ajit Singh (of DGPC) Delhi Gurdwara Prabandhak Committee (DGPC) was set up under the Delhi Sikh Gurdwara Act, 1971. It manages 16 large historical gurdwaras in Delhi, besides 400 smaller gurdwaras in the city, which are outside its purview. The DGPC carries out three main kinds of philanthropic activities: the *laṅgar* (community kitchen) where everyone is welcome; running of schools, colleges and hospitals, and; running welfare fund for the poor and the needy. The *laṅgar* provides good quality food to many thousands of people everyday. The largest *laṅgar* is at Bangla Sahib Gurdwara, where 2500-3000 people are provided free meals everyday; this number goes up to 25,000-40,000 on Sundays. Besides this, a few thousand people are provided meals at the other gurdwaras run by the DGPC.

The DGPC administers 11 senior secondary schools, five government-aided schools (where the DGPC contribution is 5 per cent of the finances), four colleges, including one women's college, one polytechnic institute, one industrial training institute, and one institute of technology. It runs two hospitals, the Bangla Sahib Hospital, which caters to OPD patients and the 50-bed Bala Sahib Hospital. The welfare fund is used to provide assistance on a case-to-case basis to the needy, such as assistance to poor families for marriage expenses. Twelve hundred widows of the 1984 riots in Delhi were provided regular assistance by the DGPC until recently.

Mother Teresa Missionaries of Charity

Nobel Prize winner Mother Teresa founded the Missionaries of Charity in 1950, based on the belief that in serving the poorest, she was serving God. The organization has provided, till date, 62 homes for the dying poor all over India. It runs numerous *śiśu bhavana*s for the poor, orphaned, and abandoned children. Over the years, about 10,000 children have been brought up at these *śiśu bhavana*s. The third area of work of Missionaries of Charity has been homes for leprosy patients. Today the organization has over 500 convents, spread over 120 countries, and runs educational establishments, clinics, homes for the poor and hospices for AIDS patients.

R H Lesser, an English Priest

R H Lesser, an English Priest, has made India his home for the last 60 years, living and working among some of the poorest and most backward people for 14 years. While staying in Rajasthan, Father Lesser was instrumental in the digging of

40 wells, building of a few houses, setting up of schools, and helping complete a *kaccā* (mud) dam. He has also founded the "Sare Dharm Maitri Sangh" as an inter-faith fraternal association where representatives of different faiths meet regularly to discuss each other's religion. The objective is to contribute to communal harmony and peace.

The Bahá'í International Community

The Bahá'í International Community has recently enunciated "five spiritual principles" or spiritually-based indicators for development, that should guide "five priority" policy areas. The five spiritual principles are Unity in Diversity; Equity and Justice; Equality of the Sexes; Trustworthiness and Moral Leadership; and Independent Investigation of Truth. The five policy areas include economic development; education; environmental stewardship; meeting basic needs in food, nutrition, health and shelter; and governance and participation. These ideas have been put forward in a concept paper written by the Bahá'í International Community for the World Faiths and Development Dialogue, organized at London in February 1998 by the World Bank (Bahá'í International, 1998). Development, guided by the five spiritual principles, would lead to a "just, united, and sustainable global civilization." The Bahá'í community has proposed bringing representatives of the world's religions under the aegis of an organization, like the World Bank, or an international development agency, like the United Nations Development Programme, to discuss and develop these principles or indicators.

Bhoodan

Although Bhoodan (the donation of land) is not a religious organization, it is one of the most important instances in Independent India of a movement for social transformation and development inspired by religion. Acharya Vinoba Bhave, who was the moving spirit of *bhūdāna*, *grāmadāna*, and *sarvodaya*, used to quote the *Iśopaniṣad* saying: "Whatever exists in the world is the possession of God Almighty." He coined the slogan

— *sabai bhūmi gopāla kī* (every piece of land belongs to Śrī Kṛṣṇa or God); one is just a trustee and not the owner of the land, therefore, one should give a voluntary gift of some portion of one's land to the landless. Vinoba Bhave perceived the relationship within communities as an extension or reflection of the perennial relationship between God and his devotees.

According to Vinoba Bhave, the Bhoodan movement aimed at the spiritual transformation of man by awakening in him the spirit of sacrifice and love. It aimed at collective liberation instead of individual salvation. The inspiration for Bhoodan had come to Vinoba in 1951 when he was touring the Telengana districts in Andhra Pradesh. Through Bhoodan he aimed to show the peasantry that there was an efficacious alternative to the communist programme.

The philosophical basis of Bhoodan movement is the concept of *sāmyayogī* society. In the words of Vinoba Bhave,

> All land, all property, and all wealth should belong to society. Only Viṣṇu can be the lord of Lakṣmī. Today we aggrandize ourselves as her lord, which is a denial of religion. None can claim ownership of air, water, sunshine, land, even one's own body. I demand one-sixth of land in Bhoodan. The objective of Bhoodan *yajña* is threefold. Firstly, power should be decentralized from village to village. Secondly, everybody should have a right on land and property. Thirdly, there should be no distinction in the matter of wages, etc. I am not interested in governmental legislation; rather I am interested in reducing the governmental authority itself in the creation of a new social order. None can profit from an unequal and unbalanced society.

Assuming that there were 50 million landless peasants in India, Vinoba Bhave set himself the task of collecting 50 million acres of land in land-gifts so that each acre could be given to each landless peasant. Roughly, 300 million acres were under cultivation in India. From 1952 to 1954, more than 3 million acres of land were received as *bhūdāna*. The largest part of this was collected in 1953 in Bihar. Later on, Vinoba Bhave also included in the Bhoodan movement the concept and practice of *grāmadāna*, or the gift of a whole village, which was most successful in Rajasthan.

Although this experiment in social transformation was unique and very significant, it was only partly successful. Evaluating the Bhoodan movement, Daniel Thorner has written that in Bihar much of the land donated as *bhūdāna* was rocky, barren, or otherwise agriculturally poor or was under dispute in litigation. In other states, people donated land that was already in excess according to the recently passed or under-consideration Land Ceiling Acts. Even greater difficulties were encountered, in practice, in distributing such donated lands (Thorner, 1969).

Positive and Negative Aspects of Religious Philanthropy

There are both positive and negative aspects associated with religious philanthropy, which may discussed.

Positive Aspects of Religious Philanthropy

Building a moral community: The most important positive contribution of religious philanthropy is that it creates a universe of moral community. It promotes peace and mutual love between the receivers and givers of charity. In traditional societies like India, religious philanthropy is a form of redistribution of wealth and *bhūdāna* exemplifies this spirit in the modern context. However, the failure of *bhūdāna* underlines weakening of the traditional *jajamānī* system and community ethos as also the strengthening of the market economy and individual interest.

Alternative to state intervention: The second most important positive contribution of religious philanthropy is that it provides an alternative to state intervention in society. In contemporary societies — both dictatorial and liberal — the state has become very powerful. In dictatorial societies, individuals and families are hopelessly dependent on the state. In liberal economies, of the modern or the post-modern variety, "the flawed consumers" or the poor are also hopelessly dependent on the state. In this context, religious and other kinds of philanthropy has a very important role in taking care of some of the welfare needs of the poor and the disabled.

Mediating role of religion: Individual, face-to-face charity is a process that places the receiver on a lower level *vis-à-vis* the giver. When a religious institution mediates, the collective donations become a fund that is available to society at large. The relationship of superiority and inferiority between an individual giver and beneficiary is avoided through this mediation. While the motive of the donor remains religious (whether devotion, thanksgiving or asking for a favour) the institution transforms this into an organizational initiative to carry out well-defined activities, both for religious and social or developmental purposes.

A related aspect here is that the diverse forms of religious philanthropy provide channels of contribution to all — high and low, rich and poor. Even those who make small contributions, or contributions in kind or through voluntary service, have the satisfaction of contributing in a positive way.

Sustainability: The large number of donors involved in religious philanthropy and its widespread nature ensure that social development activities that are based on religious philanthropy have a sustainable base.

Promoting voluntarism: Another positive contribution of religious philanthropy is that it creates alternative employment for people with social commitment. It sustains social workers and missionaries. It gives autonomy to such individuals or groups to fight for noble causes.

Negative Aspects of Religious Philanthropy

Misuse and misappropriation of religious funds: Unfortunately, many organized endeavours in mobilizing charity have become corrupt and politicized to the extent of misusing and squandering away the religious funds and resources (see section on legal aspects below). It is for this reason that the state has often intervened in the control of religious institutions in India. Alternately, religious lands and properties have also been encroached upon by others and used for their private benefit. Due to this, sometimes people are suspicious about organized philanthropic efforts in India. A reported instance is of the Vadtai Swaminarayan Trust based in Kheda district of Gujarat, which manages 30 large temples and handles donation of Rs. 4 crore every year. The chairman of the 200 years old sect was kidnapped and murdered in May 1998, reportedly due to internal divisions and money grabbing (See Desai, 1992).

***Ad hoc nature of religious philanthropy*:** Another negative aspect of religious philanthropy is that very often it provides superficial or *ad hoc* charity or relief, which may mitigate immediate need or hardship, without in any way addressing the social–structural circumstances underlying poverty, hunger, disability, or destitution. In fact, feeding the hungry or giving alms to beggars may only perpetuate an unhealthy dependence of the receivers, rather than giving them any incentive to break out of their circumstances.

***Little impact on unequal social structures*:** C.G. Shah argues, in the context of *bhūdāna*, that it aims at the redistribution of land, the basic means of production in agriculture; in contrast *sampattidāna* (charity or philanthropy) does not aim at the redistribution of the basic means of production, such as factories and others, but of income derived on the basis of that ownership. *Bhūdāna*, as a concept, challenges private ownership of land. This argument can be extended to charity or philanthropy in general. Indirectly, philanthropy endorses capitalist private property, which enables the owners of capital to exploit the workers, but appeals to them to set aside a portion of their profits for relieving the distress of the exploited poor.

C.G. Shah concludes, "The charity or philanthropy of the capitalists is motivated consciously or unconsciously by individual or class interests. The chase for limelight drives some to start or endow institutions. Others build hospitals, schools, workers' *chawls*. Capitalist production needs trained cadres, therefore technical and other educational institutions must be financed. Starvation is not infectious; therefore no capitalist charity strives for elimination of starvation. It is not the change of heart, which motivates the capitalist for charity and philanthropy; it is mostly the craze for fame or conscious or unconscious class interest. In fact, Paul Lafargue is right when he argues, 'Charity is robbing wholesale and giving retail'" (Shah, 1969).

Proselytization: Religious philanthropy is often associated with religious conversion. For instance, according to a report in the *Times of India*, Christian missionaries and allied groups received 75 per cent of the total (charitable) foreign funds, which came into the country during the first quarter of the financial year April-June 1999 (Sawhney, 1999).

Although Christians have given more in the way of schools, colleges, and hospitals than all other religious communities in India, they have also been involved in converting individuals, largely from the poor and deprived sections of Indian society. Although this is a highly controversial matter, religious conversion has often been associated with religious philanthropy by the Christians. It is reported, for instance, that during his visit to India in late 1999, the Pope said that the Church in Asia would forever remain restless until all have received peace in Jesus. A stand like this is bound to lead to social tensions, divisiveness in society, and a reaction from other religious communities.

III

Legal Aspects

The history of legal regulations related to religious institutions in India is outlined below. In general, there are few central laws that provide for control over religious institutions and their properties and funds at all-India level. State-level enactments in this regard are more important. In addition, the various laws provide for control primarily over the Hindu religious institutions and to a lesser extent over Muslim religious institutions and Wakfs. (The Wakf Act 1954 is the main legislation covering Muslim Religious Institutions. "Wakf" is defined as the permanent dedication of any property by a person professing the Muslim faith. It is recognized by the Muslim law as religious, pious or charitable.) There is minimum state control over Christian churches, which are run as organized corporations and are controlled by their higher religious authorities (Mudaliar, 1976).

During ancient times, temples and *maṭhas* received the patronage of Hindu kings, noblemen and wealthy people, who endowed temples with landed property in order to receive religious blessings and merit. This system of patronage, however, declined during the medieval period. The situation deteriorated with time and the properties were increasingly misused and considered as "private property" by many of the temple priests and heads of *maṭhas*. Some of the malpractices in which temple priests (in recent times trustees) have indulged are:

(1) Alienating the endowment property to third parties or treating it as their own property, to be passed on to their children,

(2) Misappropriation of funds and mortgage of the property, and

(3) Mismanagement of the property and squandering of funds by giving grants and loans to individuals for their private interest, rather than for the benefit of the community.

In order to safeguard the religious institutions from abuse and exploitation, the British government passed the following Acts.

(i) Regulation 19 of 1810 for Bengal province

(ii) Regulation 7 of 1817 for Madras province

(iii) Regulation 17 of 1927 for Bombay province

However, in 1863, following a policy of non-interference in religious institutions, the Religious Endowments Act was passed to transfer control of religious endowments from the Board of Revenue to trustees or other managers of religious institutions such as temples or mosques. The provision was also made for the filing of suits, by any interested individual, against the trustees for breach of trust.

The Charitable and Religious Trusts Act, 1920 enabled interested individuals to apply to a competent court to get information about a trust and to get its accounts examined and audited. The court could also direct the trustees on certain matters.

The next major development in this area was the enactment by the Madras Legislature of the Madras Hindu Religious Endowment Act, 1925, which was amended several times and finally replaced by the Madras Hindu Religious/ Charitable Endowments Act 1959. These Acts were the basis for most of the states for passing similar Acts. For instance, the Government of Madhya Pradesh passed a Public Trust Act in 1951 for trusts having public, religious, or charitable purposes. It covers temples, mosques, churches, Wakfs and other religious/charitable endowments. Other states, which passed similar legislation, are Andhra Pradesh, Bihar, Gujarat, Kerala, Karnataka, Madhya Pradesh, Maharashtra, Orissa, Rajasthan, and Uttar Pradesh. Some of the important states, which have not passed any Legislature in this regard, are West Bengal, Punjab, and Haryana.

There are some states like Andhra Pradesh, Maharashtra, Madhya Pradesh, Gujarat, and Karnataka where legislation has been enacted for dealing not only with Hindus but also with Christians, Muslims, Jains, and other endowments connected with non-Hindu religions followed in India.

Acknowledgement

I am thankful to Rakesh Kapoor for his comments and suggestions.

References

Bahá'í International Community, 1998, *Valuing Spirituality in Development*, New Delhi: Bahá'í Publishing Trust.

Bauman, Zygmunt, 1998, "Postmodern Religion?", in Paul Heelas, et al. (eds.), 1998, *Religion, Modernity and Postmodernity*, Oxford: Blackwell.

Bhaskara, Rao, V.K., 1992, *Organisation and Financial Management of Religious Institutions*, New Delhi: Deep and Deep Publications.

Bhave, Vinoba, 1955, "Bhoodan Yagna", in A.R. Desai (ed.), 1969, *Rural Sociology in India*, Bombay: Popular Prakashan, pp. 629-32.

Desai, Darshan, 1999, "Tainted Brotherhood", *The Indian Express Magazine*, April 25.

Juergensmeyer, Mark, 1996, *Radhasoami Reality: The Logic of a Modern Faith*, Princeton: Princeton University Press.

Mudaliar, Chandra, 1976, *The State and Religious Endowments in Madras*, Madras: University of Madras.

Samuel, John, 1999, "Only Those Have Received Who Have Given", in *Humanscape*, vol. VI, issue 3, March.

Sawhney, Inder, 1999, "Christians Get Lion's Share of Foreign Funds", in *The Times of India*, 16 August.

Singh, Bhupinder and S.L. Batra, 1995, *Management of Lands with Religious and Charitable Institutions: A Case Study of Madhya Pradesh*, New Delhi: Har-Anand.

Shah, C.G., 1969, "Sampatthidan and Bhoodan Movement", in A.R. Desai (ed.), 1969, *Rural Sociology in India*, Bombay: Popular Prakashan, pp. 636-41.

Shah, Vimal P., N.R. Sheth and Pravin Visaria, 1998, "Swadhyaya: Social Change Through Spirituality", in M.L. Dantwals, Harsh Sethi and Pravin Visaria, 1998, *Social Change Through Voluntary Action*, New Delhi: Sage.

Sharma, Arvind (ed.), 1993, *Our Religions*, New York: Harper San Francisco.

Thorner, Daniel, 1969, "Bhoodan, its Evaluation", in A.R. Desai (ed.), 1969, *Rural Sociology in India*, Bombay: Popular Prakashan, pp. 633-35.

Williams, Raymond, 1983, *Keywords: A Vocabulary of Culture and Society*, London: Fontana Paperbacks, pp. 54-55.

World Bank, 1999, "World Faiths and Development", Background Paper for World Faiths Development Dialogue, Bhubaneswar.

9

Travellers and Pilgrims

Susan Visvanathan

LÉVI-Strauss begins his *Tristes Tropiques* with the damning statement that he hates travelling and explorers. This is probably based on the assumption that the records of missionaries, administrators, and travellers are dangerous for anthropological writings. In 1955, when *Tristes Tropiques* was first published, the author had a terror for nostalgia or for describing the routine dangers, the "periods of hunger, exhaustion, sickness perhaps," an anthropologist must face. As he continues with the task of documenting the manner in which he collected the data on Brazil in the mid-1930s, he becomes bold enough and chronicles the truly terrorizing incidents of fieldwork. I will not go into the details of these incidents but only list them for the curious. Strauss describes the bees which did not sting but sucked at the eyes, lips and nostrils (353); a "putrid opthalmia" which affected the victims, tribals, and ethnographers (including his wife who was a team member) with the dread of blindness and paralysis (395); jokes and distancing mechanism which included mumbling and pronunciation distortions (366); the extinction of the group studied (382); and worm-infested food, dreadful hunger, or survival by eating lizards and armadillos (420). There was also the question of transport over rivers and through jungles, "Moreover, out of the thirty-one oxen I had started off with, I had only seventeen left, and they were in such poor condition that it was impossible for them to carry on even overeasy territory" (422). Part of the team with Claude Lévi-Strauss a member, shifts to boats to complete the journey.

> All we had to do was to follow the Rio Machado downstream. Months of drought had made us careless, and the first evening we did not bother to put our hammocks under shelter, but merely slung them between trees on the river bank. The storm broke in the middle of the night with a noise like a horse galloping; before we were even fully awake, our hammocks had been transformed into bath-tubs; we fumbled about in the dark trying to unroll a waterproof canvas sheet to serve as a roof, but it was impossible to fix up in the torrential rain. Sleep was out of the question: crouching in the water and supporting the canvas with our heads, we had constantly to keep an eye on the folds which kept filling up with rain, and empty them before it came through. To pass the time, the men told stories.

It is one of those stories, transcribed for us in the volumes on kinship and aesthetic representation, particularly narratives, which is the backbone of anthropology courses. We might have been tired of binary oppositions, preferring Marcel Mauss' early preoccupation with tripartite structures, or Victor Turner's focus on mediation as a central heuristic device, yet the hold that Lévi Strauss has on our imagination is renewed by reading *Tristes Tropiques*, which is truly the celebration of the spectacular. It deals with questions as diverse as body painting and its aesthetic dimensions, to questions of love and family, the relationship between the colonizing impulse and the decimation of the natives. Interspersed among these very carefully crafted chapters is a digression, which takes us to a recently partitioned subcontinent. It is to the content of those chapters that I will draw attention. The years of the visit are not certain (1948-50). It is a newly partitioned country, and the traveller captures it in the 30 closely printed pages titled "The Magic Carpet, Crowds, and Markets." Like most popular writing on the Indian subcontinent, the themes are garbage, beggars, sycophancy, corruption, and exploitation. Karachi, Dacca, Calcutta merge in this one exhalation. Like Katharine Mayo before him, his report describes the alienation of the city as "filth, chaos, promiscuity, congestion; ruins, huts, mud, dirt; dung, urine, pus, humours, secretions and running sores: all the things against which we expect urban life to give us organized protection, all the things we hate and guard against at such great cost, all these by-products of cohabitation do not set any limitation on it in India. They are more like a natural environment, which the Indian town needs in order to prosper. To every individual, any street, footpath, or alley affords a home, where he can sit, sleep, and even pick-up his food straight from the glutinous filth. Far from repelling him, this filth acquires a kind of domestic status through having been exuded, excreted, trampled on and handled by so many men" (169).

The anthropologist as traveller encounters a world quite unlike any he has attempted to capture in his painstaking records on Amazonia. He sees this as "clinical symptoms of a life and death struggle." We have heard this voice from V.S. Naipaul in *An Area of Darkness*, but when it comes from Claude Lévi-Strauss we take closer professional note.

In case the reader feels that a flying visit is an obstacle to recording social life, Lévi-Strauss assures us:

> I have visited all kinds of markets: in Calcutta, the new and the old ones; the Bombay Bazaar at Karachi; the markets of Delhi and the Sadar and Kunari in Agra; Dacca, which is a series of souks, with families living huddled in the nooks and crannies between the stalls and craftsmen's workshops; Riazuddin Bazaar and Khatunganj at Chittagong; all those at the gates of Lahore: Anarkali Bazaar, Delhi, Shah, Almi and Akbari; and Sadr, Dabgiri, Sirki, Bajori, Ganj and Kalan at Peshawar. At country fairs in the Khyber Pass along the Afghan frontier, and at Rangamati near the Burmese frontier. I have visited fruit and vegetable markets, with their piles of egg-plants, pink onions and burst pomegranates releasing a heady guava-like smell; flower markets where florists intertwined roses and jasmine with tinsel and angel hair; the displays of dried-fruit merchants, brown, tawny heaps on a background of silver paper; I have

> seen and smelt spices dry and curried, pyramids of red, orange and yellow powder; mountains of peppers, emitting a pungent odour of dried apricots and lavender which was enough to make the senses reel. I have seen meat-roasters, the boilers of milk-curds, the pancake-makers — *nān* or *capāttī*; tea and lemonade sellers, whole-sale date merchants with their produce piled up in sticky mounds of pulp and stones suggesting the excreta of some dinosaur; pastry-cooks, who might have been mistaken for vendors of flies, presenting their wares on a base of cake; tinkers who could be heard a hundred yards away because of the loud rumble of their hammers; basket makers and rope-makers with their yellow and green straw; hat-makers who had arranged the gilded cones of *kalla*s, resembling the mitres of the Sassanid kings, in rows interspersed with turban cloths; textile shops, hung with lengths of freshly dyed blue or yellow material, as well as with saffron and pink artificial silk scarves in the Bokhara style; cabinet-makers, wood-carvers and laquerers of bedsteads; knife grinders pulling on the cords of their grinding-wheels; scrap-iron fairs, separate from the rest, and cheerless; tobacco vendors with their heaps of golden leaves, alternating with russet masses of *tomabak*, alongside bundles of *cilam* tubes, vendors of sandals, stacked in hundreds like bottles in a wine store; sellers of bracelets or bangles like pink and blue glass intestines lying higgledy-piggledy as if they were the products of a recent disemboweling; potters shops, with oblong, varnished, *cilam* water vases arranged in rows; jars fashioned out of micaceous clay, and others painted brown, white and red on a background of tawny earthenware, with vermicular ornamental markings; and *cilam* bowls strung together like rosaries; flour vendors sieving flour all day long; gold and silver-smiths weighing tiny fragments of precious braid in shopfronts which were less brilliant than those of the nearby tin smiths; calico-printers striking the white cotton fabric with a deft, monotonous movement which left a delicate coloured pattern and blacksmiths working in the open air. All this formed a swarming and ordered world above which rose a forest of multicoloured children's windmills, mounted on sticks and fluttering like leaves stirring in the breeze.

If one accepts the virtue of these thousand words, which

even today can be captured in a photograph, without much change of its visual content, Lévi-Strauss' intentions to record, therefore, must be accepted, to be without malice.

Over the last ten years, in my published journalistic essays on the pilgrim town of Tiruvannamalai in south India, I too have noted the garbage accompanying the great symmetry of the mountain Arunachala and the temple dedicated to Śiva and Pārvatī in their consummation as "Ardhanārīśvara." In subsequent visits, I note that the temple, now very clean, resembles in fact photographs from the 1930s, when the crowds were fewer. An essay by a devotee in the *Mountain Path*, the official journal of Ramaṇa Ashram, describes the garbage and noise as the chief detriments to meditation, but that skimming it or delving beyond it, the devotee recognizes the meditational joy of being with the Lord. To me it seems that anthropology is still dependent on traveller's accounts and we merely need to bring to it the objectivity of our gaze. A resident of Ramana Ashram brilliantly describes the activities pertaining to the lighting of the beacon, and then prosaically says,

> The old order gives way to the new, yet the devotion of the people has remained the same. In fact, it has increased manifold, for amidst such noise and bustle, the devotee is able to inwardly experience peace and tranquillity. . . .
>
> — *Ramana's Arunachala* 78

As an anthropologist and traveller, who participates in the nature of pilgrimage, my notes for 2003 are given below.

Winter's Light in the Year 2003

> Sunlight too, on a winter's day in Delhi. The days have been volatile — rainy, windy, cold and suddenly the sun bursts again. I've just returned from three days in Tiruvannamalai.
>
> I was driven down to this temple town from Bangalore, at hundred miles an hour by a young knave who didn't know the way, and had us trapped for one hour and more at a toll-booth. He did not know that transport officials in India take lunch-breaks with no substitutes functioning in their place. When we

reached the gate, at Hosur, there were about thirty trucks and as many cars and vans. I was at a pitch of exhaustion, after having finished correcting examination scripts before setting out on my journey, and therefore, succumbed gracefully to fatalism. In any case, I was carrying with me Thor Heyrdahl's *Kon–Tiki.* This is a fabulous anthropological work on how Nordic sailors, retracing the route of ancient Peruvian sailors to the Easter islands, found serenity and wonder in isolation and danger. One of them had taken around 80 Sociology books on the raft, which he proceeded to read with the waves sloshing around him.

Finally, we reached the Ashram at night instead of dusk. The roads were jammed with people, hundreds of them, jubilant that after three years of drought, the rains had at last come, and the wells were full, nearly to the brim. It was almost impossible to cross the road.

"It's an agricultural fair," Dr Srinivasamurthy informs me, "The local farmers sell their produce, including cattle." Indeed, there is a 14 km rural market that encircles the hill.

A fire is lit on the Arunachala Mountain. It is a fire so intense, so immense, that it can be seen for miles. Peasants and urbanites throng to this sacred pilgrimage town, from all parts of the south and the rest of India and the world to see the flame, thought to be present from the earliest times.

The librarian at the Ashram, J. Jayaraman, explains the significance of the fire. It commemorates the conjoining of Śiva and Pārvatī, it also symbolizes the unitary principle that sets aside hierarchy, when Brahmā and Viṣṇu quarrel over supremacy with one another, and Śiva appears to them in a column of fire. "It's an eternal fire, which requires some human help to keep stoked," he says. "The pilgrims bring their share of ghee to pour in the cauldron at the top."

On this trip, I feel full of an intense sense of purpose. I have my camera, notebooks, and several pens. I arrive early in the morning looking purposeful at the Ashram office. V.S. Mani is busy, but he laughs when I tell him that I want to engage with the rituals at the temple. "I'll have to make a very important phone-call" he says reassuringly, but then he realizes that the crowds are such that it will be impossible for me to reach the sanctum in the temple without standing for several hours in the queue. I see the truth of this myself, later in the morning, when I venture out and the crowds are so multitudinous, that there is no negotiable space. I will have to leave it for another time. *The Mountain Path* has a completely new format, which I enquire about. I am told by one of the residents that,

> Many of the old subscribers have died, and their children write in, saying that they don't want to continue with the *Mountain Path*. The new devotees have different needs, they are from different parts of the world, they have more sophisticated and cerebral needs, and the *Mountain Path* was beginning to cut and paste from earlier issues, so the Ashram felt that the new editor was the best person to steer the magazine into a new space. Besides he knows many people and has many friends everywhere.

Just then, the editor walks into the air-conditioned, book-lined, computer-endowed office. He agrees to give me an interview at 4 p.m. probably thinking how obdurate the anthropologist is. It is difficult to get access to anything unless people trust you. I'm not yet sure if that trust in me as a person or as an anthropologist has yet been established.

A man and a woman come into the office. The man is very disturbed, and the woman is weeping. Their pockets have been slashed and they have lost Rs. 1800. The man wants Rs. 50 to go home by bus. The woman is dressed in fine silk, the only thing the man has in his pocket is his identity card, to which he keeps pointing, and says, "I will money order the amount on my arrival in my home-town." The chief accountant, who was a resident during Ramaṇa's time, listens to the story, then as I wondered nervously whether the couple would be refused, he took out Rs. 300 and gave it to the husband and wife, and said, "Return it after you reach home." The evening before, Dr Murthy had said to me, "Go out if you must, but be careful of your bag and your keys. Be careful of knives." Alas, the morning proved, quite conclusively that the doctor was being as practical as always.

Chastened by my experience of the real world, where robbers

strike where they will, I set out to go on the *pradakṣiṇā* (circumambulation of the hill). I am caught in a web of laughter, talking to eager people. It is a pilgrimage of joy, successful harvest perhaps to look forward to, for the rains have been miraculous and after the hard summer, when the water in the wells had touched rock bottom, the damp earth and the filled wells are a miracle. *Poṅgaḷ* is around the corner.

I move in step with the people, the women who have brought grass fodder for sale, smile and clutch the green stalks as a tribute to the art of perseverance — they look like they are from the third-century poems that Rāmānujan translated for eager English-speaking readers. There is laughter and voluptuousness to them, a sense of love and the memory of war. I often think that the people of India, the peasants and the poor, are never put out by the vagaries of the State. They live out their lives in a particular space, and in ways, which are adaptative to time, nevertheless, communicate resilience to homogenization. Three hours later, jostled by lakhs of devotees, I see only one man who wears the saffron of Togadia's club. He is holding a movie camera and looking at the potential harvest of lakhs of devotees for his cause. The rest are concerned only with the essential tasks of pilgrimage, oblivious to any other subtext.

The 14 km route of the *giri pradakṣiṇā* is lined with shops on either side. This is the real heart of the town's commerce. At festival times, the peasants of the hinterland and the merchants of Tiruvannamalai rake in enough profits to allow them to subsist for the remaining part of the year, which is also focused around the pilgrimage to the great Śiva temple — the Aruṇācaleśvara temple. There is rentier capital as well, besides shops, and agricultural land, which is either owned or laboured upon.

I walk and walk, first with the intensity of the anthropologist's gaze . . . a vision which records details, which is observation and classification, compounded by the delight in people's differing ways of life. The hill seems very distant to me, compounded as it is by the multitudes who are calling out to one another, to the vendors who shout louder than them and the general sense of food, flowers, ribbons, books, audiocassettes blaring. I see, however, that without this effervescence of people's belief . . . happy memories which they take back home, the revitalizing aspects of people's pilgrimage cannot be understood.

The crowds are immense. Mothers carry overgrown children who do not wish to walk anymore, young husbands hold the hands of their even younger wives, there is a surge of people, but none of it is mildly threatening. Clearly, pilgrimages are states of holidaymaking, and the ardour of faith is matched by the delight in the locale itself. I am convinced that this is due to the myth itself — the unification of two volatile lovers, Śiva and Pārvatī, and also perhaps the unifying of three principles, Viṣṇu, Brahmā and Śiva. Why annihilation is more powerful than creation or preservation — I will never quite understand, but practically I suppose it is something, which is affirmed on a daily basis.

At 6 o'clock that day, the lamp is going to be lit in the narrow space directly outside the large hall. People have gathered while a space has been cordoned off for the objects of ritual. These are placed on a table — a lamp which is but a wick placed in a bowl dripping with ghee, a large portrait of Ramaṇa Maharṣi, and a pair of binoculars along with the begging bowl which had belonged to him. Kanakammā, one of Ramaṇa's devotees told me that *Bhagavān* would sit on his chair and watch the flame, without moving, through the binoculars. The people gathered there would watch without speaking, and his concentration was so focused/total, that there was not a whisper, not a floating leaf to disturb him in his meditative gaze.

On 7 December 2003, the people have gathered in anticipation of the moment, seeing the flame. There are devotees in the crowd who have never met before, but are immediately engaged in conversation about the primacy of devotion. One says, *modallae Bhagavān* [First, Bhagavān] and the other says "modallae Arunachala [First, Arunachala]." The mysteries of non-dualism have escaped them for the moment. But when the fire is visible, that first moment, when it comes into view on the mountain, the sense of beauty and calm is as visible as the love between two people who will never be separated. It is the suddenness of the fire that takes everyone by surprise, though many of them would have seen it many many times before. From where we

> are, it is not a large flame, it is a *dīpam* — the light of a candle, but so consistent with Jesus' saying "A light on the hill that cannot be hid. . . ." I understand that people like to believe in the idea of eternity and their part in it.

A pilgrim is often the best of travellers. He or she carries with her the idea that the place of pilgrimage is one goal among other greater transcendent ones. One of the best writers in the genre called *pennu ezhuttu*, or a woman's writing, is a devotee of Ramaṇa Maharṣi called Nāgammā. She was born in August 1902 in a village in Guntur; she was married at eleven years of age and widowed at twelve. She spent many years in religious devotion, gradually educating herself in the vernacular religious literature. She had a vision of Dakṣināmūrty, who is associated with Arunachala, as early as 1913. She began to practise visible religious austerities from 1918 onwards, while staying with her brother who was a lawyer in Vijayawada. Her brothers were progressive, and did not stand in her way, though others were censorious, since she did not shave her head. While her family was supportive, yet her desire to be an ascetic was so strong that she became fatally ill. She went to her father's ancestral home in Kolanukonda, which had been empty for a long time. "Hence, snakes, scorpions and other poisonous reptiles had made it their home and were freely roaming about. We had to live together, but we did not interfere with one another. They used to come out in the night time and left me in peace during the day. Our life together was very amusing and it gave me ample opportunities to lead a life of friendliness towards all living beings." During this time of recuperation which included natural foods (jowar, flour, vegetables, no spices), performing *pūjā*, reading and explaining the *Bhāgavatam* to those who assembled at her house, she prayed for a *guru*. Her brother, D.S. Shastri had met Śrī Ramaṇa Maharṣi on one of his travels, and encouraged his sister to meet him. In July 1941, she boarded the train to get to Tiruvannamalai. It was 8.30 p.m. when she reached the town. She slept on the verandah of the house of a lady she had just met and whose husband served at the Ashram. "I woke up early in the morning, bathed in her house, and as my luggage was being placed in the *jutka*, her husband came in. He told me that there was a Telugu lady called Varanasi Subbulakshamamma in the Ashram and that she would look after me."

The record of her days, in *My Life at Ramanasramam* conveys the sense of a deep happiness and a life well spent. What we have here is the pilgrimage of interiority.

> After I got the grace of Bhagavān, like Ahalyā getting rid of her past ignorance with the touch of the dust of the holy feet of Śrī Rāma, my mind became clear with the dispelling of its darkness. It turned inwards and began a sort of Self-Enquiry. I now realized that whatever spiritual practices I had followed until then were only the paths leading to this Self-Enquiry. — 21

Whenever she had a problem, she would ask Ramaṇa Maharṣi, who had very early admired her intellectual and spiritual verve. He had once introduced her, saying, "Look. Her name is Nāgammā, it seems. These are verses on *śaraṇāgati*. Paste them in the book." (15). Four days afterwards, she wrote three verses on Ramaṇa and the Ashram. To her delight, these were also accepted and pasted in the book. Her prowess as a writer became confirmed when she started writing a record of Ashram life in the form of letters to her elder brother. He had gifted her a diary to record everyday events, since he enjoyed hearing about it, but it was not an oeuvre she felt comfortable with.

He said,

> Never mind about writing a diary. You are anyway writing to me now and then about various happenings in *Bhagavān*'s presence. In the same way write letters addressed to me but keep them with you. We will decide what to do with them in due course. We shall change them suitably if necessary. Accordingly, he brought a pen and a bundle of writing paper and left them with me — 31

Other visitors to the Ashram also begged her saying:

> We all come and go. Please take up the writing work as your

> duty, assimilate, and pass on to us the voice of *Bhagavān*. I agreed and accordingly commenced writing the letters in November 1945 after praying to *Bhagavān* for success inwardly, as I had not the courage to tell him openly about it. —31

Devaraja Mudaliar, another devotee was writing a diary at the same time. One day, he came across Nāgammā polishing her letters of which she had written five or six, read them, was delighted with their quality, and told Maharṣi about them. He asked Nāgammā to read them to him. She then made fair copies of those letters and carried them to the Ashram.

> In the first letter, I had written about *Bhagavān* as follows: "What is there for him? Should he bundle up his belongings?" A walking stick, a *kamaṇḍala* and *kaupīna*; that is all he has. When he heard this, *Bhagavān* said jokingly "Ayyayo. What about this towel? She has forgotten all about this." Everybody laughed.
>
> — 32

By July 1947, a dozen advance copies of *Letters from Sri Ramanasramam* published in Madras were ready. Two weeks later a thousand copies were received in the Ashram along with favourable reviews in the newspapers, and orders for copies began to come. However, along with it came jealous responses, which grew so vivid, that Chinnaswami (the brother of Ramaṇa Maharṣi) requested her to "Stop with this now." Since the practical matters of the Ashram were run by him, she stopped reading on the next afternoon itself. When *Bhagavān* asked her why she did not read, she said, "Chinnaswami asked me not to." "Is that so?" he said and looking at Rajagopala Iyer, who was nearby remarked, "Our asking someone to read and their asking them not to do so is curious. It means we should not ask anybody to read."

Chinnaswami explained that he only wanted her to stop writing letters. To maintain peace in the Ashram, under pressure from jealous witnesses, he took away the library keys from Nāgammā, and copies of the unpublished letters. She was unconsolable and told Maharṣi, who comforted her saying, "Never mind. Let that work go."

> I gave up the library work without much regret but I was very sad indeed that I had to give away all the letters I had with me. I had heard that some years before, the Ashram authorities had confiscated the diary of Sri Venkataramayya and so, as matter of caution, the original letters which formed Part 11 of the series had been taken away to Madras by my brother a week earlier. Hence, I had with me only carbon copies.
>
> Anyway, I felt I should obey orders. . . . We found *Bhagavān* sitting leisurely with outstretched legs. There was absolute quiet in the hall. I entered trembling all over, placed the bundle at the feet of *Bhagavān*, folded my hands, and with shaky voice said, "Here are the letters. I have been asked to hand them over to the Ashram. I have bundled them and brought them here. It is not merely a bundle of letters. It is my heart's treasure. *Bhagavān* may do whatever he likes with them. I never did the work for fame or wealth." As I said that, tears rolled down my cheeks in abundance. *Bhagavān* looked at me with sympathy and received the bundle with both his hands. He turned it over and giving it to Rajagopala Iyer remarked, "Here it is. She has brought all the letters duly bundled. Take them and give them to the office." Meanwhile, I wiped my tears and sat in the front row reserved for the ladies. — 49

The tears did not stop, however, and Nāgammā stayed away from the Ashram for ten days, since all the work she used to do has been taken away from her. She describes this as a period of tears and madness, which broke only when she started writing verses in honour of Maharṣi and offered in person to him.

On the third of these occasions, he broke his silence, and gave her a *stotra* someone had dedicated to him, to read.

> After I finished reading, he began telling me all that had happened in the last ten days as if he had tied the news up in a bundle which he was opening for my sake. He went on like that for over an hour. All were surprised at the sudden change. I felt happy and contented. From then onwards, he himself used to call me and talk to me. I showed him the song I had composed, namely "Palukave okasarei Ramaṇa" (won't you speak for once, O Ramaṇa!) thinking he did not know anything about it.

> Laughing at me for my foolishness, he said, "Yes, I know. Keep it." I felt ashamed of my stupidity. — 51

These letters describe the details of life at the Ashram with such lucidity and tenderness that the identity of the writer and her subject enter an osmosis. One of the most powerful of such writers was Paul Brunton who brought many pilgrims to Arunachala by the verve of his writing. It is not unusual in the Ramaṇa archives to come across a writer who says "I had read Brunton's book, *A Search in Secret India*."

Brunton's work is of significance even today because we get a marvellous and literal line-drawing of the topography of Ramaṇa's Ashram and the vicinity of the Arunachala temple.

See for example, the description of Maharṣi's *darśana*:

> The divan is but a few paces away from a broad high window in the end wall. The light falls clearly upon the Maharṣi and I can take in every detail of his profile, for he is seated gazing rigidly through the window in the precise direction whence we have come this morning. His head does not move, so thinking to catch his eye and greet him as I offer the fruits, I move quietly over to the window, place the gift before him, and retreat a pace or two. A small brass brazier stands before his couch. It is filled with burning charcoal, and a pleasant odour tells me that some aromatic powder has been thrown on the glowing embers. Close by is an incense burner filled with joss sticks. Threads of bluish grey smoke arise and float in the air, but the pungent perfume is quite different. (141). . . . There is something in this man which holds my attention as steel filings are held by a magnet. I cannot turn my gaze away from him. My initial bewilderment, my perplexity at being totally ignored, slowly fades away as this strange fascination begins to grip me more firmly. But it is not till the second hour of the uncommon scene that I become aware of a silent resistless change which is taking place within my mind. One by one, the questions which I have prepared in the train with such meticulous accuracy drop away. For it does not now seem to matter whether they are asked or not, and it does not seem to matter whether I solve the problems which have

> hitherto troubled me. I know only that a steady river of quietness seems to be flowing near me, that a great peace is penetrating the inner reaches of my being, and that my thought-tortured brain is beginning to arrive at some rest.
>
> — Brunton 2003: 141

Another passage records their further meeting:

> On one hot afternoon, when most people are resting, I enter the large hall and sit down near him. He half reclines upon some white cushions placed on the divan. An attendant pulls steadily at the cord which operates the *puṅkhā* — fan. The soft burr of the rope and the gentle swish of the fan as it moves through the sultry air sound pleasantly in my ears.
>
> The Maharṣi holds a folded manuscript book in his hands; he is writing something with extreme seriousness. A few minutes after my entry he puts the book aside and calls a disciple. A few words pass between them in Tamil and the man tells me that his master wishes to reiterate his regrets at my inability to partake of their food. He explains that they live a simple life, and, never having catered for Europeans before, do not know what the latter eat. I thank the Maharṣi, and say that I shall be glad to share their unspiced dishes; for the rest, I shall procure some food from the township. — Ibid., 143

In this essay, I am concerned with the resources provided to social scientists by those who record pilgrimages. I do not enquire into the nature of indoctrination as Barbara Goodwin would have us do (1978), or the critical light-hearted interpretation of "pilgrims and other travellers." My concern in juxtaposing different fragments of pilgrimage accounts, is to argue that while we do have methodologies for taking care of biases, the data provided by such writers goes a long way to establish the primacy of certain kinds of data. As anthropologists in the field, we are subject to sense experiences that we call "subjectivities" and sometimes these pervade our accounts. To be ashamed of them is unnecessary in the new genres of writing that are increasingly made available to us.

Acknowledgement

My grateful thanks to the publishers and Dr Amit K. Sharma for reprinting an essay which previously appeared in *Think India Quarterly* and *The Children of Nature* (Roli 2010). I also thank my friends at Ramanasramam for their hospitality and use of library and archives.

References

Brunton, Paul, *A Search in Secret India*, London: Random House, 2003.

Lévi-Strauss, Claude, *Tristes Tropiques*, Harmondsworth: Penguin, 1976.

Meister, Michael W., *Ethnography and Personhood, Notes from the Field*, Jaipur and New Delhi: Rawat Publications, 2000.

My Life at Sri Ramanasramam, Tiruvannamalai: Sri Ramanasramam Publishers, 1993.

Paranjape, Makarand, "Pilgrims and Other Travellers", *IIC Quarterly*, Spring 1999.

Suri, Nagamma, *Letters from and Recollections of Sri Ramanasramam*, Tiruvannamalai: Sri Ramanasramam Publishers, 1992.

10

Khāsī Religious Beliefs and Practices*

Tiplut Nongbri

KHĀSĪ religion has been interpreted differently by different scholars. According to Dalton, the Khāsī do not appear to be strong in theology, although they believe in a Supreme Being, *U Blei,* they pay more devotion to inferior spirits who reside in hills or in forests. They have no temples or idols connected with their ancient faith. . . . But they are much addicted to consulting auspices, especially in the appearance of eggs on being broken (1973: 57). In a similar vein, Mathur expresses the opinion that magic, medicine and religion are interlinked in the religious system of the Khāsī. According to him a striking feature of Khāsī religion is the use of divination, which the Khāsī resort to on almost all occasions to ascertain the cause of their problems particularly in the event of misfortune, illness and premature death. The diviner makes auguries by breaking eggs and predicts good and bad omens by examining the fall of the shells (1979: 63). This preoccupation with egg-breaking has made Western observers view Khāsī religion as animism or spirit worship. In the words of Gurdon, "the religion of the Khāsī may be described as animism or spirit worship, or rather the propitiation of spirits both good and evil on certain occasions principally in times of trouble" (1975: 105). Bivar even went as far as to say that "Khāsī religion is demon worship, or a jumble of enchantments muttered by priests who are sorcerers" (ibid.: 107). Khāsī

* The Khasi is a matrilineal community situated in the state of Meghalaya, North-East India.

scholars have, however, strongly denied the idea that Khāsī religion is spirit worship. Refuting the claim of Western scholars, Bareh asserts that the Khāsīs have a strong conception of God and the various prayers and sacrifices that they perform are merely means to find the way to Him (Bareh, 1967: 378). To understand the significance of this sharp polarization of opinion we need to look at how the Khāsīs conceptualize religion.

The Khāsī Concept of Religion

To the Khāsīs, religion is a set of beliefs and practices that are designed to restore their link to God. The belief centres on the covenant that governs man's relation to God. The Khāsīs believe that originally humankind had direct interaction with God but due to man's sin the direct link between them was broken. Hence to find their way back to God the Khāsīs had to take recourse to prayers and sacrifices. This is the *raison d'être* of their religion. In the Khāsī language this idea is conspicuous in the very content of the word "religion."

The Khāsī word for religion is *niam* or *ka niam*. It is derived from the words *nia* (reason or argument) and *im* (live). When put together the words mean living reason, that is, the reason that is eternal and timeless and ordained by God Himself. The latter is made explicit by the word *jutang* (covenant) that accompanies the word *nia*. The Khāsīs say *ka nia ka jutang* (the reason, the covenant) not only to emphasize the importance of the idea inherent in the word *nia* but also to establish that the reason (*nia*) itself is an outcome of the covenant (*jutang*). The covenant refers to the agreement that the Khāsīs are supposed to have entered with God following the severance of the link between them, that henceforth they would look for His will in the signs of eggs and sacrificial animals. Though how and in what manner the agreement was made is not clear various versions of this tradition coexist in the society. According to one tradition, following man's fall from the grace of God, the cock, acting as the mediator between the two, offered to lay down his life on behalf of humans in order to secure God's forgiveness for then sins. God accepted the offer and the cock became an important sacrificial object from which time the Khāsīs look for God's will by reading the signs in its viscera and entrails.[1]

What appears ambiguous in empirical terms the Khāsī make explicit through language. This becomes clear if we are familiar with the Khāsī language and the way in which the Khāsī makes use of imitatives to emphasise a point, qualify or add weight to the idea inherent in the word, or to broaden its meaning. By pairing the words, *ka nia ka jutang*, in the form of imitatives the Khāsī concretizes the tradition of the covenant that dispels any possibility of doubt or quarrel on this score. What follows from this is the message that language is a powerful medium that serves not only to communicate but also to legitimize and reinforce the norms and values of a society. The use of language as a means to objectify the subjective experience and norms valued by societies is clearly brought out by Berger and Luckmann:

> Language analyses, recombines and "fixes" biologically-based subjective consciousness and forms it into inter-subjective, typical and communicable experiences. The metaphorical and analogical potential of language facilitates the crystallization of social values and norms by which experience is interpreted. It is this edifice of semantic fields, categories and norms which structures the subjective perceptions of reality into a meaningful, cohesive and "objective" universe. — 1985, 66

In like manner, when the Khāsī speaks of religion it is always accompanied by the imitative *ka rukom* (custom or practice). The Khāsī says *ka niam ka rukom* (the religion the practice) to underscore the fact that an idea cannot attain the status of a belief unless it has the force of a custom which is put into regular practice. In the conception of the Khāsī a belief that is not acted upon is a dead belief and would have no chance

1. The same myth is narrated differently in different regions. Mention of this particular myth has also been made by Bareh (1967), and Natarajan (1977).

of survival even for a single generation. The importance attached to practice not only imposes serious responsibilities on the people making religious duties an integral part of their everyday existence it also adds richness to the system. In practice Khāsī religion is replete with diverse ceremonies and rituals touching on almost every aspect of a person's life.

The above account suggests that the Khāsīs not only have a clear idea of God, they also believe that it is God Himself who gave them their religion; their rites and ceremonies are but means to find their way back to Him. Hence to the Khāsīs religion is not a purposeless belief but an important system of communication that holds a promise of reunification with God. Man's fall from the grace of God had snapped the link between them, but God's generosity and loving kindness still kept the way open for them to communicate with him, through prayers and sacrifices.

But while religion seeks to re-establish Khāsī's link to God it also serves to reinforce solidarity with their fellow beings. That is why the Khāsīs describe their religion as *ka niam tip briew tip blei* (a religion that knows humankind and knows God). This is the quintessence of Khāsī religion. The Khāsī firmly believes that human beings are born into the world not for any mundane purpose but to earn righteousness by living a pious and honest life towards their fellow beings (*u briew u wan sha ka pyrthei ban kamai ia ka hok*). This is the one and only way through which a person can find favour in the eyes of God and thereby "earn" his/her salvation.

The Khāsī Idea of God

While the Khāsīs have a clear conception of God, He is an abstract entity with no physical representation or form, but reveals Himself through his creations. Thus when the Khāsīs speak of God, it is usually in terms of his fundamental attributes such as, *U Blei Trai Kynrad* (God the Overlord), *U Blei Nongbuh Nongthaw* (God the Creator and Maker), *U Blei Nongda Nongker* (God the Protector and Carer), etc. as acknowledgement of his supreme power. In the conception of the Khāsīs God is the Supreme Being who is above all things; he created and regulates the universe, gave the laws to mankind, judges their actions rewarding or punishing them according to their deeds, and is the source of all goodness and justice. That is why when the Khāsīs fail to arbitrate on a dispute they take recourse to ordeals, trusting that God's justice will favour the innocent. Highly cosmopolitan in their outlook, the Khāsī sees God as a universal figure who transcends time and space and is accessible to all those who believe in him. Similarly, in recognition of his transcendental character they associate God both with the feminine and masculine gender, which explains why they simultaneously address Him as *U Blei* (He God) and *Ka Blei* (She God)[2] or at times speak of God in honorific plural *Ki Blei* (The Gods). The Khāsī conception of God as the Supreme Being that is omnipotent, omnipresent and omniscient lends strong weight to the idea that Khāsī religion is monotheistic in nature. Though the Khāsī religious pantheon includes a plurality of spiritual beings, which are regularly propitiated, these are considered to be lesser beings who are subjected to the control of God.

Spirits and Deities

But before we jump to any conclusion on the nature of Khāsī religion it would be prudent to first take a close look at the spirit world. Broadly, two kinds of spirits are discernible in the Khāsī religious pantheon, the good or benevolent spirits and the evil or malevolent spirits. The former primarily comprised the souls of the dead who could not find the way to their heavenly abode due to the improper performance of their mortuary rituals. Dr Homiwell Lyngdoh describes how the soul of those persons whose mortuary rituals are not

2. Ehrenfels attributes this bi-sexual conception of God to the influence of matriliny. Discussing at some length the Khāsī mode of sex determination, he draws a parallel between the Khāsī idea of *U Blei* and *Ka Blei* with the Śiva-Śakti complex, the Hindu divine couple (U.R. Ehrenfels, in Vidyarthi, 1961).

satisfactorily executed by their living relatives turn into spirits which wander about in the atmosphere with no proper dwelling place. However, as these spirits comprise the souls of persons who lead good lives in their lifetime they are basically friendly spirits which cause no harm to humans (1962: 24).

Malevolent spirits on the other hand are antagonistic to humans, and are of two types. The first are made up of the souls of persons who because of their evil deeds during their lifetime have no room for them in heaven but are forced to remain on this earth, seeking shelter in dark, haunted places frequented by demons. These spirits are prone to trouble the living in various ways. Just as in their lifetime wrongdoers are a threat to the society; similarly, after death their spirit continues to be a source of trouble for humans. These spirits come under the control of *Ka Tyrut*, the queen of demons, and serve as her agents visiting humans in the form of illness, accidents, misfortunes, etc. And, it is not just the living alone who are susceptible to their attack, particularly vulnerable are the souls of the newly departed which are their most sought-after victims and whom they try to ensnare as they make their way to heaven. To ward off their evil influence and to ensure that the soul of the dead reaches its final resting-place in the other world without any mishap on the way the Khāsīs perform a series of sacrifices at the death of a person. These rituals start right from the time the soul leaves the body till the bones of the deceased are safely deposited in the clan cromlech.[3]

The second category of malevolent spirits are those which reside in nature, usually in secluded spots, deep rivers and streams that are considered dangerous for humans to venture into. These spirits cover a wide range, from the whimsical to

3. The latter, however, could take years to be completed, till the family could make the necessary arrangements to transfer the bones from the temporary shelter (cairns or *mawshieng*) kept after cremation to the clan cromlech (*mawbah*) where the bones of all clan members are kept.

the dangerous. Some may indulge in petty pranks with humans making them walk in their sleep or get them mentally disoriented while others could bring about serious diseases, infertility, famine and pestilence. To counter their evil powers these spirits are regularly propitiated by means of animal sacrifices, such as pigs and fowls. Since these spirits directly affect the daily realities of life their propitiation assumes an important place in Khāsī religion. Some of the spirits that are feared are, *u rih* which causes fever, *ka niangriang* which causes pus formation in the ear, *ka puri* which causes lunacy, *u kla* and *u tynjang* which cause people to wander about in the dark.

Besides the belief in spirits another distinctive feature of Khāsī religion is the institution of *ki phan ki kyrpad*. These are deities instituted by the family or clan for a particular purpose. Specifically, the practice is directed to address an immediate problem faced by the family/clan and usually takes place after first seeking the approval of God (Rabon Singh, 1950: 4). According to Mawrie *ki phan ki kyrpad* came into being because of the incessant inadequacies humans experience in their existence. Human life is such that it rarely brings total fulfilment of one's needs — if one is fully equipped in one part, there is want in the other. There might be wealth coupled with illness, health with barrenness, etc. This led man to concentrate his prayers and sacrifices only in that direction where there is an immediate and more urgent need. This concentration of prayers and sacrifices in that particular direction is a sort of deification of that particular issue. For example, *ki phan long kur* are invoked to secure the progress of the clan, *ki phan long ing* for the welfare of the family and household and *ki phan eh rngiew* to enhance the luck and fortune of an individual. If by worshipping such deities they achieve their objective thanks are given to God. At the same time, in extreme distress when propitiation to all lesser divinities fail the Khāsīs fall back on their last resort, *U Blei*, the high God (Mawrie, 1973: 114).

It is this supreme power that vests in *U Blei* that, notwithstanding the glaring duality in the Khāsī religious pantheon, the Khāsīs strongly maintain that their religion is monotheistic in nature. In a bid to justify this theory Mawrie sought to explain the presence of the myriad spirits in the Khāsī belief system by attributing it as a falling away from monotheism to polytheism. He observes that originally the Khāsī believed in a singular God but it was only with the increase of evil among humankind that they started to attribute godly qualities to natural objects (ibid.: 37). Bareh too is of the view that belief in spirits is a later development that occurred as an outcome of evil and pollution in the society (1967, op. cit.: 355).

In the course of my discussion with various informants, I inquired whether the Khāsīs believe in a single God or plurality of them. It is interesting to note that even those who still profess the traditional faith strongly uphold the view that the Khāsīs believe in only one God. Some of the answers supplied by my informants regarding the Khāsī belief system illustrate the rationality with which the people look at the matter. Confronted with the question to explain why the Khāsīs propitiate innumerable deities with different names one of my informants (a farmer who has read up to class V aged about 50 years) replies, "You are right there, yes we Khāsīs seem to have a variety of deities. But they are not different gods, it is God himself addressed in different ways in relation to the different roles and purpose for which he is invoked. For instance we say *ka blei ing* (family Goddess) this means it is God himself but referred as such in his role as the protector of the family, similarly, *ka blei synshar* (the ruling Goddess) denotes God as protector of the state."

This line of thinking closely approximates to what Evans-Pritchard describes as "the social refractions of the idea of God." In his discussion of Nuer religion, Evans-Pritchard outlines a similar pattern of religious thought. He observes that,

> The Nuer conception of God (*kwoth*), with a great variety of meanings attached to it in different contexts and the manner in which the Nuers pass, even in the same ceremony, from one to another may bewilder an observer. The Nuers, however, are not confused, for the difficulties which perplex the observer do not arise on the level of experience but only when an attempt is made to analyse and systematize Nuer religious thought.
>
> — 1960: 55-57

Religion and the Problem of Meaning

While there is no doubt that Khāsī religion is highly monotheistic in orientation the preoccupation with isms in academic and popular discourse tends to overshadow the real significance of the system. In this regard both the indigenous and Western observers appear to be bogged down with the same fault. Though rich descriptions are available on the system there is little explanation about why the Khāsīs believe the way they do. To arrive at a realistic understanding of the problem it is vital that we try to unravel the underlying logic that structures the system. In this context we need to relate the subject under consideration not only to the native categories of thought and meaning but also to the existential conditions under which they live. Religion is a system of meaning, which helps the believer to make sense of the empirical reality within which he/she is embedded. Human beings in all stages of history continuously seek answers to problems that affect their everyday reality. Problems of sickness and death, scarcity and want demand explanations not only to counter their adverse effect but also for emotional assurance and stability. Religion is one way through which they do this. Indeed, according to Max Weber for the adherents religion with its set of beliefs and practices, provides the ultimate answer to the problem of meaning. What this meant to the believer in concrete terms has been sharply summed up by Beattie:

> On the cognitive level, they provide satisfactory answers to otherwise insolvable questions: they fill gaps in human

> knowledge and experience and so diminish areas of doubt and uncertainty. Thus religious belief and practice may give confidence in the face of dangers, and even if these means are generally scientifically ineffective, they are satisfying morally and emotionally. — 1977: 238

Clearly, religion has to be understood as a symbolic system that is not only concerned with the Ultimate Truth but also with the transitoriness of earthly existence and man's vulnerability to the uncontrollable powers of the cosmos. Through religion man tries to counter his own powerlessness and uses his intellect to conceptualize the power that lies beyond his immediate environment, thereby creating a sacred world which he himself is simultaneously a part of and excluded from it. To borrow Durkheim's terminology, while man belongs to the profane world (empirical reality) religion connects him to the sacred world (cosmic reality). This construct not only enables man to satisfy his emotional and intellectual quest for making sense of the things that defy mundane rationality, also by locating him within the wider ordering of the sacred universe it endows his existence with greater meaning and purpose. Thus life becomes not an end in itself but a journey into a better world. The proximity between the two worlds is especially close in simple societies where the exigency of existence makes the experience of illness and sufferings more dramatic. This not only increases their dependence on the supernatural but also makes them perceive the supernatural world in a manner that is more real to their experience.

Looked at from this perspective it would be presumptuous to undermine the presence of spirits in Khāsī religion by attributing it simply to the effect of evil and pollution. Such an interpretation not only tends to denigrate the system, it also ignores the emotional, social and ethical concerns that are central to the belief.

A careful consideration of the problem shows that belief in spirits represents one of the ways in which the early Khāsīs tried to explain, predict and control the events that take place in their life. For instance, ascribing illness and misfortunes to be the handiwork of spirits not only helps the affected to look for appropriate ways to address the problem, it is also an acknowledgement of the power that the supernatural have over humans. To the Khāsī, the line separating the natural from the supernatural world is a thin one. Every event that takes place in this life is believed to be directed from above and spirits are the agents through which the divine interventions operate. Yet spirits by themselves have no power over humans unless God allows them to do so. But it is man's actions in the first place that invite God to intervene in their earthly affairs. When humans fail to live by the ordained laws God steers them to the right path by using the agency of spirits. That is why whenever suffering or misfortune strikes an individual or a family the Khāsī immediately takes recourse to divination to ascertain the cause of the malady and after locating the cause proceeds with sacrifices to appease the offended spirits and then offers prayers to God to seek his forgiveness.

Belief in spirits also helps the Khāsī to infuse moral and ethical values in the minds of the people. By alluding that the souls of wrong doers turn into evil spirits the Khāsī indirectly seeks to control the adverse consequences of evil ways, which inevitably lead to instability and anomie in society. By personifying the souls of such persons as evil beings in the clutches of demons and who must forever remain estranged from God, the imagery exerts a powerful influence especially in the minds of the young and the impressionable about the horrifying results of sinful lives.[4]

4. Though there is no conception of heaven as in Christianity, the Khāsī believe that the souls of the dead go to the house of God (*ha dwar ka blei*), which is conceived as a beautiful mansion with massive grounds where people sit around in leisure. That is why whenever the Khāsī speak of the dead they use the phrase *bam kwai hu ing U Blei* (eating betel nut in the house of God) to signify their happy state in the other world. Wrongdoers, however, find no place in this divine sanctuary.

What follows from the above is that belief in spirits is nothing short of a system of rationalization of a variety of human experiences, needs and values. By conceiving them in relation to spiritual or supernatural entities the Khāsīs not only try to arrive at answers for things that are seemingly inexplicable but also make use of divine injunction as a means to enforce order and stability in the society. The latter is by no means unique to the Khāsī. The use of religion as an instrument to enforce ethical standards is a widely prevalent phenomenon. Even established religions like Christianity and Islam use religious tenets and metaphors to impose moral standards on their believers. The same explanation applies to the attribution of sacredness to natural spaces and objects among the Khāsī.

The Ecological Dimension of Khāsī Religion

As noted earlier, Khāsī religion exhibits a deep respect for nature. Natural phenomena like sunshine, lightning and rainfall are not only seen as a manifestation of God's power but nature itself is regarded as sacred. In the conception of the Khāsī all natural objects (animate and inanimate) are sacred, since they are all the creations of God (*ki long ki jingthaw jong u Blei*). Central to this conception is the principle of the unity of all existence, which finds lucid expression in the Khāsī view of the universe, or more appropriately their cosmic vision. A brief examination of the Khāsī idea of creation would make this clear. In the words of Juanita War:

> In the beginning *Ka Hukum* (the commandment or law, that is, God the law-giver) made *Ka Ramew* (the Earth/*terra firma*). Initially it was covered with water. *Ka Hukum* then created *U Ryngkew* (dry land). The big rivers (*umbah* or *ka shor*) and the small streams (*ka suit*) cleansed the earth, bringing out the stone and earth (soil). Since that time the earth and the dry land became one. This is figuratively narrated as the marriage of *Ka Ramew* and *U Ryngkew*. . . .
>
> *Ka Hukum* also created the heavenly bodies — the sun, moon

> and stars which rest on *U Mawsiang Bneng* (heavenly slab/stone), and nature (*mariang*), water (*um*), fire (*ding*), air (*lyer*) which stand on *U Mawsiang Khyndew* (earthly slab/stone).
>
> The whole of creation operates according to the universal law of *Ka Nong Hukum* (the law-giver) and everything runs according to their appointed course. Thus the sun invariably rises in the morning at sunrise, and sets in the evening. The waters in the oceans and in the streams run within their given boundaries. The wind blows according to the direction of the Almighty. . . .
>
> There is equality among all things, since all things originate from *Ka Mei Ramew* and *U Ryngkew*. Also all created things are under the rule of *Ka Hok Ka Ktien* and *Ka Hukum*. The loving and caring hands of mother nature reach out to all, great or small. The tiny ant has as much right to live its life as the huge elephant. The gentle deer can graze on the same meadow as the wild bison. Man, however, has a special place since he was sent from heaven to steward the earth. — 1995: 55-56

Implicit in the above lines is the unity and mutual dependence of all things. Since all things originate from the same source and subject to the same laws ordained by God the law-giver (*na U Blei Nong ai hukum*), this not only renders all beings equal but also fosters close relationship and interdependence between them. In the Khāsī conception, all beings are part of one cosmic body (*Ka metbah*). Hence humans cannot have a monopoly over nature. On the other hand, humans have a responsibility towards the preservation of nature, as the survival of the universe and their very own survival depend upon their ability to adhere to the ecological principle that demands amicable coexistence of all beings and judicious use of its resources. In other words, as creatures that are endowed with greater intellect than others, it is imperative upon humans to act as the custodian of the environment to ensure that the bounties of nature are not abused or misused.

A point of clarification, however, needs to be inserted at this juncture. The concept of custodianship used above has to be read ontologically as it does not have the same meaning as is often understood in the West (see for instance Lynn White Jr., 1967). In the conception of the Khāsīs, custodianship does not confer superior claim on the holder(s) over the things under their custody, rather it imposes a responsibility upon them to ensure distributive justice and equality of access to all the stakeholders, which includes both human and non-human users. The concept carries the same meaning as the custodianship of ancestral property held by *ka khadduh*. Just as *ka khadduh*'s right to the custody of the ancestral property gives her no proprietarial right over it but rather has to fulfil numerous obligations towards the wider family by virtue of her role, the same kind of responsibilities rest on humans *vis-à-vis* the natural environment.

The institution of sacred groves and the deification of *U Ryngkew U Basa*[5] are practices that uphold this perspective. Variously known as *Law Lyngdoh* (Lyngdoh forest), *Law Kyntang* (Sacred forest) or *Law Niam* (Religious forest), sacred groves represent a long tradition of environmental conservation that recognizes the right of all beings. By treating sacred groves as the habitat of gods and deities it ensures the protection of the flora and fauna that abound in nature. Till recent times elaborate rituals are carried out in many parts of the Khāsī and Jaintiā hills to propitiate the deities that are believed to reside in these sacred sites. Though the rites vary from place to place, in some cases they may be restricted to specific families and clans, the ecological benefits accrue to the community as a whole. Notable among such rites is the propitiation of *U Lei Shillong* (the Shillong god), a deity of the Khyrim state which resides in the sacred grove at the Shillong Peak. The Shillong god is believed to be the progenitor of *Ka Pahsyntiew*, the ancestress of the *Syiem* of Khyrim who was

5. Though in some parts *U Basa* is seen as a distinct entity the name actually refers to *U Ryngkew*, the consort of *Ka Ramew*. The word *U Basa* is an imitative of the word *U Ryngkew* and the two refer to a single entity. In Khāsī religion, *U Ryngkew U Basa* is a deity that protects the village or clusters of villages from enemies, diseases or any other calamity.

captured by a man of the *Mylliemngap* clan from a cave near Nongkrem. Every year the *Syiem* of Khyrim offers animal sacrifices to the Shillong god during the *Pomblang* festival. Other deities of special significance in Khāsī religion are those which reside in the Kyllang and Symper rocks, *U Mawlong Syiem* in the Mawsmai sacred grove near Cherra-punjee, *Mih Myntdu* in the Jaintiā hills and at the *Law Lyngdoh* in Mawphlang. Besides the land-based deities, the Khāsī also propitiated deities, which reside in rivers and streams. *Ka Kupli* in the Jaintiā hills and *ka Rilang* in West Khāsī hills are regarded as important water deities which were regularly propitiated in the past (cf. Bareh, op. cit.: 359-61).

Significantly, most of the sacred groves present in the region are located on the catchment areas of important rivers and streams or in highly fragile ecological conditions. According to one study, about 60 sacred groves in the state of Meghalaya, covering an area of 6,500 ha are located at the source of perennial streams. For example, the sacred grove at the Shillong Peak is the origin of as many as 10 streams, which serve as the main source of water supply to the citizens of Shillong (Syngai, 1999: 71). This clearly shows that the early Khāsīs not only had a high level of environmental consciousness but were also equipped with an efficient sytem of conservation technique. Evidently, by couching the practice in the idiom of religion conservation of nature becomes part of the social and cultural life of the people.

What emerges from the above discussion is that Khāsī religion is based on a set of social, ecological and normative principles, which are built on the people's experience and expectations culled through generations of interaction with their social and natural environment. Their myths and legends are a dramatic assertion of this fact. Hence any attempt to understand the Khāsī religious system cannot afford to view the problem from without and dismiss it as a blind belief in spirits devoid of inner logic or rationality. Khāsī religion goes beyond animism or the simple attribution of soul to inanimate objects but encompasses the people's vision and philosophy of what in their perception they consider an ideal state of things to be achieved.

While the Khāsīs propitiate a number of spirits they worship only one God, *U Blei* (the Supreme Being) who they believe controls the universe and all that includes in it. The former arises because of the exigencies of human life, which is subjected to the interplay between two opposing forces, sickness and health, suffering and happiness, darkness and light, falsehood and truth. Although God is perceived as the source of all goodness his remoteness and the society's lack of technological facilities to address the practical problems of health and sufferings that afflict human existence made people's perception of the power of spirits more real. Believed to have immense power on vital aspects of their daily life such as children, health, crops, etc. they are regularly propitiated and ritualized.

It would not be too wrong to say that the Khāsī belief in spirits is directly tied up with their location within a harsh and hostile surrounding. To protect themselves from diseases and pestilence that abound in abundance people took steps to counter them in the way they knew best, by appealing to supernatural forces and appeasing them through offerings and sacrifices. In this regard the supernatural world became the world of spirits. Nature itself became both a foe and an ally. While it personifies the power and magnificence of God where he manifests in various forms it also gives shelter to evil spirits who lurk in dark dingy corners, in whirlpools and streams and in the angry winds and thunderstorms. The principle of peaceful coexistence demands that humans should not encroach upon their precincts; survival needs, however, make this practically impossible. Forests had to be cleared for cultivation, jungles and rivers crossed for game and fish, springs and streams had to be tamed to get water for domestic use, in short all the items of everday use, wood, water, air, medicine, food, etc. come from nature. So what is the solution? How should man act so as not to annoy the spirits which reside in nature? Functional theory sees man in society as characterized by two kinds of needs and two kinds of propensities to act — man must act upon the environment either by adjusting to it or mastering and controlling it, to ensure their own survival (O'Dea, 1969: 4). While the Western man evidently opted for the latter by using science and technology to subdue nature the Khāsī clearly opted for the former. Taking recognition of the rights of other beings they take recourse to divination and reading of omens in an attempt not to intrude into their precincts, and if by chance they do so then appease them through offerings and sacrifices. However, when everything is well with the world the Khāsī give their thanks and praise to God.

To understand the nuances of the Khāsī belief system it is important to take a close look at the native categories of thought and symbols that are salient to their religion. One such category is the word *mane* (pronounced as *ma-ne,* i.e. worship), which is used only in relation to God and never to other spiritual beings. The Khāsīs say *ngi mane is U Blei* (we worship God) and never *ngi mane ia ki ksuid* (we worship spirits). Spirits are propitiated and appeased for their capacity to trouble humans but are never worshipped. Neither is the word *mane* ever applied in relation to the ancestors. Although propitiation of the ancestors constitutes an important part of the Khāsī ritual complex they are not worshipped in the way in which the act operates in relation to God. As supernatural beings, ancestors (more on this later) are believed to possess immense powers to intercede with God on behalf of the living but they are never objects of worship, as the act is understood in Khāsī. Hence the use of the word "ancestor worhip" to describe the ancestor cult amongst the Khāsī by some scholars is misplaced. In the conception of the Khāsī only *U Blei,* the Supreme Being, commands or is worthy of worship. Although the linguistic distinction between propitiation and worship is rather thin in the English language, the way in which the term *mane* operates in Khāsī makes the distinction between the two acts fairly clear. As a frame of action, the word *mane* sharply divides the supernatural entities into those which command unqualified reverance and devotion (*U Blei* alone) and those which are objects of ritual attention for other purposes (spirits and ancestors). It is this conception of *U Blei* as a Being who stands apart from, and above all other beings that make the Khāsī claim that their religion is monotheistic.

Rituals and Ceremonies

An analysis of beliefs without looking at rituals is incomplete. If beliefs mirror the way in which the people perceive their social and natural universe, rituals represent the way in which they act upon their belief. Though not entirely devoid of instrumental content rituals are basically symbolic in nature. Rituals not only express the anxieties, fears and hopes of the participants, they also serve as strong social pointers to their status and status relations and of the world they live in. How and in what manner this is manifested will become clear as we look at the various rituals practised by the people.

Broadly, any event that affects the well-being of the individual and/or group(s) calls for ritual attention. Illness and calamities that threaten to disrupt the normal tenor of existence need to be countered by rituals. Events such as birth, marriage and death are attended to by rituals. Similarly, assumption of social and political office or mundane activities like constructing a house, sowing of seeds and harvesting are sanctified with rituals. Anthropologists distinguished the rituals performed on these different occasions into piacular and confirmatory rites (Evans Pritchard, 1956: 272; see also Mair, 1972: 232-44). Piacular rites are those which are performed in situations of danger such as illness and calamities. As is the case with the Khāsī, in many simple societies illness is not seen simply as a natural process that affects an individual, but is believed to be caused by supernatural forces due to some fault committed by the affected or by his/her family members. Hence to ward off the danger the offence has to be amended by expiatory rites. In many instances this involves the appeasement of the offended spirits and deities with live offerings in which case it takes the form of a sacrifice.

Confirmatory rites, on the other hand, are those which are performed during life crisis events associated with birth, marriage and death or during periods of status change, as in institutions of kingship and age grades and/or during an individual's passage from childhood to adolescence or from youth to adulthood. These are what the French scholar, Arnold Van Gennep described as the "Rites of Passage" almost a century ago (1908/1960). Van Gennep argues that human life is made up of a succession of stages/events — birth, marriage and death — that mark an individual's passage from one status position to another. For every one of these events there are ceremonies whose essential purpose is to enable the individual to pass through the transitional phase. The ceremonies are important not only for the social recognition of the individual's newly acquired status but also for his smooth integration into the new status position. According to Van Gennep an individual does not merely pass through the successive stages of life; each transition has to be validated by society otherwise his integration into the next stage would not be complete. To Van Gennep what is important is the transitional stage, which he defines as liminal or threshold and the crossing of which assumes a sacred character because it unites the one who passes through it with a new world. To emphasize the importance and multi-dimensional aspects of this transition he further distinguished the rites of passage into rites of separation, rites of transition and rites of incorporation. Though there is some minor disagreement on the terms used by the translator in the English version of the book Van Gennep's schema provides a powerful conceptual framework for the analysis of rituals.[6]

6. The British scholar, John Beattie, disagreed with the translators's use of the word Rites of Passage and prefers to call it "transition rituals." He also substitutes the word "transition" in rites of transition noted above as rites of Segregation because at this stage the individual occupies no recognized status in society but is, as it were, betwixt and between (op. cit., 211).

This brief excursion into theory provides the necessary prelude for a systematic analysis of Khāsī rituals. This, however, is not to suggest that the above classification exhausts the full possibility of rituals found in the society. For instance, while propitiation of the ancestors constitutes an important part of piacular rituals among the Khāsī, their ancestor cult cannot be strictly classified as piacular rites. In the following paragraphs we shall take a close view at Khāsī rituals, focusing in particular on divination, birth, marriage and death rituals, and intercessionary and thanksgiving rituals.

Divination

As would be obvious from the preceding discussion, divination occupies a prominent position in the religious practice of the Khāsī. This is a technique that the Khāsī invariably employs to find out the cause of illness, misfortune or sufferings that afflict an individual or a family and to ascertain the auspiciousness or otherwise of an event or a thing. In the past, divination was an everyday occurrence in the life of the Khāsī. A Khāsī would not venture into any activity without first taking recourse to divination to ascertain whether the intended activity concurs with God's will or not. In the ritual complex of the Khāsī, divination usually precedes all other rites. For our purpose, however, we will look at how divination operates specifically in the diagnosis of illness and misfortune.

As a diagnostic procedure divination is usually conducted by a senior male member of the subject's family, or in the absence of one, a close relation or any person whom the family trusts and considers to be well-versed in the technique. A variety of devices, egg-breaking (*shat pylleng*), fowl slaughter (*khad syiar*), cowrie shells (*khan sbai*), rice grains (*khan khaw*) or a lime container (*khan shanam*) may be used in divination. But irrespective of the means employed the rite begins with the diviner asking for the sign (*pan ia ka dak*) from God and then proceeds to interpret the same (*it ia ka dak*) from the positions or appearance of the ritual objects used. Where egg-breaking is the means employed the diviner reads the auguries from the positions of the shells that fall on or around the wooden board against which the egg was broken. If the signs obtained are negative, the diviner proceeds with the task again asking for fresh signs or focusing on new causes till the desired result is achieved. Although there are no fixed rules about how the signs should be asked and interpreted (the accuracy of interpretation primarily depends upon the signs asked) years of practice has given rise to a standardized pattern of interpretation. The position of the shells right or left of the board, or the manner in which the fragments fall face turned upwards or downwards, are supposedly taken to indicate good or bad omens accordingly. Any impending disaster that may befall the family such as sickness, death or other calamity could also be read from the fall of the shells.

Similar procedures are followed where fowls are used in the place of eggs. Here the diviner reads the signs by examining the entrails and viscera of the slaughtered bird and predicts favourable or unfavourable outcome from their appearance. The colour, shape and health of the internal organs, such as liver, heart, kidney and spleen indicate concurrence or otherwise to the signs asked. The position of the intestines especially is crucial as the Khāsīs believe that God's response to the rite can be inferred from the distance of two protuberances in the intestine, which are appropriately distinguished as God and man. If the two points move towards each other or if the membrane connecting the two is not fractured the sign is taken as positive and if the reverse occurs the result is considered to be negative.

Central to divination is the firm belief that nothing happens without a cause (*ka daw*). Hence solution to a problem can be arrived at only if we could identify the causal factor that gave rise to it. This demands a close scrutiny of the problem and the life and actions of the affected person. Broadly, causes are classified into two distinct categories: internal cause (*daw ing*) and external cause (*daw lum*). Internal cause is linked to the family and the clan and external cause to the outer domain or the natural world at large. Briefly, internal cause occurs because of the breach of socially stipulated rules by the afflicted or any of his/her family members. External cause, on the other hand, is attributed to problems that are brought about by spirits that lurk in nature.

In empirical terms, however, the two causes are closely interrelated. If the internal domain is above reproach, that is so long as the members adhere to the laws (both human- and God-given) the powers of the external domain are kept at bay. However, breach of the stipulated norms by any of its members reduces the immunity of the family, thereby exposing them to external dangers. That is why whenever illness or misfortune strikes a family, the Khāsī first of all looks into the domestic domain to see if any of its members had violated the prescribed norms which enable the external forces to cast their power over them. Once the cause is located the diviner offers prayers and sacrifice to God and to the ancestors, seeking their forgiveness and help to restore the afflicted person to the normal state and to extend their protection over the family. To emphasize the seriousness of the matter the Khāsī appropriately defines this ritual act as *ka khein ka bishar* (*khein* means to calculate, examine or evaluate and *bishar* means to judge). By couching the ritual in the language of law the Khāsīs emphasize the importance of arriving at the root (truth) of the matter through a careful examination of all evidence available. And, once the truth has been established it calls for proper atonement through rituals. Failure to do this would not only make the violators stand condemned in the eyes of God but also render them vulnerable to evil forces.

The description of divination given above is based on first-hand observations of a series of rites conducted by U Ein Warlarpih (alias *u kpa ka Rial* or Rial's father) in Nongkrem village where he was the diviner of the Lyngdoh family when I was carrying out my doctoral research. Except for the incantation that accompanied the ritual, which slightly differed from case to case depending on the problem addressed by the rite in question, the procedure remained largely the same and broadly conformed to the descriptions given by Gurdon (1975). However, Gurdon made no attempt to spell out the implicit meaning of the rite. It needs to be noted that what is significant about divination is not the procedure or means adopted, but the meaning that underlies the act. Broadly, two things stand out in divination. Firstly, it brings out the close link that exists between Khāsī religion and the family. Secondly, it highlights the tacit trust that the Khāsīs have in the supernatural to provide them the solution to the problems they confronted. Indeed, at the higher level of abstraction divination not only reflects the Khāsī's deep faith in the supernatural but also a reaffirmation of the idea, implicit in the covenant of the cock and the tales of U Hynniewtrep, that their empirical world is but an extension of the sacred world. Man's sins had fractured the link between the two and divination is an attempt to restore that link. This objective finds clear expression in the incantation, "I have sinned" recited by the diviner during egg-breaking and/or cock sacrifice and his asking God not to forget the covenant pledged, but to accept the ritual offering as a sign of his atonement for the wrongs committed.

Rites Associated with the Ancestors

As stated in the previous section propitiation of the ancestors constitutes an important feature of Khāsī religion. In fact, it would not be far wrong to say that invocation of the ancestors is an integral part of most Khāsī rituals. Besides invoking them in divination and in the life cycle rituals the ancestors are regularly propitiated by means of feasts and sacrifice by the family and the clan over whom they extend their protection. To the Khāsī ancestors are not just dead relatives, more importantly they are the guardians and protectors of the living. The primordial ancestress of the clan Ka Iawbei, her husband U Thawlang and brother U Suidnia are particularly revered and are invested with spiritual qualities that raise their status to the level of deities. These are the three cardinal figures that formed the cornerstone of the Khāsī family. To commemorate their memory and immortalize the important position they occupy in the family and the clan megalithic structures depicting the ancestors are erected during funerary rituals and bone burial ceremonies. But while the Thawlang is venerated in his conjugal family his figure is excluded from the megaliths of his wife's clan. In keeping with the matrilineal principle and the ideology of the ritual unity of the sibling group he finds representation in his own clan in the role of the maternal uncle. That is why Khāsī megaliths usually comprise a group of three spherical stones (menhirs) standing vertically on the ground representing the maternal uncle and his sister's sons and a flat oval stone (dolmen) lying in front of the menhirs, which stands for the ancestress of the clan and lineage. However, to commemorate the memory of the father a man's children occasionaly set up a single stone that is known as *mawnam* or *maw kpa*. According to the late mother of the Lyngdoh of Nongkrem this memorial is usually instituted to mark the transfer of the father's bones (*ai kpa*) to his natal family. Today remnants of these stone monuments are visible in many parts of the Khāsī and Jaintiā hills.

An important component of the ancestor cult is *ka ai bam*, the offering of food and sacrifice to the dead. The rite is usually performed as thanksgiving to the ancestors for blessings that the family experienced during the preceding years or months. The rite normally involves the sacrifice of a hen or a pig and assumes the form of a feast between the ancestors and the living members. To the accompaniment of a prayer, wherein they simultaneously thank and solicit the ancestors for their continuous blessings, food particles are symbolically offered to the dead by dropping small pieces of meat, pinched from the organs of the sacrificial animals, at the altar especially constructed for the purpose. The internal organs are purposely chosen as these are regarded as most delicious and treated as delicacies in the Khāsī cuisine. The number of pieces offered vary usually from five to nine or depending upon the number of families which take part in the rite. The left-overs from the pieces and the rest of the sacrificial meat are consumed by the clan members and their guests who are invited for the rite. Gurdon compares the *ai bam* of the Khāsī with the offering of rice balls (*piṇḍa*) in the Hindu funerary rituals (*śrāddha*) and to the ancient Shinto cult of the Japanese, which possessed several features in common with the ancestor cult of the Khāsī (op. cit.: 110-11).

Reverence of the ancestors has its roots in the high respect the Khāsīs accord to the senior members of the family. Although the system of age grade, which exists among many African tribes, is absent among the Khāsī, age and generation play an important part in determining a person's position in the society. An elderly person of an ascending generation is associated not only with maturity and wisdom but also with integrity and moral worth. Parentage and a responsible dispensation towards the wider family and the clan add merit to a person's status and overall standing both within the family and the community at large (though the weight definitely swings in favour of men). Elders in the family, such as the father and the mother's brother are regarded as protectors, guides and counsellors whom the junior members of the family must give due respect and obedience.

It is considered a sacrilege for a Khāsī to fail to honour their dead members. Such a lapse would not only hurt their sentiments but would also bring bad luck and misfortune to the family. As members who have gone ahead to the house of God (*kiba la leit ha shwa sha dwar u Blei*) ancestors are believed to possess considerable power over the living. That is why whenever a Khāsī fails to resolve a problem the help of ancestors is solicited. Two other practices that are occasionally followed by families in the rural areas are *ka kynruh shang kwai* (shaking of the betel basket) and the use of *ka jing phong* (a small strip of cotton cloth) to call on the ancestors in times of trouble. In the first, the practitioner ceremonially holds the betel basket (an integral item in practically all Khāsī homes) in her lap, tilts it slightly as if looking for some ingredient and speaks to the ancestors as she would to a living person sitting next to her. Acting as if the ancestors are physically present she prepares the betel leaves and betel nut to offer them while she recounts the problem that afflicts the family and calling upon them to intercede with God on their behalf. This ceremony is usually resorted to in case of protracted illness, family disputes or indebtedness. It can be carried out at any time of the day but is usually done in solitude to avoid distraction and to maintain privacy.

The second practice is adopted when a child in the family suffers from perpetual ill-health, throws tantrums, or exhibits extreme irritability. This is taken as a sign that the ancestors lament (*ki ud ki iam*) over some acts of omission and commission made by the living. To appease their spirits the affected child is made to don a *jing phong*. If the child is a female the cloth is pinned over the shoulder the way adult women wear the *jain kyrshah* (the outer apron that is worn to protect the dress from getting soiled while working) and if the child is a male it is worn as a sleaveless jacket. Alternatively, the cloth can be spread out over the pillow used by the child. Interestingly, this practice is associated with the ancestors on the paternal side of the family and appears to be a re-enaction of the customary gift of a *jainit* made to a newborn child by the father's mother or his sister. The *jainit* is a long cloth made of thick unbleached cotton, the same material as the *jingphong*, and is used to strap the baby to the mother's back while she works. The gift is not only a show of affection but symbolizes the close bond that exists between a man's mother and sister (*meikha* and *nia kha*) on the one hand and his children (*khun kha*) on the other. While matriliny attaches the child to the mother's clan it is morally and socially bound to the father's clan by a strict code of conduct that demands deference and honour to the father's kin. The bond is not confined to this life only but continues even after death. Children and grandchildren are expected to pay homage to their father's and grandfather's kin for generations.

Rituals of Birth, Marriage, and Death

Among the Khāsī all life cycle events are occasions for rituals. Rituals are performed to confer social recognition on a newborn child, rituals are also necessary to sanctify a marriage and in death rituals are needed to aid the soul of the departed to reach its final resting place. In short, from birth to death life is marked by a series of rituals.

Indeed, in the past rituals preceded an individual's entry into this world. When a gestating woman reached the third or fourth month of pregnancy a rite known as *tap kpoh* used to be conducted to ensure safe and easy delivery of the child. A white hen was sacrificed to invoke the blessings of God for the mother and child. To ensure that the prayer offered had been accepted by God the priest looked for the sign in the entrails of the hen sacrificed. If the signs show a favourable response he would offer his thanks to God, otherwise he would proceed again with another hen till he obtains the positive answer.

Birth itself is not marked by the performance of rituals although it is an occasion for rejoicing for the family. Irrespective of the sex of the baby its arrival is greeted with joy and best wishes bestowed on its health, luck and happiness by all those present on the occasion and by friends and relatives who visit the mother and child. However, extreme precaution has to be taken so that evil spirits do not get a chance to harm the baby. A newborn baby is not only physically delicate but is also highly vulnerable to mystical forces; it is particularly susceptible to attack by water-dwelling spirits. To prevent such an eventuality from taking place special vessels are bought before the delivery to keep and heat water for the baby's bath. Taboos are also imposed on parents from crossing streams and rivers till the umbilical cord of the child has fallen off and its stump carefully tucked in the loft of the house. The child itself is kept indoors till after a sacrifice of appeasement to the spirits of the wild is made to secure their protection over the child.

In the perception of the Khāsī a newly born baby is not a social being but a godling (*khun Iawbei or khun Blei*). The child acquires its identity as a social being only after it has been duly named. Till the child is named the placenta is kept in the house covered in an earthen pot and not disposed of for fear that the spirits will whisk away its soul. To expedite the incorporation of the child into the social world the naming ceremony takes place directly the morning after birth. The ritual itself is simple and is carried out in the presence of the father's mother or the father's sisters besides the parents and other family members, friends and relatives. The priest or any person knowledgable in the task conducts the rite by setting out a few pieces of dry fish, powdered rice and a little turmeric on a plantain leaf. Then he picks up a gourd of rice beer and offers a prayer to God and the ancestors making known to them the addition of another member to the family and seeks their blessings on the newborn child. Calling the ancestors to bear witness to the occasion he utters a name and turns the spout of the gourd downwards to pour out the rice beer waiting to see whether the beer remains suspended at the mouth of the gourd or drops down. If the beer remains in suspension at the utterance of the name it is considered acceptable to the gods and so suitable for the child. But if the beer flows down freely then it is considered as a negative response from the gods and another name is selected. Usually three names are uttered to see which of the three is ritually suited for the child. If all three names result in the flowing out of the rice then other names are chosen till the positive response is achieved.

After the naming rite is over, the father takes the pot in which the after-birth (placenta) is placed and goes to leave it in the jungle, usually keeping it inside the hollow of tree trunks or nested between branches covered with thick foliage (cf. Ghurye, 1963: 72). On his return from the mission his feet are ritually washed with water by a close relative before he enters the house to ensure that no evil spirit followed him from the forest. On entering the house he takes three helpings of the powdered rice which has been prepared beforehand to feast on the occasion. After this the priest marks his right foot with the rice powder and left foot of the child and mother as a sign of the formal incorporation of the infant into the (mother's) clan. All those present are likewise marked. To distinguish their different relations to the child the clan members (*kur*) are marked on the left hand or foot and the paternal kins (*kha*) are marked on the right hand or foot.

Although the ritual act *per se* is the same for both male and female babies, interestingly, a sharp distinction is made with respect to their domestic role. When the child named is a male a bow and three arrows (*ka ryntieh bad lai tylli ki khnam*) are kept closeby. If the child is a female these implements are substituted by a *dāo* (*ka wait*), a conical basket and a cane strap (*u star*), utility items that are used for cutting and carrying things. These tools and implements signify their future callings in life. A male is primarily seen as a warrior who protects the family and the community from the enemies and as a hunter who brings home the game, hence the bow and arrows. A female, on the other hand, is seen not only as a carer and nurturer whose duties are to attend to the domestic tasks of cooking, washing, fetching water and fuel but also as a worker in the field. This explains the presence of these items in the naming rite of a female child, as a symbol of the multiple roles she is called upon to fulfil. The *dāo*, the basket and the strap are indispensable items in a Khāsī household, they are not only crucial for clearance of the *jhum* plot but also for cutting fire wood, chopping fodder and for bringing water from the springs and agricultural produce from the field.

This work arrangement lent a distinctive character to the position of Khāsī women. While the Khāsī gender ideology clearly defines the female as physiologically and mentally inferior to men and thereby exclude them from important areas of decision-making, interestingly, in their domestic role women are saddled both with reproductive (nurturing) and productive (economic) functions.

Marriage Rituals

To the Khāsī marriage is the first step towards a union not only between the two individuals who enter into the relationship but more importantly between the two families and clans to which the couple belong. Marriage amongst the Khāsī is not a civil contract but a sacred union that is necessary to perpetuate the family and the clan. Hence failure to get married is a matter of serious concern not only for the individual but also for the family as a whole. However, unlike the Hindus the system of arranged marriage is absent among the Khāsī though parents and relatives assist their children in various ways to find a suitable mate. Once the prospective partner is found and the match meets with the family's approval rings are exchanged to confirm the engagement and divination conducted to obtain an auspicious day for the solemnization of the union. As marriage is seen as an arrangement ordained by God so that man could prosper and procreate, there is no money payment or exchange of expensive gifts between the families of the bride and groom to lend legitimacy to the relationship. However, the ritual itself is flexible to accommodate the different economic capacities of families.

Traditionally, three different kinds of marriage rituals are found among the Khāsī: *Ka pynhiar synjat*, which involved the exchange of gold or silver rings between the bride and the groom. This is carried out amidst elaborate sacrifice of cocks and pigs and is usually adopted by the rich. Next is *Ka Lamdoh,* which is also marked by elaborate feasts but in the absence of the exchange of rings and animal sacrifice. The third type of marriage ritual that primarily caters to the common man is *Ka Iadih Iad Um*. This is solemnized only with simple libation and drinking of rice beer devoid of elaborate feasts. Though ritually distinct these different forms of marriage have the same degree of religious and legal sanctions.

Essentially, the different forms of marriage rituals possess certain common features which can be classified as follows:

(a) the exchange of betel between the parties of the bride and the groom as a form of greeting;

(b) the exchange of the marriage vows or contract by two senior males (*ksiang* or go between) who act on behalf of the bride and the groom,

(c) the use of rice beer to sanctify the union, and

(d) the exclusion of the groom's female kin from the wedding ceremony.

By custom the Khāsīs always perform the marriage ceremony at the bride's house in the presence of her parents, siblings, mother's brothers, other family members, friends and relatives. From the groom's side only his male clan members, his father's brothers along with friends and well-wishers attend the ceremony. Neither his mother nor her sisters, his own sisters or other female clan members could accompany the groom to the bride's house. It is a taboo for the female kin to do so as this would amount to *die khaw duh*, that is, outright sale of the son or brother to the bride's group.

Typically, on the day of the wedding as the groom and his party make their way to the bride's house they are met at a little distance before the house by her male relatives and friends where betel is exchanged and then ceremonially escorted for the rest of the way. This practice bears a close resemblance to the *milni* of the Punjābīs where a groom is not supposed to directly enter the bride's village where the wedding is held unless they are first met by the bride's kinsmen and exchange of gifts takes place (Hershman, 1981: 164). Among the Khāsī, on reaching the bride's house the groom and his party are greeted by her maternal uncle and father at the door with words of welcome and cheer while the female kins offer them betel, which is duly reciprocated by the groom's side. After the exchange of betel and pleasantries are over and the bride and the groom are seated next to each other the two mediators recite the terms of the marriage on behalf of the two sides. The terms bind the couple to conjugal fidelity and charts out the rights and responsibilities that each spouse has towards the other. As a mark of acceptance the couple exchanges gold or silver rings with each other. The union is then sanctified by mixing the fermented beer kept in two gourds one from the bride and one from the groom's side and pouring the same on three pieces of dry fish kept on the floor. The libation is carried out to the accompaniment of a prayer to God and the ancestors to shower their blessings on the newly-wed and a call to all those present to bear witness to the newly formed union (cf. Lyngdoh, 1962: 152-54).

Three days after the wedding the groom takes the bride, who is duly accompanied by her relatives, for a ritual visit to his mother's house. For the couple, the visit marks the beginning of the kin-affine relationship (*ka jing ia dei kha dei man*), without which a household's kinship universe is incomplete. The bride and her entourage make a round of the house of each of the groom's aunts and sisters presenting them with gifts of rice cakes (*pu tharo*) and bananas specially brought for the purpose, the latter in turn would saturate them with betel, tea and goodies. Traditionally, this is an important part of the marriage ritual — it not only socially seals the alliance, but also provides an opportunity for the extended families on both sides of the line to interact with each other, thereby expanding their ever-widening kinship networks.

The alliance established at marriage gains permanency with the birth of children. A childless marriage brings an end to the relationship between the two clans with the death of the couple or their divorce. But if there are children the relationship between the two continues for generations through the bonds of complementary filiation (Fortes, 1949 and 1953), in fact in a way that is not unlike what Louis Dumont calls genealogical affinity (1957 and 1983). Although cross-cousin marriage as a norm is absent among the Khāsī, the alliance established between the two clans at the time of marriage gets institutionalized with the birth of children through social injunctions, premised on the age-old adage *tip kur tip kha* (know thy clan know thy affine). Among the

Khāsī the affinal bond that binds the parents in holy matrimony is reinforced by the children on each ritual occasion. Although matrilineal ideology excludes the non-kin from the rituals of a clan, a man's children and their children are expected to pay obeisance to their father's/grandfather's ancestors and ancestresses, particularly the figure which represents the *meikha* (father's mother). Similarly, on the mother's side the mother's father and mother's mother's father and so on beyond the line are revered. This is clearly reflected in the invocation of *U Thawlang* in the ancestor cult and the tributes (*nguh meikha*) that the son's children offer at the funerary rites and bone internment ceremonies in the father's family or clan.

However, unlike birth rituals where the incorporation of the child into the clan and the cosmic world is the dominant theme of the rite, marriage rituals confer no membership rights on either spouse in the clan of the other. In accordance with the exogamous principle adopted in the society, that marriage should be outside the clan, husband and wife retain their respective clan membership even after marriage. This contrasts sharply with the patrilineal ideology of Hindu society where a woman after marriage is assimilated into the husband's patrilineage as an inmarrying affine. However, marriage gives a man right of residence in his wife's group and access to her sexual and domestic services. It also binds the wife to conjugal fidelity, which extends beyond the husband's death. If a man dies in the married state and his wife (widow) and children keep his bones in their possession tradition forbids the widow from remarrying till the bones are transferred to his natal kin.

Among the Khāsī marriage sanctifies sexuality and parenthood. Sex is seen as a biological need which every mature person naturally has an urge for, but which should be channelized through the institution of marriage. Hence marriage is a desired state that every adult aspires to achieve, failure of which can render his/her life incomplete. This explains the performance of the mock marriage for the spirit of the dead who died in an unmarried state at the bone burial ceremony. To fulfil their "unquenched desire" a poor man or woman is hired to act as the bride or groom of the ghost and after enacting the marriage ritual made to cross over a wooden mortar (*thlong*) and pestle (*synrei*)[7] as a symbol of the consummation of the marriage. The Khāsīs believe that the spirit of a person who died in an unmarried state is more dangerous than the spirit of the married ones, so to pacify its soul what could not be fulfilled in life has to be compensated for after death (Rabon Singh, 1950: 34).

The above idea about sex and sexuality also explains the apparently liberal attitude that the Khāsīs exhibit towards non-ritualized union or cohabitation. While loose sexual congress is frowned upon in the society cohabitation is a common phenomenon. The Khāsīs believe that sex is a sacred act that should take place only within the institution of marraige. Hence when a young boy and girl become sexually intimate before marriage the two families usually try to limit the damage by formalizing (*pynbeit ne pynskhem*) the relationship. This step not only serves to bestow social recognition on cohabitation but also to bring back the deviant within the jurisdiction of marriage.

Death Ritual

While marriage rituals are geared towards cementing the alliance between groups death rituals are primarily directed at aiding the soul of the departed reach its final resting place without any hitch on the way, so that it can be "reunited" with God and with the ancestors who had gone before. The ritual involves a series of sacrifices starting from the time life ceased in the body till the bones are interred in the clan cromlech. Although the invasion of Christianity has reduced the Khāsī death ritual to a mere shadow of what it was in the past some orthodox families still stringently adhere to the practice. Given their importance in the past and the light

7. These articles represent the female and male genitals respectively.

they throw on the Khāsī religious belief, it would be useful to take a close look at the rites. The account, however, will touch only on the salient points of the ritual and leave out the minor details, as our idea is not to describe procedures but to bring out the sociological significance of the practice. To begin with, let me narrate a case I witnessed some years ago in Shillong:

> The case concerns the death of U John Dkhar (name changed to protect the privacy of the family), a widower of about 62 years of age. John was a healthy man and was not expected to die for many years yet. As is the custom among the Khāsī when death occured John was living with his youngest daughter, her husband and their children in a house which he and his late wife had constructed. His elder daughter, also married, lived separately with her husband and family. John's youngest daughter had followed her husband to Christianity. John and the elder daughter, however, continued to follow the Khāsī religion. On his mother's side, both his sisters and a brother had adopted Christianity. After John expired, and after the initial heart-rending cry of mourning the loss of their loved one had temporarily subsided and the body arranged and kept in state, his family sat down to discuss plans for the funeral. His elder daughter expressed the view that as a Khāsī (that is a non-Christian) John's body should be cremated just as her mother was. The younger daughter with whom he lived was, however, in favour of burying the body, so were one of his sisters and the brother. His younger sister, though a Christian, wavered and stated that they should respect John's loyalty to the traditional religion and in keeping with its tenets they should cremate his body. John himself had never expressed what his family should do with his body after his death. After much discussion, the lid was put by John's elder sister who opined that it is meaningless to cremate the body without following the proper rites and procedures, which include the collection of the uncalcined bones from the pyre and their internment in the clan cromlech. To cremate John's body without collecting the bones would amount to *thang lum* or *thad ha lum*, that is, exposing his spirit to the four winds, which she claimed is not proper. She suggested burying the body, because even though the associated

> rites are absent this would save her brother the indignity and "danger" of having his bones left out in the open. As both his sisters had adopted Christianity they had ceased to observe the *niam* (Khāsī religious practice) so there was no one to take charge of the bones and complete the rites. According to the Khāsī tradition even though John had lived with his children and his body cremated by them, after a reasonable period of time his bones would have to be returned to his natal family to be deposited by his kin in the *mawbah* or cromlech of the clan.

The case cited above not only illustrates the dilemma that many Khāsī households today experience when confronted with death, it also brings out the social and religious significance of the event. To the Khāsī death is not the end of life but a door into the other world. Hence it is incumbent upon the living to ensure that the soul of the deceased reaches its final destination in the house of God. This demands the proper execution of all the funerary rites to prevent the soul of the dead from being held up by evil spirits.

The Khāsīs never dispose of the body immediately after death. Depending upon the age and status of the deceased the body is kept either for one or three days in the house, till the near and dear ones are informed to enable them to attend the funeral.[8] Death itself is a social occasion where lavish feasts are thrown up in honour of the dead. Immediately after a person dies the bed on which the deceased expired is stripped of its matress and quilts and replaced with a cane mat spread over with a fresh white sheet to keep the body cool. Likewise the body is sponged and donned in fresh garments and kept in state till the day of the funeral. The body is screened from public view with sheets attached to the four poles of the bed over which rich fabrics of silk, *muga* and *endi* that are used by

8. In their description of the Khāsī death rituals both Gurdon and Homiwell Lyngdoh observed that the body is never kept in the house for an even number of nights such as two or four but in odd numbers, such as one or three. This custom is, however, rarely strictly adhered to nowadays. High expenses and fear of decomposition of the body has made even the orthodox to cremate the body after the second night.

men and women on festive occasions are hanged in a line folded vertically one over the other. A lighted wick candle is kept in the screened enclosure to keep evil spirits away. From the time of death and throughout the mourning period the main door of the house is kept unbolted to enable the spirit of the dead to come and go.

Traditionally, while women of the family sit with the body in mourning, the males consult the family diviner and make the necessary arrangements for the rituals. An egg is placed on the belly of the deceased to signify his/her link to God. This is followed by a cock sacrifice (*u iar krad lynti*) to pave the way for the soul of the dead. As long as the body remains in the house food offerings are made to the spirit of the deceased during the morning and evening meals. Friends and relatives who come to pay their last respects to the departed likewise bid their last farewell by offering betel nuts and betel leaves to its spirit, which they put in a brass plate placed at the head of the bed. Like the Coorgs of south India the offering of food to the dead is a dominant motif in Khāsī rituals (on the Coorgs see Srinivas, 1952). The Khāsīs believe that just as the living subsist on food the dead too should be accorded their share of the victuals. In ritual terms the act is conceptualized as *noh dkhot* (piece offerings). This ritual act symbolizes the communion of the living and the dead through the sacrifice and finds its full expression in the *Ai bam* celebrated in the ancestor cult.

On the day of cremation, which usually takes place on the second or third day of death, early in the morning the body is bathed by close relatives and friends and then clothed in new garments. But in contrast to the living the dead are clothed in a reversed form. While the living wear their undergarments on the right side up the dead are made to wear the wrong side up. Similarly, the upper garments are arranged in the reversed order, what is worn from right to left among the living is arranged from left to right on the dead. The body is then placed on a wooden bier (coffin nowadays) decked with gold, silver and silks on which it is taken to the cremation ground in a precession of mourners and sympathisers. In the distant past it was common for the rich to engage drummers and musicians to play during the funeral procession and scatter copper coins as the procession wound its way from the house to the cremation ground.

Before the body leaves the house for the cremation ground friends and relatives file past the bier to pay their last homage. Close family members express their feelings to the departed by offering cash tribute, which is known as *bai lynti* or road money for the soul. To distinguish their respective relations to the deceased the affinal kin puts (*pynkham*) the money in the right palm and the matri kin in the left palm of the deceased. Then a cock is sacrificed (*u iar syngkhong*) to purify the soul of the dead from any fault he/she may have committed in his/her lifetime. As an act of purification the blood of the cock is smeared over the bier and on three small pieces of wood, which are thrown away on the way to the cremation ground as a sign that the sins, if sins there were, had been cast off. Among the well-to-do a pig is also sacrificed on this day in honour of the dead.

At the cremation ground the belly egg is cast at the head of the pyre and another cock (*iar padat*) is sacrificed. The sacrificer smears the blood over the pyre and throws the cock three times across the flames. This act is believed to aid the soul of the deceased to go straight from the pyre to the abode of the dead. Next, he takes three arrows, which is the symbol of a man's calling at the naming rite, and shoots them in three different directions west, north and south to scare away the evil spirits. Then he throws the bow into the burning pyre as a sign of the final severance of the dead from their worldly duties. When the body is fully burnt, the burners sprinkle water three times over the pyre while the sacrificer calls out to the spirit of the deceased to go in peace and unite with the spirits of the ancestors as he pours out libation of fermented beer. Then the nearest family members, who are also the main mourners, begin to collect the bones moving from the foot of the pyre to its head three times. The rest are collected by other relatives and any ornaments or gold worn by the deceased are collected by the burners. The ornaments and gold which is known as *siar iap* go to the burners who sell them and divide the proceeds among themselves. It is also customary to present the burners with bottles of liquor to help them ease the fatigue and heat they had to bear in making the crematorium and burning the body. After all the bones have been collected they are washed and tied in a white cloth. The bundle is then deposited in a rough stone structure or ossuary (*mawshieng*) where it remains till the family could arrange for the transfer of the bones to the clan cromlech, which may take several years to be completed.

Close relatives of the deceased observe mourning for three days during which period food offerings are placed at the stone ossuary where the bones are kept. Till the mourning period is over (*lait miet or lait ia*) the affected family members are to abstain from all normal duties. However, the day after the funeral the floor, clothes and other washable items are thoroughly washed and cleaned, and accounts taken to find out the expenses incurred and the contributions made by friends and kin. It needs to be noted that Khāsī funerals are highly expensive affairs. Apart from the items necessary for the ritual and for use on the dead the family has to feed the funeral guests from the time of death till the end of the mourning period. Though the lavishness of the feast varies with the age and status of the deceased, a family that fails to treat its funeral guests properly can be accused of showing disrespect to their dead relative. As a show of solidarity with the bereaved family friends and relatives who attend the funeral make their token contribution by giving a small amount of money to the chief mourner before taking their leave. Depending upon the proximity of relationship and their financial capacity close kins, however, usually give a larger amount to help the family meet the expenses incurred.

The account given above is an ideal type of Khāsī funerary rituals, many elements of which are still found among the orthodox. While the main concern of the rite is the smooth transmission of the soul from the human body (natural or profane world) to the abode of the dead (spiritual or sacred world) it also helps the living to restore their world to its normal state. Though death is seen as an inevitable fact of life that every individual born into the world has to pass through, when it actually occurs it brings about a discontinuity, a kind of anomie, in the ordered pattern of normal life. Rituals help the affected family to cope with the anomic situation firstly, by ensuring that the soul of their loved one goes into a better world and secondly, by helping them overcome the emotional void suffered by the loss. The first is achieved by the series of rites and sacrifices that are performed from the time the soul departs from the body to the deposition of the bones in the stone ossuary. The second is provided by the support of friends and relatives who come to mourn the loss with the family.

Among the Khāsī death is not only perceived as a liminal phase, a threshold "betwixt and between" two worlds in the Van Gennepian sense of the term, it is also seen as the most critical event that any family encounters in its life history. Hence death becomes not a private concern in which the bereaved family alone mourn their loss but a public matter where the entire community must rise up in solidarity with the afflicted. In practically all parts of the Khāsī and Jaintiā hills community norms make it compulsory for each family in the locality where a death takes place to come forward and render their services to the bereaved family. It is interesting to observe that even the most reserved family brings down their "fences" in the event of death. When death takes place in a family the entire task of informing the distant relatives, shopping, cooking, constructing of the crematorium, etc. become the responsibilty of the community. This transformation of death from a private to a public event not only helps the bereaved family to mourn their loss without having to bother about practical matters it also acts as a theraphy that eases the pain they suffer. The continuous flow of guests into the house of the dead and the social necessity of providing them food and refreshments that are symbolic of a feast provide a therapeutic effect that acts as a restorative, which helps the bereaved to overcome their grief and get on with life.

The effect that this practice has on the psyche of the Khāsī finds lucid expression in a statement made by Mr Phrang Roy, Director, Asia Division, International Fund for Agricultural Development, Rome, at a recent conference at the Asian Institute of Technology, Bangkok.[9] To a query about his post-retirement plans made by one of the participants in a post-dinner chat he replied that he would surely like to go back to the Khāsī hills as he would not like to die anywhere else in the world. As one who has lived in different countries of the globe for more than half of his life there is no society in the world he observed that gives a more honourable send-off to their dead as the Khāsīs do. This sentiment is shared by many Khāsīs and explains why despite the erosion of the religious elements under the impact of Christianity the social aspect of Khāsī funeral continues more or less unchangd till today.

Beyond Cremation: From Spirits to Ancestors

The process outlined above does not mark the end of the Khāsī death ritual. In the past, the process extended beyond the cremation of the body till the bones of the dead are interred in the clan cromlech. This is the final rite that integrates the spirit of the dead with the host of ancestors who died since the inception of the clan and brings it in the company of Ka Iawbei and U Suidnia, the two mythical ancestors who are deified and propitiated by the clan. The Khāsīs believe that till the bones of the dead are deposited in the *mawbah* or clan sepulchre together with the bones of the other dead members of the clan their soul will not find complete rest and is liable to be troubled by myriad mystical forces. Hence to ensure peace for their soul the bones of the dead need to be relocated from the *mawshieng* to the *mawbah* to join the community of ancestors in the clan sepulchre (*shi khrum ka maw*).

9. At the time of writing this chapter Mr Roy was the Vice President of IFAD.

In analytical terms, the ritual of bone burial hinges between a funerary rite and an ancestor cult and marks the transformation of the dead from spirits to ancestors. Unlike cremation which is basically organized to dispose of the body of an individual the bone burial ceremony involves the internment of the bones of all the members of the lineage or clan who died during the period in question, which could range from some months to a few years. The rite is also marked with all the elements reminiscent of an ancestor cult. Ancestors are propitiated and effigies are made to represent Ka Iawbei and U Suidnia, the mythical ancestors of the clan. Goats and bulls are sacrificed as offerings in their honour. Also the rite marks the final separation of the kin from the affine and non-kin members. This is symbolized by the erection of the *mawkjat* (megalith), a halting point from where the affinal kin (*ki kha ki man*) together with friends and well-wishers (*ki lok ki jor*) must turn back and only clan members are allowed to the cromlech for the final internment of the bones.

The bone burial ceremony is, however, a rite of the past. None of my informants whom I interviewed could recall when the last rite was held. Gurdon attributed the extinction of the bone burial ceremony partly to the inability of the clan members to come to a common agreement and partly to the high expenses involved (1975: 140-44). Empirical evidence, however, suggests that the disappearance of the bone burial ceremony has less to do with the inability of the clan to arrive at a consensus or the cost of the ceremony as with the intrusion of colonialism and Christianity into the society. This brings us back full circle to the case I cited at the beginning of this section.

It is important to note that the bone burial ceremony shows that the Khāsī concept of death goes beyond Van Gennep's idea of liminality. Although like Van Gennep the Khāsīs see death as a liminal stage, which locates the deceased between two worlds the natural and the supernatural, it extends beyond the cremation of the body and the rites associated with it till the bones are interred in the clan cromlech. What gives rise to this unique situation is the Khāsī ideology of the unity of the clan. As members who descended from a common ancestress, clan members are not only expected to remain united in their lifetime but also after death. To deny the dead this unity is to deny their soul eternal peace. In symbolic terms, the bone burial ceremony marks the dramatic separation of the kin (clan members) from the non-kin (non-clan members). Indeed, the entire ritual complex that surrounds the life crisis events shows the stark opposition between these two social entities which are represented by the contrasting categories kin and affine.

Analysis shows that while the bond of alliance demands that kin and affines co-operate with each other on all ritual occasions, at the same time their different structural positions are clearly distinguished. In both birth and death rituals their difference is registered in terms of the lateral positions left and right, left for the clan members and right for the affines. Further, in death the bones of affinal kins have to be kept separate, for example a man's bones cannot be kept together with his wife's and children as they belong to separate clans. The separation culminates in the bone burial ceremony where the rite not only unites the spirit of the clan member with its community of ancestors but also excludes the affine (non-kin) from witnessing the final internment of the bones at the clan cromlech.

This sharp opposition between kin and affine is rooted in the Khāsī ideology of the ritual unity of the sibling group, which excludes affines from the rituals of their conjugal families. In keeping with the matrilineal principle of descent brothers and sisters must remain in close co-operation with each other to maintain the solidarity of the descent group. The stipulation is necessary because uxorilocal residence tends to erode consanguineal bond under the countervailing pull of affinal ties. Hence to maintain the unity of the descent group religion is organized round the clan. The arrangement not only seeks to ensure the continuity of matriliny but also gives brothers permanent right in their natal family. This also explains the dominance of the ancestor cult in Khāsī religion. As protectors of the family and the clan ancestors are duly recalled and propitiated on all ritual occasions.

Conclusion

The sets of beliefs and practices outlined in this chapter not only bring out the interesting manner in which the Khāsī organize their religion but also its vulnerability to the forces of change. Whereas Khāsī religion is based on sound ecological and social principles, many of their rites and ceremonies are reflective of a people at a lower level of technological development. Piacular rituals, in particular, have borne a heavy brunt with the introduction of modern medicines. Exposure to Christianity and process of modernization have also taken a heavy toll of the life cycle rituals, particularly those related to death. Hence what has been presented in this chapter are more in the nature of Weber's ideal types than the current reality. This, however, is not to suggest that Khāsī religion has faded into oblivion. While there is a definite process of de-ritualization the system of belief remains firmly entrenched, aided in part by its monotheistic orientation. Also the importance of cultural symbols in the making of identity has contributed to its resilience, leading to a process of re-definition or adaptation of elements that clash with new ideologies and processes. This is demonstrated by the tendency to underplay the religious aspects of public festivals and project them as cultural events that add distinctiveness to the people. Guided by this intent, a few years after Meghalaya came into existence Syiem Olim Singh, the late ruler of Khyrim in a broadcast over All India Radio on the eve of the Pomblang[10] in November 1975 categorically stated that the Pomblang is not a religious but a cultural festival. Such rationalization is not only critical

10. Ka Pomblang is a social-religious festival of the Khyrim state dedicated to the Shillong God which is believed to be the progenitor of Ka Pahsyntiew, the mythical ancestress of the Khyrim royal family.

for the survival of the practice but also politically beneficial for the people.

REFERENCES

Bareh, Hamlet, 1967, *The History and Culture of the Khasi People*, 3rd rev. edn., Guwahati: Spectrum Publications.

Bareh, Hamlet, 1979, *A Short History of Khasi Literature*, 3rd rev. and enlarged edn., Shillong: Selbstverl.

Bareh, Hamlet, *The History and Culture of the Khasi People*, Calcutta: The Author, 1967.

Beattie, John, *Other Cultures: Aims, Methods and Achievements in Social Anthropology*, London: Routledge and Kegan Paul, 1977 (first published, 1964).

Berger, P. and T. Luckmann, "Sociology of Religion and Sociology of Knowledge" in Roland Roberston (ed.), *Sociology of Religion*, Hamondsworth: Penguin, 1985, (first published 1969), pp. 61-73.

Dalton, E.T., 1973, *Tribal History of Eastern India*, Delhi: Cosmo Publications, previously published as *Descriptive Ethnology of Bengal*, Calcutta, 1872.

Dalton, *Tribal History of Eastern India*, Delhi: Cosmo Publications, 1973.

Dumont, L., 1957, "For a Sociology of India" (adapted by D. Pocock), in *Contribution to Indian Sociology*, vol. 1.

Dumont, Louis, *Affinity as Value: Marriage in South India, with Comparative Essays on Australia*, Chicago: University of Chicago Press, 1983.

Dumont, Louis, "Hierarchy and Marriage Alliance in South India", Royal Anthropological Institute, Occasional Papers, no. 12, London, 1957.

Durkheim, Emile, *The Elementary Forms of Religious Life*, Joseph D. Swain (tr.), Free Press of Glencoe, 1956.

Ehrenfels, U.R., "The Double Sex Character of the Khasi Great Deity", in L.P. Vidyarthi, *Aspects of Religion in Indian Society*, 1961, pp. 268-79.

Evans-Pritchard, E.E., *Nuer Religion*, Oxford: Clarendon Press, 1956.

Evans-Pritchard, E.E., "A Selection from Nuer Religion" in Charles Leslie's, *Anthology of Folk Religion*, New York: Random House, 1960, pp. 55-57.

Fortes, Mayer, "The Structure of Unilineal Descent Groups", *American Anthropologist*, **55**, 1953, pp. 17-41.

Fortes, Mayer, *The Web of Clanship among the Tallensi*, London: Oxford University Press, 1949.

Fortes, Meyer, 1949, *The Web of Kinship among the Tallensi*, London: Oxford University Press.

Fortes, Meyer, 1953, "The Structure of Unilineal Descent Groups", *American Anthropologist* 55, 1741.

Gennep, Arnold van, *The Rites of Passage*, tr. from French by Monika B. Vizedan, London: Routledge and Kegan Paul, 1960 (first published 1908).

Ghurye, G.S., 1963, *Anatomy of a Rururban Community*, Bombay: Popular Prakashan.

Ghurye, G.S., *Anthropological Papers*, Bombay: Popular Prakashan, 1963.

Gurdon, P.R.T., 1975, *The Khasi*, Delhi: Cosmo Publications.

Gurdon, P.R.T., *The Khasis*, Delhi: Cosmo Publications, 1975, p. 105 (first published, 1907).

Hershman, P., 1981, *Punjabi Kinship and Marriage*, Delhi: Hindustan Publishing Corporation.

Hershman, Paul, *Punjabi Kinship and Marriage*, Delhi: Hindustan Publishing Corporation, 1981.

Juanita Havill, 1995, *Jamaica's Blue Marker*, illustrated by Anne Sibley O'Brien, Houghton (Boston, MA).

Lucy Philip Mair, 1972, *Marriage*, New York: Pica Press (distributed by Universe Books).

Lyngdoh, Homiwell, *Ka Niam Khasi* (The Khasi Religion), George M. Lyngdoh, Shillong, 1962.

Lyngdoh, Homiwell, *Ki Syiem Khasi Bad Synteng*, 3rd edn., Shillong: George M. Lyngdoh, 1964, Getr. Zīhlung, Khāsī.

Lyngdoh, M.P.R., 1991, *Festivals in the History and Culture of the Khasi*, New Delhi: Vikas Publishing House.

Mair, Lucy, *An Introduction to Social Anthropology*, Oxford: Clarendon Press, 1972 (first published, 1965).

Mathur, P.R.G., 1979, *The Khasi of Meghalaya: Study in Tribalism and Religion*, New Delhi: Cosmo Publications.

Mathur, P.R.G., *Khasi of Meghalaya*, Delhi: Cosmo Publications, 1979.

Mawrie, H., Onderson, 1973, *Ka Pyrkhat u Khasi*, Shillong — IX, 110 S., Khāsī: Khāsī — Customs and Religion.

Mawrie, H.O., *U Khasi Bad la ka Niam (The Khasi and his Religion)*, Shillong: The Author, 1973.

O'Dea, T.F., *Alienation, Atheism, and the Religious Crisis,* New York: Sheed and Ward, 1969.

O'Dea, Thomas, *The Sociology of Religion*, New Delhi: The Prentice Hall of India Ltd., 1969.

Pritchard, E.E., 1951a, *Kinship and Marriage among the Nuer*, Oxford: Clarendon Press.

Pritchard, E.E., 1956, *Nuer Religion*, Oxford: Clarendon Press.

Sing, Rabon, *Ka Kitab Niam-Khein ki Khasi*, Ri Khasi Press, Shillong, 1950.

Srinivas, M.N., *Religion and Society Among the Coorgs of South India,* London: Oxford University Press, 1952.

Syngai, D., 1999, "Sacred Groves of Meghalaya", in *Biodiversity : North East India Perspectives* (eds. B. Kharbuli, D. Syiem, and H. Kayang), Shillong, Meghalaya: North Eastern Biodiversity Research Cell, North-Eastern Hill University.

Syngai, D., "Sacred Groves in Meghalaya", in B. Kharbuli, D. Syiem and H. Kayang (eds.), *Biodiversity: North-East India — Perspective,* Shillong, North-Eastern Biodiversity Research Cell, North Eastern Hill University, 1999, pp. 70-76.

Trautman, Thomas R., *Dravidian Kinship*, Delhi: Vistaar Publications, Delhi, 1995 (first published, 1981).

War, Juanita, "The Khasi Concept of Nature", *Religion and Society*, **42** (3), 1995, pp. 55-59.

Weber, Max, *The Sociology of Religion*, Ephriam Fischoff (tr.), Beacon Press, 1963.

White, Lynn, Jr., "The Historical Roots of Our Ecologic Crisis", *Science*, **155**, 1967, pp. 1203-07. Reprinted in Ian G. Barbour (ed.), *Western Man and Environmental Ethics*, Addison Wesley, Reading-Mass, 1973, pp. 18-30.

Part III
Culture in India

11

The Composite Culture of India
The Need for a Better Appreciation

C.N. Venugopal

THE empires of the past several centuries such as Babylonia, Assyria, Egypt, Rome, Greece, China and India were characterized by religion working in tandem with the nation-state. Religious pluralism was the mainstay of these empires. They were mostly ruled by dynasties, although a few such as Egypt and Rome had other central political figures such as Pharaohs (king-priests) or Caesars at the helm of affairs. To cite a few examples: Egypt had the widespread polytheistic cults of gods and goddesses existing together. The same was true of Greece. Rome had a far-flung empire which extended over several parts of Europe, Asia and Africa — the Roman policy was to encourage the worship of local cults in religion. The subordinate states paid for the maintenance of Roman garrisons and also gave a tribute to the Roman state. They were free to pursue their own religion.

China and India retained for a long time a tolerant outlook. In China, Confucianism, Taoism and Buddhism lived together often side by side. In India, Hinduism, Buddhism and Jainism were complementary to each other. In these ancient states not only the rulers but the common people accommodated religious diversity without feeling any loss of freedom. In the words of Arnold Toynbee, religion was ecumenical: it provided a broad structure of religious or moral authority under the auspices of which the various activities of the state were conducted. The rise of the state or citizenship as a secular entity is purely a modern notion. In the Greek city state of Athens, for example, the religious and civic freedoms were one and the same. If a person was excluded from participation in the public cult, he was also excluded from civil rights. Fustel De Coulanges has shown that religion and citizenship were inseparable in the ancient city.[1]

The notion that religion could be dispensed with arose only during the French Revolution. But Bonard, Durkheim, Hegel and others did not go along with the French Revolution. They held that religion was the cementing factor in most modern societies, although it might take different contours. The debate between those who uphold religion in society and those who oppose it has continued up to the present. Till now, i.e. the modern times, religious tolerance was a moral virtue. In India Aśoka's edicts composed in the third century BCE proclaimed that the state should protect and honour different faiths, but contemporary India has been facing the dilemma; it has many religions but the spirit of tolerance has become evanescent. It will be my endeavour to show that the spirit of accommodation is still widespread in India in spite of political aberrations.

In this article I would like to highlight some of the major salient aspects of religious pluralism in India. Mostly, I will be referring to religious coexistence in terms of concrete, embodied and tangible aspects. Indeed, anyone can traverse India and witness the phenomenon of religious accommodation at the gatherings at holy rivers, sacred complexes and the far-flung monasteries.

Culture of Tolerance

India has sheltered not only different religions but also different sects within these religions. There are amidst us Hindus, Buddhists, Jains, Sikhs, Muslims, Christians, Parsis and Jews. Many of these religions are sub-divided into various

1. See F.D. Coulanges, *The Ancient City*, Boston: Willard Small, 1873.

sects. For example, Hindus have Śaiva, Vaiṣṇava and Śākta sects and sub-sects. Muslims have Sunni, Shia and a variety of sub-sects. Christians too are divided into various sects. Sometimes, there is more friction between two sects of the same religion than between two different religions. Frictions in religious life have arisen from ideological, institutional, historical and cultural factors. These frictions have been overcome or made less explicit by the expansion of the mental horizon of tolerance. Two anecdotes given below will illustrate it.

When Parsis arrived in a boat (*c.* eighth century CE) on the coast of Gujarat they sent an appeal to the king for providing them shelter. The king sent an emissary with a pitcher of milk to which the Parsi leader added sugar and sent it back to him. When Guru Nanak was camping in the north-western area of Punjab in the *c.* fifteenth century CE, a Sūfī saint who was dominant in the area sent him a vessel of milk in which the milk was up to the brim. Guru Nanak floated a few flowers on the milk and sent it back to the Sūfī saint. In both instances the message was clear. The new creed was not superfluous but could thrive with the existing religion without turmoil. The above instances bear ample testimony to the spirit of accommodation.

Swami Vivekananda has emphasized that sects in India did not *per se* contribute to religious disharmony.[2] They merely expressed different viewpoints on divinity. They shared the common heritage of Vedānta although they argued from different perspectives. Further, they gave birth to different patterns of reform in Indian society. The Buddhists and Jains did not express total opposition to the Vedic path but only to certain beliefs and practices which were not conducive to a humane outlook. Thus animal sacrifice was a point of contention. Vedic rituals were often engrossed with

2. Speaking on sects Vivekananda said: "In India . . . in spite of those jarring sects that we see today and all those that have been in the past, the one authority, the basis of all these systems, has yet been the Upaniṣads, the Vedānta" (see *The Complete Works of Swami Vivekananda*, vol. 3, Calcutta: Advaita Ashram, 1939, p. 322).

materialistic desires — for example, desire for progeny or prosperity. Instead they focused on the knowledge content of the Vedas: their spirituality. In sum, sects did not detract from religious pursuit in spite of their differences. In fact, the *ṛṣis*, *munis* and *sādhus* associated with various sects modified the meanings of original texts (Vedas, Upaniṣads, Dharmaśāstras, etc.) in order to develop a more pragmatic outlook. Hence, instead of setting aside the heritage of the past, the sects contributed to a dynamic awareness of India's religious philosophy.

In the pre-colonial times, war and violence were certainly causing social disintegration in Indian society. Fields where crops grew were laid waste; towns were razed to the ground; innocent people were killed. These conflicts did not stem from religious partisanship. They were due to aggressive demand for territory or for wreaking political vengeance. During Mughal rule, Muslim rulers fought against each other (Babur and Lodi, Humayun and Sher Shah Suri), while Hindu kings did not lag behind in internecine warfare. Aurangzeb was the governor of Deccan wherein the famous Kailāsa temple and Ajantā caves were located; he left them intact. He also financed the building of Śiva temple and Jain temple near Red Fort in Delhi. Yet it was the same ruler who destroyed Hindu temples at Banaras and Mathura.

Śivājī's case was also illustrative of the times. He spent a number of years fighting against Mughal rule. He overtook their forts and territories in Deccan with a fiery zeal. His personal life was marked by not only tolerance of Islam but by his visits to a Sūfī shrine in Ratnagiri (coastal Maharashtra) where he offered prayers. His bodyguards were Afghan Muslims and some of his commanders were also Muslims. Earlier, another Hindu ruler, Rana Pratap, spent several years in the jungles of Mewar (Udaipur district in Rajasthan) as a fugitive; he was a relentless fighter against the emperor Akbar. The chief commander of his army was an Afghan Muslim.

In antiquity, about 60 Indo-Greek dynasties ruled over

small kingdoms of north India (in the area stretching from Punjab to Madhya Pradesh). Many of them adopted Hindu or Buddhist customs and rituals. Even the Muslim invader Muhammad Ghori issued gold coins which bore the image of Hindu goddess Lakṣmī.[3]

The later Muslim rulers like Akbar also made use of some Hindu symbols. The Indian society, however, has witnessed some aberrations within the broad framework of religious co-existence. A Hindu ruler of Bengal — Śaśāṅka — destroyed many Buddhist temples due to a personal spite. Kumārila, the propounder of Mīmāṁsā School of philosophy (eighth century CE), disguised himself as a Buddhist in order to defeat the Buddhists in arguments. He encouraged the local rulers to persecute them. But he became penitent and in order to atone for his misdeeds immolated himself in the fire of husk. Around this time the Jainas of south expelled the Buddhists to Sri Lanka after defeating them in argument.

Yet these instances were minor compared to the violence of the war of Crusades, the Spanish Inquisition and the conquest of Mexico by Spain. In Europe numerous lives were sacrificed to serve the interest of religious bigotry. In Europe a systematic campaign of hate and programme of destruction were launched by the dominant sections against the minorities; for example, Catholics persecuted Protestants or one section of Protestants persecuted another section of the same faith. Especially, all over Europe the Jewish people have been subjected to violence time and again. Relatively speaking there has been religious tolerance and mutual goodwill in India in spite of some violent incidents. Till the rise of communal consciousness during the last few decades there has been no systematic campaign launched by one section against the other.

Religious Interactions

Among Indian religions Hinduism, Jainism, Buddhism and

3. See P.L. Gupta, *Coins*, New Delhi: National Book Trust, 1996, III edn., Chapters III, pp. 23-42 and XI, p. 107.

Sikhism have mutually enriched each other. Sri Aurobindo's writing on Vedas has made some striking observations. Firstly, if we go to the Vedas on the verbal level mostly they are not intelligible or at least they are susceptible to multiple interpretations. Secondly, the European Indologists — Max Mòller onwards — systematically distorted the Vedic message by focusing on philology or purely textual interpretations. Thirdly, India's own academic researchers in Oriental studies vied with each other to excel in the European type of scholarship. He, therefore, stated that the time has come to wake up and understand Vedas and Upaniṣads in intuitive rather than in scholastic terms. Sri Aurobindo[4] cited Buddha, Nanak and Ramakrishna Paramhamsa as some of those who grasped the Vedas intuitively.

Ananda Coomaraswamy[5] noted that in the sphere of art there was nothing exclusively Hindu, Buddhist and Jaina. Broad similarities have marked the temples (inclusive of architecture and sculpture) belonging to these faiths. According to him, Indian art does not represent the naturalistic design but it is only a symbolic art centred on sacred themes. This is especially true of Gupta art which reached its perfection between sixth and eighth centuries CE. The gods and goddesses are not anthropomorphic but they represent the ideals, symbols or values. (Gaṇeśa, for example, is a personification of Praṇava Mantra or Oṁ symbol.) It was the lack of understanding that led Muslim invaders to destroy Hindu temples mistaking their idols as human or animal images.

In Islamic art, the geometric and floral motifs are incorporated in the structures of mosques, tombs of Sūfīs,

4. See *Sri Aurobindo: A Chapter,* on the Veda translated into Kannada by K.H. Krishnamurthy, Bangalore: Sahitya Sindhu Prakashan, 1999, p. 14.

5. See A.K. Coomaraswamy, *A History of Indian and Indonesian Art*, New Delhi: Munshiram Manoharlal, 1972 (rpt.) pp. 105-19; also his other work, *The Transformation of Nature in Indian Art*, New Delhi: Munshiram Mahoharlal, 1974 (rpt.), pp. 1-57.

etc. In fact, the Vedic art (altar used in fire sacrifice, etc.) has a geometric pattern. Again, early Buddhist art (found in Sāñcī, Amarāvatī, etc.) depicts Buddha not as an icon but as a symbol (Parasol or begging bowl). According to Coomaraswamy, the Uniconic Islamic art is not different from the iconic medieval Christian art or the ancient Indian art which is not *realistic* but *symbolic*. The many-armed gods and goddesses found in Indian art, the fiery dragon, the unicorn and the sphinx found elsewhere are examples of religious symbols transformed into art. Vivekananda averred that Hindus in India did not regard the idols or icons as an end in themselves; they merely pointed to an underlying spirituality. They were used to grasp the religious ideas in a concrete form.

It is a matter of concern that today a political interpretation of what a particular religion stands for has led to a biased thinking. As a matter of fact both Islam and Christianity have been an integral part of India for a long time. Christianity entered the south in the first century CE; the pre-Islamic Arabs reached the south in sixth century CE. They pursued peaceful occupations as traders, artisans, farmers, etc. In north India, the Muslim rulers from eleventh to seventeenth century CE often employed force to convert people to Islam. However, Sūfīs acted as a countervailing power by their message of peace, compassion and goodwill. Besides, they exerted a benign influence on the northern *bhakti* sects. In south India, in contrast to the early Christian settlers, the Portuguese who came to Goa in seventeenth century used force to convert people. In other words, only certain sections of Muslims and Christians have acted contrary to the principles of religious tolerance. As mentioned elsewhere the colonial rule gave rise to divisive forces in the Indian subcontinent.

Another sensitive area is Islamic education. For centuries, madrasas have existed in all parts of India. According to J.P.S. Uberoi the madrasas among other things enculturated the Muslim groups by bringing them from marginality to the core of Islam in terms of doctrine. But political tendencies have crept into many of them at present. The Taliban of Afghanistan claimed that they were the products of Deoband Academy in north India. In the recently set-up madrasas there is a growing fundamentalism which has adopted a rigid pro-Islamic stance.

The spirit of India is essentially manifested in religious tolerance. Radhakamal Mukerjee[6] noted that Hinduism and Buddhism spread to many countries such as Sri Lanka, China, Japan, Indo-China, Indonesia, Cambodia, Thailand, etc. in different waves, starting from Aśoka's rule in third century BCE. No force or violence was used in the propagation of these religions beyond India. Further, Hinduism and Buddhism blended with the local cultures and thereby promoted religious pluralism. To this day in Malaysia and Indonesia, in spite of Islam, the Hindu or Buddhist influences are present in their culture.

Clifford Geertz's work *Religion of Java* has provided abundant instances to show the zeal with which Indonesians participate in the enactment of plays based on *Rāmāyaṇa* and *Mahābhārata*.[7] The Hindu and Chinese Buddhist neighbours are often invited by Muslims to participate in *siametan* feast which is held to mark the life crises. Neither Malaysia nor Indonesia has witnessed communal frenzy.

The numerous festivities that take place in India have revealed a non-sectarian and non-communal participation. Men and women drawn from different religious backgrounds have taken part in them. Both Muslims and Hindus visit the Sūfī *daragāhs* situated in different parts of India. The Christian shrines dedicated to Virgin Mary in the south draw a number of Hindus and Muslims. In recent years the cult of Infant Jesus in Bangalore city has attracted numerous people from among Christians, Hindus and Muslims. The major Hindu temples such as Tirupati, Vaiṣṇo Devī, etc. — are open to all

6. See Radhakamal Mukerjee, *The Flowering of Indian Art*, Bombay: Asia Publishing House, 1964, pp. 108-41.

7. Clifford Geertz, *Religion of Java*, Glencoe, Ill: Free Press, *c.* 960.

no matter what their religious affiliation is. Likewise, the Sikh gurdwaras provide food and lodging to all who come without any restriction. An important aspect of religious participation in India is that religious centres never seek publicity through media. It is the people themselves who induce each other to go on pilgrimage to a temple, church or *daragāh*.

Although it is paradoxical, whether in the past or present, the secular and the religious aspects have been interdependent in India. The Dharmaśāstras (composed by Manu and others) showed a disdain towards secular governance of society because they were preoccupied with the salvational aspect (liberation to ancestors, etc.) and the normative control of Hindu society. But *Arthaśāstra* of Kauṭilya and the *Nītisāra* of Śukra dealt with statecraft predominantly in secular terms. Even Bhīṣma's Śānti-Parva address in the *Mahābhārata* prepared the ground for these two writers. While Kauṭilya gave importance to commerce, agriculture and state control of production, Śukra laid stress on the governance of subjects by the ruler in accordance with the laws of the realm. Thus, in their texts the esoteric and mystical were marginalized but religion was not discarded.

The rulers gained merit in Indian society in proportion to the religious works taken up by them. The *stūpa*s of Aśoka, the temples of Coḷas, Pāṇḍyas, the Candela and Orissan kings were built by the use of enormous resources of the state. Many of these monuments have survived to this day in full glory. But the palaces of rulers of antiquity disappeared long back. What added lustre to the king's rule, was his zeal as manifested in religious activity. Usually, rulers regarded themselves as upholders of *dharma*.

During the prolonged freedom struggle, right from the violent campaign of Bengal extremists till the non-violent programme of M.K. Gandhi, religion inspired people to stand up in protest against the foreign rule. This was true of mass mobilization also. Religious symbols were used in political campaigns by B.G. Tilak, B.C. Pal and M.K. Gandhi among others. Secular ideology of liberation was mainly confined to some towns and cities of colonial India. In the post-Independence period, *Sarvodaya* movement started by Vinoba Bhave and the *Svādhyāya* movement initiated by Pandurang Athavale have used religious symbols to motivate people. The secular problems of land reform, poverty amelioration, and upliftment of weaker sections have been addressed through a religious perspective in these movements.

M.K. Gandhi, B.R. Ambedkar, Narayana Guru and many other reformers of Indian society did exemplary secular work (spread of education, social reconstruction, rural development, etc.) mainly within a religious framework. Earlier, Jyotirao Phule in his Bahujana Samaj movement sponsored secular causes without discarding religion. The one exception was Ramasami Naicker of the Draviḍian movement in the south. He stood for an anti-religious political programme. Broadly speaking, in India, secular accomplishments have attained effulgence if they are accompanied by a religious orientation. The Indian Constitution upholds secularism mainly as a bulwark against interference in the religious affairs of others.[8]

According to the Constitution, religious freedom is guaranteed with the proviso that the practice of religion does not place any obstacle in the path of the secular development of the country.

---

8. In its recent judgement on NCERT textbooks, the Supreme Court observed: "The lives of Indian people have been enriched by the integration of various religions and that is the strength of this nation. Whatever kind of people came to India either for shelter or as aggressors, India has tried to accept the best part of their religions. As a result composite culture gradually developed in India and enriched lives of Indian people. . . . This process should continue for the betterment of multi-religious society which is India." The court, however, ruled that in schools there should not be any attempt to negate India's religious pluralism. See *The Hindu* (Bangalore edn.), 12 September 2002, p. 11.

Limits to Communalism in India

In the last five decades India has witnessed communal violence on a large scale but the damage is confined to about twenty urban centres. The urban conglomerates of people tend to be conducive to the disinformation campaign by fundamentalist groups (Hindu or Muslim). The urban media often disseminate rumours and unverified stories. During communal riots, people impulsively resort to violence in which innocent lives are lost. Such conditions are rare in villages where the existing social bonds cannot be easily set aside by communal campaign. To this day most parts of rural India have remained outside the communal frenzy. In villages nearly all people — men, women and children — know each other through the networks of family and kinship. But in the urban centres the outsiders can sneak in large numbers and indulge in violence. For example, in Ahmedabad the rioters have often come from tribal belt which has little connection with the city.

It is a fact that only during partition of the country and the recent destruction of Babri Masjid in Ayodhyā was the rural–urban divide dissolved. Spatial proximity of different groups in urban India — Hindu, Muslim and Christian — is endangered by ideological opposition which often gives rise to animosity. There are thousands of urban centres which are not affected by communal violence, although there may be underlying tensions in these places. But it is a puzzle as to why cities such as Ahmedabad, Moradabad, Kanpur, Mumbai and Delhi have remained susceptible to communal outbursts in free India. In the urban belt throwing a bomb on innocent folk does not seem to create pangs of guilt in those who indulge in violence because of the anonymity. The studies of crowd behaviour in the West have shown that in mob behaviour discrimination or moral judgement is suspended. It is replaced by indifference towards other beings. The rioters even derive pleasure from assault, rape or arson.

It is to be averred that religion *per se* is not associated with the communal hatred. It is a fact that in purely religious places such as the hill shrines of Tirupati, Vaiṣṇo Devī or the temple towns of Madurai, Kāñcī and Śrīraṅgam the communal outlook has not gained prominence. This is also true of *daragāhs* at Nagore in Tamil Nadu and Ajmer in Rajasthan.[9] Thus, it can be stated that communalism is a national problem but not a nation-wide problem. There is no doubt that the communal frenzy will fade away in the years to come. Just as Europe is less anti-Semitic today, the present antipathies among Indian communities will be losing their destructive edge in the future. But fundamentalism may take other forms such as electoral battles or ideological projections on a wider scale; these developments will definitely damage the composite culture of India.

Religious Reforms and Cultural Integration in India

Compositeness in Indian religion has been derived from certain institutionalized beliefs and practices. Since antiquity Indians have traversed across the land in order to visit holy rivers, sacred spots and temples associated with mythological events. In *Bhāgavata* there is a detailed description of Balarāma — elder brother of Kṛṣṇa — visiting holy places as a pilgrim. *Ṛṣis*, *munis* and *saṁnyāsins* of diverse religious backgrounds have been moving across the country as pilgrims. Most ordinary householders — Hindus, Jainas or Sikhs — have visited holy places at one time or the other. In pilgrimage distinctions of rank and privilege are sidelined. Anyone can bathe in the holy river or receive the blessings of deities in any temple. The pilgrims make no distinction between one

9. Although Islam is a universal religion from eighth century CE up to the present in many Islamic states such as those found in Middle East and West Asia religion has worked in tandem with the state. But in the North African Islamic states the levers of political control are held by two opposing groups: the urban-based *ulemā* supported by the sultanate and the rural based Sūfīs (Shaiks) who have drawn support from their peasant or tribal followers. See. E. Gellner, *The Muslim Society*, New York: Cambridge University Press, 1983.

religious place or the other. For instance, holy places like Tirupati, Vaiṣṇo Devī, Dilwāṛā, Amritsar, Maṇikaraṇ and Badrīnāth are visited by people irrespective of whether they are Hindus, Sikhs or Jainas.

In the medieval age the rise of *bhakti* movements in different parts of India had also contributed to shape the composite culture. Nanak in Punjab, Shankaradeva in Assam, and Caitanya Mahāprabhu in Bengal, drew followers from different religious backgrounds into a fellowship based on devotion. In north India apart from Guru Nanak, Kabīr, Dādū and Raidās played a similar integrative role. Earlier the Nāyanāṟs (Śaivite saints) and Āḻvārs (Vaiṣṇavite saints) of Tamil Nadu had also drawn followers through their poetic compositions which emphasized a personal relationship between man and God.

A reference needs to be made to a few reforms which heralded a composite existence. In the eighth century CE Śaṅkarācārya of the south welded together diverse creeds (Śaurya, Gāṇapatya, Śākta, etc.) within a common Advaitic framework. The Liṅgāyats (also known as Vīraśaivas) of Karnataka propounded a monotheism centred on the worship of Śiva by converting polytheistic groups. This was done in order to make religion more focused and purposeful. A number of tribal groups and nomadic castes in Karnataka were absorbed into the Liṅgāyat faith; these groups gave up spirit worship which involved animal sacrifice or masochistic rites. Guru Nanak's mission transformed the turbulent north-west into a peaceful place where devotion could flourish. Although these reforms did not set out to change the world radically, their "exemplary" characteristics provided an impetus to religious integration.

In the institutional framework of religion ritual purity transcends caste status. For example, in many states of India (Tamil Nadu, Orissa, etc.) the priests serving in the temples are not confined to the brāhmaṇa caste. In fact, from twelfth century onwards both brāhmaṇas and non-brāhmaṇas have officiated as priests, particularly in the Śaivite temples of Tamil Nadu. The rulers of Tamil Nadu (Coḷa and Pāṇḍya) legislated in favour of such a practice. At present in Tamil Nadu in the state-controlled temples a number of executive officers (managers) are drawn from the underprivileged groups. Even some of the priests are drawn from such a background. Some Dalits have also been appointed as priests. In the temple service ritual purity (stemming from personal cleanliness, wearing a prescribed dress and abstinence from certain kinds of food) is more important than mere birth in a particular caste.

Besides, the knowledge of liturgy is an important criterion for priesthood. In fact, the Hindu Śāstras do not limit priesthood in temples to a particular caste. In a recent judgement, the Supreme Court has ruled that the persons other than brāhmaṇas can become priests, provided they are trained in ritualistic duties. However, it needs to be pointed out that while public temples are open for all, there are private temples controlled by castes and hereditary trusts which restrict priesthood to some groups. Even these temples are becoming more liberal due to the changing outlook of their trustees.

Summing Up

Every religion has projected a political system as its by-product. As noted earlier, religion gave shelter to a host of activities in the ancient empire or ancient city. Medieval Europe was stringently controlled by the Church; its political functionaries could not remain independent of the authority of the Church. In the wars of Crusade fought between eleventh and thirteenth centuries CE. Christians and Muslims fought bitter battles against each other in order to wrest control over the Holy land in West Asia. Medieval European politics centred on land control, military domination and small states warring against each other. While nominally acknowledging the Roman Church's authority the medieval rulers in Italy, Germany, etc. engaged themselves in mutual attrition. The Crusades had brought them together because they had a common cause. In the Dark Ages of tumult and warfare, interestingly the churches and monasteries remained the safe places for fugitives or refugees displaced by war. As soldiers did not enter a monastery, it was the bright spot in the midst of feudal darkness. Here the many monastics and the lay people cultivated religion, art and science.

In India the Polity was based on the Notion of Dharma

The Dharmaśāstras composed by Hindu law-givers served to sustain ancient polity, irrespective of the personal faith of the ruler. Buddhist and Jaina rulers followed more or less the same injunctions laid by Hindu law givers in conducting the affairs of the state. In India the unique development was that the king as a person was a mere mortal; but kingship was divine insofar as it was based on *dharma*.[10] If the king failed to uphold the *dharma* he was often dispensed with. In India the king was never the source of law. He merely drew upon the ethico-judicial texts for dealing with the exigencies of the state. He used his discretion according to the needs of time but he did not deviate from its role as the defender of the Moral Law.[11]

In contrast to the macro-level or state polity the village republic depended on the collective wisdom of people and elders of the village who wielded supreme authority. Caste and religion were intricately related to each other in the village. In spite of inequality, the traditional *pañcāyat* integrated the village folk. Its decline during the Islamic and British rule weakened the village polity. This was a setback to the demotic pattern of Indian society in its micro-level.

Free India has broadly witnessed two kinds of

10. A.K. Sen writes: "To the Hindus the concept *dharma* implies an admixture of socio-ethico-religious ideas not a purely religious concept." See Sen, *Hindu Political Thought*, Delhi: Gyan Publishers, 1986 (rpt.), p. 4.

11. See Sen, ibid., pp. 49-64.

manifestation in religion. On the one hand, we have the cultural side of religion which continues to be centred on pilgrimage, *satsaṅga* and spontaneous participation of people in festivities cutting across caste and creed. On the other hand, there is a political projection in which Hindutva ideology has often confronted the *jehādī* ideology. Both forms of political mobilization are strident in politics. In Indonesia for example, the nationalist ideology grew out of the existing *slametan* culture of ethnic accommodation and mutual tolerance. The Permai cult which is engaged in the political mobilization of the Indonesians at the national level is in essence an extension of the *slametan*. Likewise *jehād* in Islam stands for two objectives: self-improvement and struggle against injustice. It excludes territorial aggression and killing of unarmed people. But it is today used by Islamic militants in India and elsewhere, as a slogan for terrorist attacks on non-Muslims.

At present the political projection of religion tends to be divisive but the cultural projection continues to be integrative. This is no doubt a simplified statement but there is truth in it. There is an abundance of goodwill in India which can overcome political rancour and herald a new beginning in our national life. As a prelude to this, *inter alia*, the contentious issues which have embittered the Hindu-Muslim relations need to be resolved within the framework of the Indian Constitution. Enormous judicial delays have continued the stalemate with reference to the Ayodhyā temple issue which has gained topicality in India's national life. It is a challenge to the resilient nature of Indian society to overcome the political impasse through a valourization of the Indian ethos of tolerance.

12

Culture in Bengal
A Small Town Diary

Avijit Pathak

RECENTLY a friend of mine wanted to know about Kolkata, a city she idealized, but for some reason or other, could not visit. I, therefore, got an opportunity to inspire her to visit her dream city. I told her the following:

> If you wish to experience this unique city you have to evolve a distinctive way of seeing. See its beauty amidst chaos and disorder, its life-energy amidst decay and destruction. Make it a point to visit the much-talked-about College Street. See the old bookshops, the grand Presidency College, the historic Sanskrit College, the statues of Raja Rammohun Roy and David Hare. Feel the Bengal Renaissance. Spend some time in the ever-popular Coffee House, visit the Rupa bookstall, and, if time permits, have a cup of tea and a piece of bread/butter in the Favourite Cabin. Feel the culture of *aḍḍā*. Go to Nandan, see a couple of films. And don't forget to see a good theatre. Come to the Sealdah Railway Station, buy little magazines, and merge yourself completely with the moving crowd on the Howrah Bridge or at the Gariahat Crossing.

I knew that I was conscious of Kolkata and its cultural heritage. Perhaps I wanted to convey a message to my friend:

> Bengal may not have economic affluence. Kolkata may not look like sleek New Delhi or hyper-modern Bangalore. Yet its cultural sensitivity is remarkable. Bengal is known for its tradition of rigorous thinking, its poetry and music, its theatre

and cinema, its political radicalism and its intense community life. And it is not yet dead!

Yet, a series of questions began to haunt me: Was I speaking of the real Bengal? Or was I constructing an image of Bengal? Was I merely nostalgic, fixated at the past because, as someone might argue, I was essentially uncertain about its present and future? Furthermore, did the culture I was talking about exist only in a tiny section of Bengal? Or did it exist even outside Kolkata, in remote and unknown corners?

I was eager to find appropriate answers to my questions. And finally came the opportunity. This time I visited my home town — a small/unknown town in the northern part of Bengal. In the process of rediscovering it I examined whether my pride in the culture of Bengal could still be legitimized.

From Poetry to Book Fair

There is poetry in the culture. Indeed, poetry can be felt everywhere: in literature, in political slogans, in wall posters. Even in these "pragmatic" times poets are adored and respected. Perhaps the Alpha Bangla Channel is the only TV channel in the country that organizes poetry competitions. And Kolkata Doordarshan often invites poets — from Nirendranath Chakravarty to Joy Goswami, interviews them and recognizes the meaning of poetry in life. This poetry can also be felt in the way these days a group of innovators (recall Suman, Nachiketa and Anjan) are giving new life to contemporary Bengali music. It is indeed difficult to find young people in Bengal who do not have aspirations for poetry. In every locality one would find someone who earns his livelihood by, say, teaching school children how to recite poetry. Each time I visit my home town I see new cassettes of Bengali poetry (in fact, my elder brother and sister-in-law who are by no means professional intellectuals surprise me when they show me their collection of poetry cassettes). I realize that to see this culture without poetry is to miss its essence.

Not solely that. What I witness is remarkable sensitivity

to Bengali language and literature. And this is not limited merely to the cultural elite. Bank employees, LIC agents, housewives — almost everyone can tell you what Sunil Gangopadhyay is writing these days, how *Desh* — the popular literary magazine — is doing, and what is latest in the list of Ananda Publications. This excessive love for one's own language, it is true, may degenerate into cultural chauvinism. Nevertheless, its positive gains are tremendous. Even in the age of television and much-pampered Indo-English literature good Bengali writers, novelists and poets have become household names. Each time I meet my elder sister (who teaches at a village school) I realize what I have missed, what I have not read and how ignorant I have become of the recent literary creations in Bengal.

She reminded me: "You, a JNU professor, it seems, are reading English and English only. Don't forget to read your own language." So she asked me to accompany her to the local book fair.

The book fair is yet another major component of the kind of cultural sensitivity I am talking about. Indeed, this is a great achievement of the Left Front government. It has succeeded in bringing book fairs nearer to the people. Book fair is no longer a Kolkata-centric phenomenon; it is being organized in every corner of the state.

I saw the festivity all around. I saw young poets persuading people to buy their latest publications. I saw the continual growth of little magazines. And I witnessed the sale of Bengali novels, stories and other literary creations. My sister came to a stall and asked me which book I would like to read. I was in a dilemma: whether to choose Joy Goswami or Bani Basu. Finally, I told her: "Give me Bani Basu's *Astam Garva*." I got the book. She told my wife: "you must read Sunil Gangopadhyay's *Sei Samay*." So she got two volumes of this great literary creation. I saw similar things taking place all around. The book fair was also an occasion to organize debates/discussions on contemporary issues. It was a cold winter evening. And a discussion on "television and new culture" was going on. I saw great interest in this discussion: ordinary people — students, teachers and activists — were listening to the debate. I also saw a local Leftist leader releasing his book (a book that he wrote after returning from Cuba), and sitting quietly for three hours to listen to the speakers. I realized that despite the all-pervasive decay, Leftist leaders continue to retain the practice of serious intellectual thinking.

Communicative Interaction and Dialogic Temper

Bengal cannot be imagined without its culture of *aḍḍā* — the process of free/relaxed communication, reflections on innumerable issues: important and unimportant, serious and trivial. This can be seen everywhere — in club buildings, in tea shops, in local trains, in schools, colleges and offices. This shows the power of communication: the way it softens the human mind, releases tensions and anxieties, and intensifies the foundations of public culture. At times, I feel that a thinker like Habermas — who is exploring the possibility of communicative interaction — should come to Bengal, and experience how the logic of instrumental rationality is often negated here. *Aḍḍā* is possible because in Bengal time has got a distinctively different meaning; it is not what modernity wants it to be: fragmented/measured time that is used for "productive" purposes — industrial growth, material prosperity, scientific knowledge and career development. In fact, Bengalis know how to free themselves from the tyranny of time. They do not mind if time is "wasted." That is why, the culture of *aḍḍā* continues. It disobeys the "discipline" of time!

The other day I went to meet my old school teacher who once taught me to see poetry even in mathematics and three-dimensional geometry. I saw happiness in his face, his eagerness to communicate and share his ideas. The *aḍḍā* began. It was a relaxed environment: free from tension, anxiety and hierarchy. We discussed many things — those "old" days when I was his student, how times had changed, the politics of

Bengal, the meaning of "situational ethics," Kṛṣṇa in the *Bhagavad-Gītā*, Immanuel Kant in his celebrated *Critique of Pure Reason*, and, above all, the possibility of yet another renaissance in this "dark" age. I didn't notice that we had already spent three hours.

I was not tired. From my teacher's residence I came to my old school. I met three teachers who once taught me and gave me some golden moments to remember and cherish. As usual, with tea and biscuits began our *aḍḍā*. We talked about many things: the state of higher learning in the Jawaharlal Nehru University, the commercialization of education, and the changing aspirations of the new generation. No wonder, I forgot to look at my watch.

It was quite late. My mother was anxious. As I returned home she asked me why I was so late. I told her everything. I saw the changing expression in her face: from anxiety to joy. Perhaps she felt: "My son, despite tremendous geographical mobility, has not become rootless."

One afternoon we three friends decided to walk. And we walked for three hours. We passed through mango groves and reached a lonely village. Bangladesh was not far away. We felt like running, overcoming the barriers of the Border Security Force (BSF) and touching the sky of Bangladesh. We felt the political absurdity of dividing the sky, the river and the landscape. We, however, could not do anything. We have already been defeated by the political rationality of modern nation-states.

But then, there was an old temple in the village that drew our attention. It was the temple with its mythologies about which we learned from our mothers and grandmothers. It was evening: a moment of intense silence. We looked at the temple, closed our eyes and contemplated.

But then, how could we resist the intoxication of *aḍḍā*? Sisir broke his silence and said: "I can't say that I am non-religious. I do have faith — faith in the supreme power that governs us, faith in humanity, faith in noble truths." And

Debasis observed: "Religion is universal. True, because of my surroundings, I may feel more identified with Hindu gods and goddesses. But then, this by no means suggests that other religions have to be disliked and hated."

It was a dialogic mood. I spoke of Sri Aurobindo's *The Secret of the Vedas*. We continued our discussion on religiosity and secularity, science and faith. We came back. My mother asked my wife to give us tea. Tea-*aḍḍā*-tea: is there any escape from this cycle?

Community Life and Intensity of Public Culture

Another striking feature of contemporary Bengal is its ethos of communal harmony. Well, it is possible to see hidden tension (for example, a Hindu woman getting married to a Muslim man is an idea society is not yet comfortable with), and particularly at a time when there has been massive communalization of politics throughout the country. Bengal cannot exist as an island. Yet, what cannot be denied is its reasonable success in retaining the culture of harmony.

I could feel this when I was observing the celebration of Eid at this small town. I witnessed the mood of festivity all around — the same mood that could be seen during *Durgā Pūjā* festivals. There was light. There was music. And there was the carnival of food. There were local clubs (consisting of Hindu participants) that came forward, organized cultural programmes, and participated in festivals. I did not notice the ghetto mentality. There was no seclusion. I also witnessed the large-scale participation of Muslim women (mind it, they were not rich, they belonged to the poorer and lower middle-class sections of society). The way they were moving, eating, celebrating and participating in the public domain of cultural gatherings enabled me to see the limitations of the dominant stereotype of the Muslim community secluding its women!

Pāṛā (neighbourhood society) is an integral component of Bengali culture. *Pāṛā* symbolizes many things: intimacy, informality, face-to-face interaction, shared memory and sense of belonging. True, because of the growing geographical/social mobility, increasing self-centredness, illegitimate politicization and resultant fractions and divisions in society, it is becoming difficult to retain the integrity of *pāṛā*. Yet *pāṛā* is not dead. It would not be wrong to say that the local club (an association of young people) seeks to keep the spirit of *pāṛā* alive.

This time in our own *pāṛā* I saw this assertion. The club was celebrating its silver jubilee. It mobilized almost every family, every individual in the *pāṛā*. Since early morning one could hear the sound of the loudspeaker: Rabindrasangeet and frequent announcements regarding the celebration. In the evening the cultural programmes attracted almost everyone.

In this public domain I could see a sense of belonging, one's ability to come out of the magic of television and enter the domain of people's culture: an intensely participatory culture in which local artists and singers perform, and a close bond is established between the entertainer and the entertained. In a way, *pāṛā* and club serve a positive function. Barriers are overcome (in clubs there is no caste/class/religious distinction), and men and women discover a common platform to share their joys and sufferings. But then, the club culture is also undergoing a speedy transformation. With increasing unemployment and lumpenization of politics, clubs have often been reduced into "entertainment centres" in which young boys spend time, derive vicarious pleasure in looking at women passing by, smoke and drink.

Directionless Youth and Distorted Religiosity

This time I witnessed the phenomenal growth of temples — the temples in which every Tuesday and Saturday devotees come and worship. In a way, this is not surprising, because as it is believed, Bengali culture cannot be imagined without Kālī temples. But then, in recent times the growth of temples does not necessarily mean the intensity of religiosity and spirituality. In fact, local clubs have constructed these temples:

the clubs that consist of unemployed young people. They seem to have realized that temples give some kind of legitimacy to their existence. Moreover, they are clever enough to understand that temples are reliable sources of earning money! In fact, the very rationality behind the existence of these temples shows that there is nothing sacred or sacrosanct anymore. It is, therefore, no wonder that near these temples one could see young boys listening to popular Bollywood music, gossiping, playing cards, smoking and drinking.

As a matter of fact, to see the mental map of these young boys is to realize the intensity of unemployment and the resultant meaninglessness confronting them. At this important juncture of their biographies when they are expected to tap their physical/mental/spiritual energy and engage themselves in life-affirming projects, they find themselves in a state of void: utterly directionless and deprived of any alternative agenda. This shows that urban/middle-class people in Bengal have not yet been able to orient themselves to new career pursuits — starting their own small-scale business, accepting the dignity of manual labour, and choosing a productive engagement in the field of agriculture or rural industry.

It seems that they are still the children of Macaulay. Except "secure" jobs in government offices and primary/secondary schools they cannot imagine anything else for them. As a result, for an unemployed young man, there are only two options (a) spending time in local clubs with tea, cigarette and alcohol, and (b) exhausting his entire life-energy by offering himself as a "private tutor" for schoolchildren. This tragedy reflects that the ruling Left Front has not been able to do much to spread the culture of sanity amongst them.

Yes, I was thinking about temples. Not all temples have got the similar kind of sanctity and sacredness. For instance, the Ramakrishna Mission and its newly constructed temple complex are "sacred" zones. Every evening devotees — retired officers, educated housewives, college/school teachers and other professionals — visit the temple, participate in the collective prayer, contemplate and meditate. But then, a careful look at the Mission shows its growing bureaucratization. To enter the Ramakrishna Mission temple (its huge structure and aesthetic beauty symbolize the material prosperity of the organization) is to come across a number of notices and instructions: don't touch this, don't touch that; in fact, a series of official/bureaucratic orders. All these made me feel the growing distance between the saints (they are often regarded as *mahārājas*) and the people. I also felt what Max Weber regarded as the routinization of charisma. The original charisma of Ramakrishna and Vivekananda seems to have been replaced by a bureaucratic structure with its hierarchies and rationalities. It is, however, possible to see a difference between this bureaucracy and the governmental bureaucracy. It has got its "sacred" character; it is more "efficient" in delivering services. No wonder, the Ramakrishna Mission School is the best school in the town. It is not that this school is committed to an alternative educational ideal. It plays the same game, and plays better. It has got a "disciplinary" regime; it assures success. What else do middle-class parents need?

From Cricket-fantasy to Capitation Fee

Cricket continues to fascinate. It is fast replacing football as the most popular game in Bengal. Cricket is not just popular; it is prestigious. In the age of television, and particularly when there is a close link between cricket and money/glamour, this game seems to have acquired a new manning. I witnessed great excitement centred on cricket. I saw young mothers sending their children to cricket coaching camps. Like computer, cricket, it appears, has become a potential career opportunity for the emergent middle class.

There was great excitement regarding the state-level cricket competition among schoolchildren. It was indeed an event in this small town. Cricket, it should not be forgotten, comes with its own symbols: the symbols to which sponsors add special value. Although schoolchildren were playing I saw big banners of Bagpiper in the playground. I saw the local cable channel taking special interest in the tournament. Indeed, this cricket-fantasy showed the changing cultural landscape in this town. Cricket meant many things: money, glamour and success. I asked myself: how long could one protect this small town from these metropolitan symbols?

These chains of aspirations could be seen in every domain of existence. For example, I saw the phenomenal growth of nursing homes (this shows the decline of the public health system in Bengal). These nursing homes looked like big business houses. Human helplessness before sickness and morbidity, the complexity of modern medicine, the increasing medicalization of the human body, the decline of the ethos of service in the medical profession and eventually the reduction of doctors into "money-making machines" could be felt every moment.

To move around the town is to experience the prosperity of doctors amidst the all-pervasive suffering of people. Indeed, doctors constitute a class: a class that tempts. Not surprisingly, middle-class parents want their children to qualify the Joint Entrance Test and enter the "prestigious" medical colleges of Bengal. Everyone — school-going children, private tutors, coaching centres — seems to be thinking how to succeed in the Joint Entrance Test. At times, one tends to feel that this has become the most important question shaping the discourse in every middle-class family. This is indeed tragic. A culture that once created its renaissance thinkers is now obsessed with this little desire. It does not seem to have a wider vision, a perspective or a cause to fight for.

This superficiality (moral void intensifies the ambition to grow rich at any cost) could be seen in many other realms. I saw the emergent phenomenon: prosperous parents — businessmen, contractors, PWD engineers — sending their children to Bangalore and other parts of south India for doing medical/engineering courses. There was a time when Bengalis used to have contempt for the "capitation fee" phenomenon; they expressed pride in "high standards" prevalent in their educational institutions. But now, things have changed. If money can buy a professional degree in the global market, why should Bengalis lag behind?

Money and success, it should not be forgotten, require English: the language of "power." Although the pride for Bengali language is still alive, the lure of English cannot be resisted. English, the new generation knows, has got tremendous possibilities. No wonder, even in this small town I could notice the steady growth of English medium schools and their new legitimacy amongst the ambitious class that seeks mobility, and is striving for a "sure" road to success.

Protest, Cynicism and Self-destruction

Bengalis, it appears, love to protest. They think that they are protesting against exploitation, against injustice, against the Centre's "discriminatory" policies. This culture of protest is all-pervasive. Everyday I could see some form of political demonstration or other: people shouting slogans, or local leaders in street corner meetings debunking the world around them.

It is not difficult to see the history of this culture of protest: the way at a crucial juncture of modern Indian history leaders like C.R. Das and Subhas Bose differed from the mainstream Congress policies, or in post-colonial times the Leftists protested against the unholy alliance of feudal landlords and industrial capitalists. It is obvious that this culture of protest has given a distinctive identity to Bengali culture. A militant trade union leader, a radical Leftist, or even an anarchist poet — everyone seems to convey the message that the road to capitalist development in Bengal cannot be easy; it has to face resistance. That Bengal continues to be a centre for an alternative political culture cannot be denied. It can be seen in many ways: in Left movements, in little magazines, in Mrinal Sen/Ritwik Ghatak films.

It is, however, sad that these days the culture of protest is losing its meaning. Far from being emancipatory it has become negative and self-destructive. The protest is always against some external enemy: be it the Centre, the capitalist class or the Gandhi-Nehru legacy! But seldom does one look at oneself: one's own follies and mistakes. This refusal to undergo the process of self-criticism is essentially an escape from one's own work and responsibility. It would not be wrong to say that in Bengal the culture of protest has become an escapist route; it seeks to hide one's irresponsibility, callousness and inertia. It is, therefore, not surprising that these days the ruling Leftists are realizing the mistakes made by irresponsible trade unionism. Almost everyday, the chief minister asserts that people must come to offices in time and work religiously.

Perhaps the nihilistic and self-destructive character of this protest can be felt in the frequent Bengal *bandha*s. Every political group — Left or Right — uses this strategy and paralyses normal social life. The other day, I realized the meaning of one such Bengal *bandha* called by Mamata Banerjee, leader of the Trinamool Congress. I moved around the town. I saw that everything was closed: banks, government offices, schools and markets. I witnessed complete chaos in the streets: three Trinamool cadres threatening an old rickshaw puller and damaging his vehicle (his "mistake" was that he brought out his vehicle to the street on that "eventful" day). I felt that these "successful" *bandha*s express the tragedy of contemporary Bengali life: cynicism, escape from work, lumpenization of politics, and a deep-rooted fear that a group of lumpens can damage public property and destroy the normalcy of everyday life.

Indeed, the Bengali mind, it appears, is becoming more and more cynical. It condemns and debunks. It sees only negative things. It does not create and construct. It does not have a positive vision to live for. This cynical/negative mindset has got many expressions: unemployed young people spending hours in neighbourhood tea shops, employees in government offices escaping from their duties and deriving tremendous pleasure in discussing the economics of cricket, and people in general obsessed with all sorts of negativities.

For Creative Self-renewal

There is despair. Bengal is not progressing. Nothing seems to have been done to reduce the intensity of unemployment. There is political corruption. Violence is all-pervasive. A friend of mine, who till now was a committed cadre of the CPI-M, shared his anguish:

> It is becoming difficult to remain in the party. The certainty of power has caused widespread corruption. The party has lost its ideal and direction. There is no democracy within the party. I wish to dissociate myself from the party for which I fought for so many years.

There is indeed a crisis. Time and again one witnesses the typical middle-class despair: "There is no hope. Bengalis are not doing well in competitive examinations!" Is there any way out? One thing has to be realized. Bengal cannot find salvation by producing more and more IAS officers. There is no hope if Kolkata imitates Mumbai and Bangalore, and Bengali girls begin to participate in the Femina beauty contest! Nor is there a possibility of self-renewal if more and more "bright" economics/engineering graduates from Presidency College and Jadavpur University migrate to the USA and become "successful" NRIs.

In fact, Bengal ought to evolve an alternative path: a path that is sensitive to the ethos of egalitarianism, a path that privileges great cultural ideals of creativity and innovative thinking, a path that draws its inspiration from emancipatory radicalism.

But then, Bengal cannot afford to remain contented with the nostalgia it often cherishes: "We have a saint like Vivekananda, a poet like Rabindranath, a revolutionary like Subhas Bose, a film-maker like Satyajit Ray, a musician like Ravishankar, and an economist like Amartya Sen." In fact, at this crucial juncture Bengal needs a rigorous exercise of self-reflection. It needs yet another renaissance to give itself the direction and confidence it has lost in recent times.

13

Saying God into Presence
Narrative Embodiment in Folk Religion

Roma Chatterji

In the anthropological study of Hinduism the term "folk religion" co-exists with other terms like "little tradition" and "non-sāṁskṛtic tradition" (Sinha, 1956; Srinivas & Shah, 1968). All three terms are used to contextualize beliefs and rituals within everyday life. Sontheimer, the Indologist and student of popular Hindu cults, is concerned with the definitional status of folk religion and its implications for the understanding of Hinduism itself. According to Sontheimer (1995) folk religion is an important component of Hinduism and is to be distinguished not so much by its specific localizations, cultic beliefs or customary practices as by the modality of its being. It is a "way of doing" rather than a "way of saying." Thus, a crucial aspect of folk religion for Sontheimer is the aspect of divine presence. The god or goddess is accessible in the form of a *mūrti* and is earth bound. The corporeality of the deity is the distinguishing feature of folk religion and may take diverse forms. Thus, the deity eats food in the form of offerings, can express her/his pleasure or displeasure at the form that the offering may take, and is attentive in a variety of ways.

In this essay I will take up one aspect of this presence that Sontheimer has not touched upon — the telling of sacred stories. Sacred stories make the divine present and give it corporeality in the mode of saying; and they do so by positing a lived synchronicism between events that occurred in sacred time and our everyday time. In Puruliā, a district in West Bengal, such narration is called *kathā* (utterable truth). The truth narrated as *kathā* is not propositional truth but the utterability given to a sacred event that may occur in cosmic time and yet relate to ordinary secular time. It is thus that every woman visiting Vrindavan may be appropriately addressed as Rādhā. As *kathā*s are personified discourses they take on different forms when they are narrated in different contexts. The dramatic conflicts between the gods and demons embodied in the Chho dance, for instance, are very different from the paradoxes encapsulated in the riddle or the accounts of the tribulations suffered by the archetypal devotee in the *vrata kathā* (the sacred story ritually narrated in the course of certain *pūjā*s undertaken as vows). Again, the *kathā* takes a different form in the songs of devotion (*jhumur*s) which express the despair of separation of the devotee from his/her god and describe his/her *līlā* on earth. In that sense the *kathā* is simultaneously the story as it is embodied in the text, the oral narration of it and the events that are retained in memory and reproduced in the social contexts when the features of a space, a person or a social activity have to be explained as indexical symbols of the activities of gods.

We have already said that each *kathā* is related to all the other *kathā*s in the universe of discourse. They are related synchronically in collective memory and during the course of narration; events that appear paradoxical or strange are explained by linking them causally through the concept of *karma* to other events that took place in a different *yuga*. To take one example — when Kr̥ṣṇa and Balarāma first leave Vrindavan and go to Mathura they want to exchange their simple clothes for more princely garb. They ask a washerman passing by to give them clothes, but he spurns them, retorting that he is taking the clothes to the royal palace. Kr̥ṣṇa cuts off his head with one sweep of his hand. This story is difficult to understand unless we juxtapose it with another story, that of the washerman in Rāma's kingdom. The washerman had been abandoned by his wife and he refused to take her back when she returned, saying that he was not Rāmachandra to take back a wife who had strayed from her home. When rumours of this reached Rāma, he was compelled to expel Sītā to the forest, although he was convinced of her innocence, for keeping her in the palace would lead to dishonour. People would say Rāma had accepted a wife, sullied by the demon king, Rāvaṇa. It was this washerman who was punished in the next birth.

There are many such stories which link the *avatāras* of Rāma and Kṛṣṇa and it is often said that what Rāma left incomplete in *Tretā-yuga,* is completed by Kṛṣṇa in *Dvāpara-yuga.* The story that is being unfolded in the course of the narration is located in plot time and therefore its episodes have an oriented character. The very act of narration, however, presupposes a synchronic relation with all other narrations that have taken place both in the heavenly and earthly domain. It occurs in the perpetual present and subsumes within itself all the narrations that have occurred in the past and will occur in the future.

During my fieldwork, this was depicted pictorially in a *Navapārāyaṇa* (a ritual reading of the text) held in Khira Bera village in Puruliā. The *Rāmāyaṇa* by Tulsīdās had to be read in fulfilment of a vow and it had to be divided in such a way that it could be read in nine days. Icons were arranged at the centre of the space where the text was being read. Rāma and Sītā sat enthroned, with Lakṣmaṇa, Bharata, Śatrughna and Hanumān in attendance. On one side of this cluster of icons were placed Kākabhuṣuṇḍī and Garuḍa as well as Śiva and Durgā, on the other side Muni Bṛhaspati and Yājñavalkya and finally Tulsīdās. All these icons depicted the narration of the *Rāmāyaṇa* in the different *loka*s — Śiva to Pārvatī on Mount Kailāsa, Kākabhuṣuṇḍī to Garuḍa on some other celestial mountain, Muni Bṛhaspati to Yājñavalkya on earth and Tulsīdās to all of humankind.

The arrangement of icons was a synchronic representation

of what happened at different times and at different places, although the icons were united by the narrative. Through the presence of Tulsīdās among the icons, the narration that was taking place in Khira Bera also became part of all the narrations of the *Rāmāyaṇa* that have taken place earlier, some even before Rāma's birth actually took place. For, the *Rāmāyaṇa* has been enacted in every age, and events in the *Rāmāyaṇa* are thus not limited by space and time.

The narration of the *kathā*s is ritualized. At one level, it can be said that the *kathā* is constituted through the act of narration. At another level, the act of narration makes the narrator and his/her audience participate in the world of the *kathā*s. In fact, the sacred texts (*pustaka*) in which the *kathā*s are compiled are thought to exist only in the context of their use. The possession of such a text imposes an obligation on the possessor for it to be read ritually, and it is felt that a sacred text never remains long in the possession of a person who does not know how to use it. It is emphasized that books get lost or disintegrate because people do not know how to use them.

Through ritual narration, the *kathā*s relate the secular to the sacred world: while participating in the unfolding of the cosmic events in the stories, the listeners are also reminded of the concrete manifestations of the divine presence in their own world. Thus, in the course of the narration of the *Rāmāyaṇa*, the listener is reminded that during their period of exile Rāma and Sītā came to Puruliā and spent one night on Mount Ayodhyā at the foot of which the village is located. The proof of this, the villagers say, can still be seen in the ruins of the hut that they built there, and in the spring in which Sītā washed her menstrual rags. A few people say that they have had the privilege of seeing the water run red on the day of the great Ayodhyā hunt on Buddha Pūrṇimā (full moon) in June, which is proof of the "truth" of the story.

Human activity is revealed to be part of the overarching cosmic design through the events described in the *kathā*s. This can be seen in the taboos that have been instituted, the ritual formalization of activities that are of fundamental importance to the society, and even in the physical states of the people. To illustrate this let me describe some of the activities associated with agriculture. In Puruliā the first ritual sowing of grain is performed on Akṣaya Tṛtīya in the month of Baiśākha (mid-April to mid-May). This date has been established as appropriate for sowing, in human time, because of its relation with an event that took place in primordial time when the form of the world had still to be set — the great god Śiva was given the responsibility of making the crops "flower" on the earth (*shoshho phota*). Śiva, in turn, asked Bhīma, the powerful hero of the *Mahābhārata* and the second of the Pāṇḍava brothers, to perform the tasks of ploughing and sowing of the grain. For this purpose he was given a tiger and bull (*baghar baulod*) to harness the plough. But where was Bhīma to get the grain (*dhāna*) to sow? Yudhiṣṭhira, his brother, sent him to Kubera, the god of wealth, who enquired whether Yudhiṣṭhira would be able to return what he had borrowed (*jemni libek ki semni dibek*). Yudhiṣṭhira, the truthful one, immediately admitted that to return the precise amount that had been borrowed was impossible. People say that this state of affairs prevails till today (*ekhuno chole ashche*). We borrow and when the time comes to return it, we say that we cannot collect together the right amount (*jogar korte pachhi nai*).

Bhīma ploughed the earth on Akṣaya Tṛtīya and his plough was harnessed to the bull and the tiger. He sowed the auspicious two and a half fistfuls (*arai mutho*) of paddy. Śiva asked him the amount he had sown and when Bhīma told him, he scoffed and said that such a paltry amount should be cast into the fire. Having said this Śiva forgot about it, till to his chagrin, he discovered the fire to be still burning after 12 or 13 years. This made him realize the power of the two and a half fistfuls of grain that had been sown in the earth, and he ordered the fire to be put out. What remained of the paddy crop then, was the *jhaura*, the black portions among the healthy grain that falls off (*jhore jae*), the *maurra*, that flower inside the paddy sheath and the *dhāna*, the actual grain. Villagers say that we can see the effects of this fire on the paddy crop that is harvested every year even today, for some of the grain is black and rotten and falls off the plant and some of it remains unripened in the paddy sheath.

How are we to read this story? Is it a fable, a social commentary or are we supposed to look for traces of divine presence in the world around us as we saw in the earlier example about Mount Ayodhyā which still bears the mark of Sītā's sojourn there? Traces of Sītā's presence both secure as well as localize place in Puruliā. Sacred places in Puruliā can establish their genealogies in terms of cosmic time. Thus the Ayodhyā Mountain can be said to have existed at least from the *Tretā-yuga*, the time when Rāma and Sītā lived on earth. It also locates it on the cosmic map so that Mount Ayodhyā becomes an extension of Rāma's kingdom, the commonality of name marking shared identity and establishing the facticity of Puruliā's sacred history. Bhīma's story is somewhat different, however. It does not specify a particular form of social activity nor does it give facticity to a particular state of being. Instead it speaks of the human condition in general terms. (We must remember that this is one of the important functions of the fable.) It uses the example of a single paddy sheaf to speak ironically about the incompleteness of the human form of life. Divine presence, that is, Śiva's presence, is seen here precisely in the gap between the goals of human endeavour and its final outcome. This story also describes human activity in terms that are very different from ritual activity, for unlike the latter, human activity is governed by chance.

There are other registers in which this story can be read. Thus Bhīma's creation of the world through hard labour and scarcity is juxtaposed with the effortless creation (*līlā*) of the gods. I am thinking here of Viṣṇu's creation of Brahmā while lying asleep on the cosmic serpent Ananta. This could also be said of Śiva's careless utterance in the story above that has such devastating consequences for the world that humans labour to create. But I want to take up another aspect of this story. The inedible parts of the paddy sheaf, the raw and rotten parts, are called *jhaurra* and *maurra* — this playful alliteration mimics Śiva's careless utterance. Irony is one of the ways in which humans address the whimsical activities of the gods that sometimes have such devastating consequences for the human world. Riddles, word-play, a gift given to humans by the Goddess Sarasvatī, is another, for this is one of the ways that humans can approximate the playful creativity of the gods, a creativity that is inherently ambivalent.

Consider the following riddle:

> *Dausho shir mauhabir*
> (The mighty hero has ten heads)
> *Loe to Rabon*
> (But is not Rāvaṇa)
> *Stri loker hate tar nischoi mauron*
> (His death at the hand of a woman is certain)

The answer to this riddle is the vegetable called *jhiṅgā* (snake gourd) in Bāṅglā. The *jhiṅgā* plant is a creeper whose fruit grows in clusters. The comparison with a common domestic vegetable not only diminishes Rāvaṇa's stature as a mighty warrior but also reduces Rāma's heroic act of killing him. Thus, Rāvaṇa's death at the hands of the divine Rāma is inevitable in the same way the death of the *jhiṅgā* is inevitable, but by the hand of an ordinary housewife. Word-play, the skilful use of analogy, creates a juxtaposition between the human and the mythic registers, reducing the dimensions of the mythic figures and adding a touch of mystery to the human and the banal.

Riddles "play" with the cognitive categories of society through the medium of the word. They collapse boundaries between different semantic categories and create new boundaries where none existed before. They create unexpected paradoxes in seemingly axiomatic relations. Thus, riddles are a mode of dialogue with society or perhaps a series of trick questions which play with all the ambiguities in language to reflect on the ambiguities that exist in society. Some of these are "real" but many are fantasies created by clothing the facts in impossible metaphors and breaking the expected relations between them and creating unexpected ones. This is a different mode of dialogue from the one that exists in the *kathā*, but related nevertheless, because the riddle takes up some of the relationships in the *kathā*s and displays them in the light of fantastic paradoxes. They juxtapose situations which would not merit intellectual scrutiny in themselves, being quite "ordinary" but which take on the qualities of the unexpected by this juxtaposition. Thus,

> *Dui brikkho ek mool*
> (Two trees and one root)
> *Tinti koli charti phool*
> (Three buds which yield four flowers)
> *Dine poti rate bhashur*
> (Husband in the day time, but husband's brother at night)
> *Nikash korle hoe shoshur*
> (But if you calculate he becomes the father-in-law)

The reference is to Draupadī's relationship with Karṇa. The two trees referred to in the first line are Yama and Karṇa both of whom originate from one "root" that is Sūrya. They are both his sons. The three buds are Sūrya and his two sons, Yama and Karṇa but they yield four flowers because Yudhiṣṭhira is Yama's son as well and is referred to obliquely in the next two lines. The woman who is the subject of the next line is Draupadī, married to the five Pāṇḍava brothers. In the day-time Draupadī is struck by the thought that Karṇa could have been her husband because he is Kuntī's son but at night she must put such thoughts aside and maintain an avoidance relationship because he is her husbands' elder brother. But because Karṇa is Sūrya's son he is also Yudhiṣṭhira's uncle and therefore Draupadī's father-in-law.

*Kathā*s talk of gods' play on earth. Riddles mimic this play through words. Riddles have no function; they too are a form of purposeless creativity in the same way as divine *līlā*.

Ke je kaumole baushe shauroje bhalo bashe na
(*Kamala* and *saroja* are synonyms for the lotus.) Who is it that resides in the *kamala* but does not love the *saroja*?

Kori niye khela kaure gauje pauroshe na
(*Kori* and *gaja* are synonyms for elephant.) Who is it that plays with the *kori* but will not touch the *gaja*?

Kr̥ṣṇo ke shaube bhoje śyāmo nautobaro teja
(Kr̥ṣṇa and Śyāma Naṭavara are both names of the same deity.) Who is it that celebrates Kr̥ṣṇa but casts Śyāma Naṭavara aside?

Rādhikā niye khela kaure gopīr majhe jae na
Who is it that plays with Rādhikā but will go amongst the *gopīs*? (Rādhikā is one of the *gopīs*.)

The answer is the letter *ka* which is missing from all the second terms in the pair of synonyms.

This riddle points to the joyous abundance of language that creates through the use of synonyms apparent differences where none exist. Riddles use word-play to re-create the phenomenal world symbolically. Therefore, in a sense they also actualize it even if only in the mode of representation. They remind us however "playfully" that creation, making something present, has unexpected consequences. Even words that seem to be mere symbolic representations can have devastating effects — I am thinking here of Śiva's careless utterance. Making god present is not always easy to cope with.

In conclusion, let me turn once again to Sontheimer's views on folk religion. Giving the gods corporeal presence is one way of domesticating orthodox and hierarchical traditions, and indeed scholars like Ramanujan (1999) who have written extensively on folklore, have said that this is one of its chief functions. However, folklore can also mythicize the mundane as we saw in the case of the first riddle presented here. Riddles are in a reflexive relationship, not only with the other narrative traditions in this society but with the phenomenal world as such. However, reflexivity is not a characteristic only of the riddle genre; it is found in all the lived traditions in India (see Ramanujan, 1999). This is so, I think, because of the specific mode by which presence is invoked. Gods are made present as sacred images or icons. Icons are signs that exist once removed from the things that they represent. They have an autonomous existence and can come to represent more than one kind of thing over time. This gives them a special efficacy in the sphere of religion because they can enter into a kind of dialogue with the community of worshippers. Thus, to give one example, take the cross as an iconic symbol of Christianity. The cross existed long before Christ was actually crucified on it. It was one of the instruments of execution and Christ was executed as a common criminal. It is only after this event that the cross becomes an icon but it does not change its form in any way. It has an existence prior to the event of Christ's crucifixion but also has the capacity to take over the image of the event completely. It has the capacity, therefore, to bridge different time periods and also to bring events that occurred in the past, whether historical or mythic, into the present. In the introduction to this essay I referred to this as a kind of "lived synchronicism." I want to end by saying that all sacred narratives have the quality of lived synchronicism because they give people the experience they would have had if they had actually been present at the event. Sacred narratives bring mythic events into "real" time and make them part of our day-to-day lives. They are part of what Sontheimer would characterize as folk religion precisely because of this feature. What is folk religion then? It is not something that can be set apart as a separate entity but rather it is that aspect of religion that is lived and therefore must be a part of sacred life *per se*.

References

Ramanujan, A.K., 1999, "Where Mirrors are Windows: Toward an Anthology of Reflection", in Vinay Dharwadikar, ed., *The Collected Essays of A.K. Ramanujan*, Delhi: Oxford University Press, pp. 6-33.

Sinha, Surajit, 1957, "Tribal Cultures of Peninsular India as a Dimension of the Little Tradition in the Study of Indian Civilization: A Preliminary Statement", *Man in India*, vol. 37 (2), pp. 3-118.

Sontheimer, Gunther D., 1995, "The Erosion of Folk Religion in Modern India. Some Points of Deliberation", in Vasudha Dalmia and Henri von Stietencron, eds., *Representing Hinduism: The Construction of Religious Traditions and National Identity*, Delhi: Sage, pp. 389-400.

Srinivas, M.N. and A.M. Shah, 1968, "Hinduism", in D. Sills, ed., *International Encyclopaedia of the Social Sciences*, vol. 6, Crowell Collier and MacMillan, p. 359.

14

Articulation of Sacred Knowledge in Dance

Nita Mathur

THE concept of "sacred" which constitutes the cornerstone of discourses in the disciplines of Anthropology, Sociology, Indology, Philosophy and Theology is enshrined in the oft-cited Durkheim's definition of religion which reads: "A religion is a unified system of beliefs and practices relative to sacred things, that is to say, things that are set apart and forbidden — beliefs and practices which unite into one single moral community called a Church, all those who adhere to them" (1965: 62). Here, the determinants of that which is sacred are contained in the expressions, "set apart" and "forbidden." The sacred, as is a well-known fact, stands in opposition to the "profane." The sacred-profane dichotomy in the domain of religion and religious behaviour has been the subject of profound discussions and debates many of which challenge the very foundation upon which the two categories are constructed (see Stanner, 1967; Saraswati, 1975).

In the Indian situation, however, such dualism in intellectual thought does not apply well enough to understand religion as a phenomenon. Madan (1991), among others, emphasizes that Indian religious thought is hierarchical rather than dualistic and that the profane, though opposed to the sacred, is included in and thus subordinated to it. The distinction between the two is extremely nebulous and that on many occasions it is hard to separate the sacred from the profane and to tell when the sacred gets rid of its sacredness and becomes profane and profane gets sacrilized. This is not to deny the integrity of the two categories but to establish that these are neither rigid nor fixed in any way.

The concept of sacred knowledge used here is derived from Madan (1991: 23) to mean, as he does, ". . . first of all, knowledge that may be considered sacred in itself — by virtue of its source, form and content. In other words, it is essentially and uncontestably sacred for the believers." It includes, among others, religious texts and scriptures and all that which relates with cosmology, moral order and the esoteric in terms of symbols, myths and beliefs. These are expressed distinctly in symbols, myths, rites and rituals, places of pilgrimage, architectural layout in places of worship, iconography and murals on the one hand and incantations, narratives and several kinds of performances on the other (see Srinivas, 1952; Vidyarthi, 1961; Turner, 1967, 1969; Mushir-ul-Haq, 1972; Das, 1977; Ostor, 1980; Gold, 1988).

Writings on religion, particularly indigenous religion, abound in the mention of dance as an integral component of ritual behaviour (see Paul and Elaine Lewis, 1984; Weber and Seaman, 1985; Walker, 1986; Dalmia, 1988). Whether in the context of effecting rain, or overcoming ritual contamination, dance has been realized as a powerful means of placating gods and goddesses and for invoking their benignity. While the chief interest of many scholars remains confined to the movements and postures in dance as also drawing parallels between dance forms and iconographic representations (see Avtar, 1984; Kothari, 1988; Visvanathan, 1984; Sathyanarayana, 1994), the essence of what dance is all about largely lies in its sacredness and being part of a knowledge system which has the potential to provide an impetus to achieve salvation or escape from worldly concerns that has been identified as the perennial urge of people and the objective of all religious practices in the final. Dance as a ritual and the ritual of dance, re-define moral relations, and make for presentation of imagery in the culture through semantics of symbols. In this paper I bring to the fore the play of rituals, symbols and myths in dance whereby the body transcends its fineness and physical limitations. What I emphasize here are the twin elements of ritual and religious belief system as constituents of Bharatanāṭyam dance form substantiated with insights from the lives of Tamil brāhmaṇas. Interestingly, Tamil brāhmaṇa culture and life philosophy envision the dance of Bharatanāṭyam as a form of ritual that renders reverence, worship and honour to deities. A brief introduction to the people and their predominant dance form is followed by the cultural theory of the origin of dance that imbues sacredness to it, and an account of myths about the origin of and reflexivity in dance that provide a framework of the analysis of symbols, meanings and values as they explain behaviour.

Tamil brāhmaṇas describe themselves as "high-caste residents of Tamil Nadu" which they refer to as *engaluadaya nadu* meaning "our country". Like brāhmaṇas in other parts of the country, those in Tamil Nadu enjoyed close access to deities in temples. Many of them have been involved in temple affairs including those related with performance of dance in temples by *devadāsīs* (literally meaning "wives of gods"). *Devadāsīs*' dance in temples was regarded as an essential part of performance of their wifely duties aimed at pleasing their "god-husband". Tamil brāhmaṇas were not mere spectators of dance, they were also engaged with temple rituals that had a bearing on the art form in many ways (discussed later). Gradually, the dance, which was initially *dāsī-aṭṭam* or dance of the women servants, evolved into what in better known in the present day as Bharatanāṭyam. In the late nineteenth and early twentieth centuries, brāhmaṇas largely pursued Western education and were able to acquire positions of power in civil services. A new middle class with keen interest in the arts emerged and came to incorporate performing arts as a fundamental component of their identity (Irschick, 1986; Subramanian, 2006; O'shea, 2003, 2009). The seeds of Bharatanāṭyam have travelled across the country with Tamil brāhmaṇas, as also others. Even as it moved out of the temples, the dance retained its religious character. The major themes that are performed in dance relate with the lives of gods and goddesses enshrined in the ancient scriptures. In fact, the origin of dance is traced to the rhythmic movements of gods and goddesses (Mathur, 2002).

One of the earliest scriptures, the *Ṛgveda* bespeaks of dance (in a general sense) of several deities as in the following hymn: "Thence as of dancers from your feet, a thickening cloud of dust arose" (X.72-vii). The occasion here is that of the birth of Aditi. The word *aditi* means, "the unbounded, the free." Aditi is the goddess who personifies the infinite universe. Often represented as a cow, she is the supporter of the sky, the sustainer of existence, the nourisher of the earth (Walker, 1983). Another hymn referring to dance reads, "With the sisters they have danced, embraced by them, making the earth re-echo with the sounding treads" (X.94). The *Ṛgveda* associates dance with occasions of birth as also death, of joy as also sorrow, and of togetherness as also solitude. Furthermore, the description of rituals in the *Yajurveda*, the Brāhmaṇas, the Gṛhyasūtras, *Rāmāyaṇa* and *Mahābhārata* incorporates dance as a significant component.

The dominant imagery in Hindu psyche derived from myths and legends is that of the court of Indra (the king of the heaven) in which *apsaras*es (heavenly nymphs) dance. In fact, Indra himself is known for his competence to appreciate the nuances of dance as also for the skill to dance. Many other gods and goddesses are known to dance in sheer ecstasy and bliss. One of the major deities is Kālī — the black goddess representing terror — who is believed to have danced in burning grounds amidst corpses and fire on several occasions. The burning ground where Kālī dances represents the interface between the gross (body) and the subtle (spirit) states of existence. People with deep insight into Hindu thought state that the element of fire that consumes the dead bodies in cremation grounds symbolically engulfs pride and anger leading to tranquility. Kṛṣṇa — the dark hued god who was raised in the village of Vrindavana — danced with the milkmaids of the village in a way that each one felt his exclusive presence with her. In dancing with their beloved, the milkmaids transcended their earthly existence. Their individual identity merged with the identity of Kṛṣṇa. The dance of bliss was the fruition of their life-long spiritual discipline. One of the themes that run as an undercurrent in the dance of both, Kālī and Kṛṣṇa is that of liminality, of interface between the physical and the ethereal body, and between sensory pleasure and transcendent bliss.

Apart from the dance of Kālī, Kṛṣṇa and other deities is that of Śiva — the Lord of dance. He dances alone and with Pārvatī — his consort, in agony and in ecstasy, in cremation ground and in the golden hall, for devotees and for ascetics. Once Śiva danced on the Himalayas. The orchestra was created by gods and goddesses. Brahmā — the creator, the writer of people's fate, and one who keeps records of people's deeds — played the cymbals. In Hindu thought, cymbals mark time. Viṣṇu — the preserver and one who makes provision for everyone's needs — played the drum that set the rhythm of the universe. According to Walker (1983), a characteristic of Indian drummers is that the beating is accompanied with vigorous movements of the head, shoulders and arms. Often the eyes look up and they reach a state of near trance. It is believed that Viṣṇu's drumming made for the pattern of the universe that repeats itself in the cycle of seasons, rotation and revolution of the earth, waxing and waning of moon, rising and falling of waters, and other processes of nature upon which all forms of existence depend. Indra played the flute known for its melody and power to draw out the best from one's inner self. Sarasvatī — the goddess of wisdom — played the *vīṇā* which is one of the oldest of Indian musical instruments consisting of seven strings. Lakṣmī — the goddess of wealth and prosperity — sang the song. The dance of Śiva and the divine orchestra consolidate the fundamental elements of existence and survival: time, rhythm, knowledge and prosperity woven together in a definite pattern. Śiva danced again at Chidambaram (in Tamil Nadu) before an assembly of deities and devotees.

Dancing Śiva appropriately described as Naṭarāja which literally means, the "king of dance" is popularly depicted by sculptors, painters and other artists as one with four arms, long braided hair, a wreathing cobra, a skull, mermaid figure of Gaṅgā carrying a crescent moon crowned with leaves (see Sivaramamurti, 1974 for a vivid description). He is adorned with earrings, armlets, bracelets, rings, belt and anklets. The right foot rests on a malicious dwarf while the left is raised. One of the right hands holds a drum; the other is configured as the *patākā-mudrā* (a configuration of the hand in which the fingers are joined together and stretched out, the thumb is bent to touch the base of the forefinger). One of the left hands carries a pot of fire; the other points to the raised foot. From the lotus pedestal originates encircling glory fringed with flames. The right hand holds the drum and the left one holds fire that touches the flames. Notwithstanding the obvious meaning of symbols as the *patākā-mudrā* denoting fearlessness and pointer to the raised foot as inviting surrender before the god, the image of Naṭarāja revels with deeper structures of thought and meaning.

The critical elements in the image of Naṭarāja that serve as significant symbols in the life philosophy and collective psyche of people are: snake, lotus, Gaṅgā (water), fire, and encircling glory. Vatsyayan (1993) mentions that the convoluted snake represents the coiling and recoiling of time. The mouth and the tail come together occasionally representing "cyclic" nature of time. They also straighten up to form a line which represents continuity and eternity. Conceptually, the lotus is to the mythical centre of the earth through its rhizomal stem, leaf and flower. The human body is conceived as constituted of seven lotuses in the form of centres of psychic energy. These centres coincide with the base-root centre of sexual experience, base of the genital organ, near the navel (lumbar or epigastric plexus), heart, throat, between the eyebrows, and head. Psychic energy passes through the six lotuses and matures in the seventh one, the head.

The snake and the lotus are dominant symbols in the collective psyche of people. It is believed that in the beginning, there was nothing but an expanse of water on the surface of which Viṣṇu reclined comfortably over a serpent. The stalk of a lotus came out from the navel of Viṣṇu. Brahmā emerged from the lotus. In fact, Brahmā is visualized with a lotus flower in his hand. Having made his appearance, Brahmā created the world teeming with diverse forms of life. According to Bosch (1994), the lotus is known for life-giving substances drawn from the water that defies the travails of old age, sickness and death and bestows fertility on women, cattle and fields. The lotus is closely associated with the snake in Hindu thought. Apart from plain morphological similarity, between the body of the snake and the lotus stalk, the snake, like the lotus, also possesses the power to absorb life-supporting energy from waters and lay it upon others effecting stimulation and prolongation of life. The lotus and the snake initiate a shift from the state of undifferentiation to one of differentiation and multiplicity.

Water is regarded as the primary source of life. It is an important element of Hindu cosmogony, continuity and renewal of life and its dissolution at one level, and of physical existence and viability at the other. Gaṅgā is the sacred river personified as a goddess by the same name. The water of river Gaṅgā is believed to be bestowed with sacredness and propensity to confer fertility, fecundity, auspiciousness and prosperity. Gaṅgā is the source of creative energies, strength and vigour. The other element is *agni* or fire. Chakrabarti and Frits Staal (1996) suggest that fire is not only the source of heat and light in the cosmos but also a mediator between human beings and gods by means of ritual fire. No ritual action is complete without a fire sacrifice. In the microcosm of the human body, fire is associated with breath (*prāṇa*), speech (*vāk*), vision (*cakṣu*), and digestive process. The last element in the imagery of Naṭarāja is glory or *tejas* which refers to energy or power associated with light. At a philosophical level, Filliozat (1996) explains *tejas* is the preferred designation of Śakti or energy, will of god. It is the property to be manifest and to make manifest. In terms of energy and heat, *tejas* may be thought of as personified in the form of the sun and fire. These are invoked on several occasions as witnesses of solemn actions and vows. It is believed that the discus of Viṣṇu; the trident of Śiva, the lance of Kārttikeya and weapons of several other deities are made out of the brilliance and radiance of the sun. In the integration of these elements as in the body of Naṭarāja (some of them forming apparent binary oppositions) cosmic order is established and human existence is made possible.

There is a legend according to which a king known for his wisdom witnessed the dance of *gandharva*s — beings of the heaven. He was convinced that this form of art begets auspiciousness and fervently prayed to Bharata and other deities to teach the dance to his subjects. Finally, Bharata conceded and entrusted the task to his sons. The sons of Bharata descended on the earth. Children born out of them and women of the earth were skilled in the art. Alternatively, it is believed that Śiva ordered Taṇḍu — one of his disciples to demonstrate the dance to Bharata. Pārvatī taught him *lāsya* — the form of dance known for graceful and gentle movements. While Bharata and few other sages trained the women, Pārvatī trained Uṣā — the wife of Kṛṣṇa's grandson. Uṣā, in turn, taught dance to women of Dvārakā in Gujarat from where it spread to other parts of the country (Avtar, 1984).

It is believed that the dance of the gods establishes *ṛta* or cosmic order. *Ṛta* is a Vedic concept which signifies the regularity and periodicity of cosmic processes, the rising and setting of the sun, waxing and waning of the moon, circadian rhythms and cycle of seasons. These are also markers for regularity, uprightness, and justice inherent in cosmic order which underlies the very genesis of life. The solar and lunar calendars marking rituals and festivals exemplify the principle of cosmic order amply. Most of the festivals consist of creating, consecrating, worshipping, and abandoning or burning of images. Temple images are, however, permanent but they are enlivened, awakened, bathed, fed, and laid to rest regularly.

Following the *Nāṭyaśāstra* (tr. Ghosh, 1950), Brahmā sifted the textual material from the *Ṛgveda*, songs from the *Sāmaveda*, histrionic representation from the *Yajurveda* and emotions from the *Atharvaveda*. Out of the essence collected from the four Vedas, he composed the Nāṭyaveda. The importance of this text lay in the fact that it was accessible to people belonging to all the castes rather than remaining the preserve of the brāhmaṇas. The sage Bharata and his hundred sons learnt the Veda and the skill to dance from Brahmā himself. Thence, *apsaras*es were created and asked to pass on the technique and style.

More specifically, Bharatanāṭyam which, as mentioned earlier, is associated with Tamil brāhmaṇa culture, marks the coming together of emotion (*bhāva*), melody (*rāga*) and rhythm (*tāla*). Interestingly, the syllables *bha*, *ra* and *ta* for *bhāva*, *rāga* and *tāla* respectively suffixed with *nāṭya* which means drama forms the complete word, *bharatanāṭyam* referring to a dance form which fuses the aforesaid components in a way that opens up possibilities for depicting innumerable characters and episodes associated with them. There are different channels of enactment or *abhinaya* namely the body, speech and costume, for the portrayal of different psychological states. There are several stances and poses, and movement sequences. These are complemented with 28 single hand gestures and 24 gestures employing both the hands (see Coomaraswamy and Duggirala, 1997). Many of them signify gods and goddesses in different situations, their ornaments and accessories and activities of worshipping and seeking boons from them. The *patākā-mudrā* (referred to earlier), for instance, owes its origin to Brahmā who first held out his hand in this gesture when he saluted other gods with a cry of victory. Interestingly, the word *patākā* means, "flag." As is well accepted the unfurling of flag evokes sentiments of victory, of national pride, and of collective identity. In other contexts the *patākā-mudrā* is used to denote clouds, forests, rivers, wind, moonlight, etc. Similarly, the *muṣṭi-mudrā* in which the four fingers are folded and the thumb rests on them was employed by Viṣṇu in fighting Madhu — a demon. The word *muṣṭi* means, the "fist." This gesture is also used to denote steadiness, wrestling, etc. In addition, there are eleven gestures denoting members of one's family such as mother, father, brother, husband, husband-wife, mother-in-law, father-in-law, brother-in-law, sister-in-law, daughter-in-law and co-wife. There are also *mudrā*s to represent particular rivers, oceans, animals and flying creatures. The dancers are equipped to perform any event in an aesthetically impressive and emotionally gratifying manner. There are several characters in a simple episode. More commonly, these episodes are myths relating to the lives and works of deities.

In the specific life situation of Tamil brāhmaṇas, dance in religious expression falls into three broad categories that are, by and large, overlapping and inclusive of each other: worship, meditation and embodiment. People state that performance is not as much about public appreciation as about rendering of reverence, devotion and veneration of the performer to the gods. Apart from the fact that dance was a part and parcel of temple rituals performed by *devadāsī*s, it was believed to bestow prosperity and auspiciousness on both the dancers and spectators. Tamil brāhmaṇas have been closely associated with dance ever since it was performed in temples for keeping the gods happy and cheerful. They arduously taught Sanskrit to *devadāsī*s and maintained relations with the gods' wives beyond temple precincts. Later when the institution of *devadāsī*s collapsed as the anti-nautch movement gained momentum (in the third quarter of the nineteenth century) threatening the very survival of dance, Tamil brāhmaṇas tried hard to retain it as a special religious ritual. Young girls enrolled themselves as students of dance, men would dress up in feminine clothes and perform before a gathering of interested people. Some brāhmaṇa men married *devadāsī*s. This went a long way in offsetting the stigma attached to the *devadāsī*s as being prostitutes and hand-maids of rich, landed clients.

*Devadāsī*s usually belonged to the Veḷḷāḷar and Mudāliyar castes. The *devadāsī*s constituted a community with a distinctive way of life predominated by love and devotion to temple deities. The essential duties of a *devadāsī* consisted of serving and pleasing her husband. She would fan the idol, dance before the idol, and put the idol to sleep. This was in addition to dancing before the idol as part of daily rituals. Young girls were initiated into the *devadāsī* fold after rigorous training in dance through a series of rituals that wedded them to the god. *Devadāsī*s as wives of gods who are immortal were regarded as the "always auspicious women" since they could never be widowed (a widow is regarded as inauspicious and kept away from important religious rituals). Their blessings were sought on important occasions. The dance of *devadāsī*s was instrumental in inviting prosperity and destroying all evil and suffering. The role of *devadāsī*s in temple and society is twofold: on the one hand they would protect the gods and community from danger and evil influences as those accruing from evil eye, while on the other they instilled dynamism into the processes of gaining livelihood and preserving well-being (Kersenboom-Story, 1990).

In the present day, when the *devadāsī* tradition is wiped out, Tamil brāhmaṇas nurture the dance as an integral part of their culture and as an important component of their cultural identity. The first encounter of most people with dance is even before birth when expectant women watch dance performances with the hope of developing interest for the art in the child resting in the womb. Girls are initiated into the tradition of dance at an early age while boys get familiarized with its nuances by attending performances. Children seek admission in dance schools usually on the day of Vijayadaśamī which is an important festival marking the victory of Lord Rāma over the demon Rāvaṇa. Vijayadaśamī follows the *navarātras* or nine nights (*nava* meaning "nine" and *rātra* meaning "night") of rigorous worship of nine goddesses.

It is believed that pleased after being worshipped, the nine goddesses become exceptionally benevolent and readily agree to confer success on all those who undertake new endeavours on the tenth day. Describing the ceremonial beginning of dance lessons in the eighteenth century, Subramanian (1982) mentions that the student would bathe after an oil massage and thence decorate herself beautifully. Older performers would bring her to the dance room where she would worship a wooden rod and invite Gaṇeśa (the god who removes obstacles in one's ventures) to dwell in it. The student would learn the first steps holding a rod at the level of her chest and trying to balance her with it and beat her feet to the rhythm of a song in praise of Gaṇeśa.

Students approach the teachers with gifts of coconuts, betel leaves and nuts, bananas, lime, sweets, flowers, and sometimes clothes. They worship the teachers as they would a deity and reverently touch their feet. One of the preliminary lessons they learn in a dance class is that of venerating the earth which is believed to be imbued with consciousness. She, therefore, has to be sought permission from before thumping one's feet on her at the beginning of each class and thanked for her perseverance after each class. Having done that, they learn to extol the attributes of different deities and worship them. It may be reiterated here that an ideal Tamil brāhmaṇa is said to be one who does regular worship and meditation, for, these are believed to prepare them for achieving higher spiritual ideals later in life.

The people believe that dance strengthens and reinforces moral values and ideals that are held high and looked up to by the people. Many of them deal with simple aspects of life such as regular prayer, compassion, obedience, co-operation, and nurturance as the following one: Morning and evening you should learn the art. Only at the sight of sun does the lotus bloom. The blessings of others are important to achieve success. The four qualities of *acham* (respect for elders), *nāṇam* (modesty), *madam* (humility) and *payirpu* (appropriate conduct and simplicity) in women are appreciable. One should uphold equality and not discriminate on the basis of caste or creed. Art of living consists of cultivating courage and honesty. One should remain prepared for contingent situations.

As the children grow older and are able to understand definite situations, they are encouraged to enact episodes out of scriptures and sacred narratives. The following are two examples from Kuppuswamy and Hariharan (1982):

> O lord of the universe with holy and alluring form and a face with a colour of the clouds, who is known to be very considerate towards your dependents and whose feet are worshipped by sages with minds full of transcendental pleasure! You promised to come back quickly. But alas! I have been cheated. Is it because you are immersed in penance? I yearn for your company, come quickly, and embrace me with the nectar on your lips. (p. 42)

> O lord, I have exclusive faith only in you. Why then are you cheating me? O Creator of the god of love who is worrying me by directing his flower arrows at my heart, save me who is struggling in the ocean of acute separation and protect me with sympathy, hear my plea. Do not be obstinate. I am dependent solely on your feet for my salvation. Like the *cātaka* bird anxiously waiting for the clouds, I am eagerly awaiting your arrival. This is the proper time for you to protect me whose pangs of separation have increased sharply on hearing the humming of bees, songs of the cuckoo bird and chirping of (other) birds. O ocean of sympathy! Anoint my body with musk and sandalwood paste and adorn my curls of hair with flowers. Talk to me in a manner calculated to assuage my pains of separation. Embrace me and kiss me on the face. (p. 47)

Seemingly, the theme related with the yearning of milkmaids for Kr̥ṣṇa has at the deeper level to do with life philosophy bespeaking of devotion to the god and connecting what seem to be oppositions and polarities between imperfection and perfection, finiteness and endlessness, confinement and freedom, and secular and sacred realms.

The training begins with simple units of dance that exercise different parts of the body and develop a sense of proportion in movements. Everyday children repeat one set of steps taught by the teacher till they are able to perform them effortlessly and with precision. It is when the children have acquired considerable competence which satisfies the teacher that they are initiated into the next stage. The rigorous training is all about acquiring control of body muscles, of breath and of expression. Control over physical body is accompanied with definite psychological processes that largely reduce the conflict between body and mind. Explaining the transmission of performance knowledge, Zarrilli (1990: 133-34) writes,

> This process is the same in the performance, the martial, and the meditative arts. After conforming to behaviour restrictions, the practitioner of classical *yoga* begins his formal path by first mastering poses (*āsana*s) and breathing (*prāṇāyāma*). Only when these have become habitualized in body processes is the practitioner ready to begin higher stages of meditation. But even in these preliminary practices, the *yogī* is beginning to free himself from the flue of the body's agitation, and from the flux of the normal, everyday psycho-mental stream of consciousness.

This is achieved at two levels: that of training in dance schools and through enactment of narratives that deal with such virtues effectively. The dance opens up alternative ways of managing a disconcerting situation amicably.

It may be recalled here that in the Hindu thought, the mind is described as volatile and as prone to reacting and dissipating its energy in unproductive ways. The dance of Bharatanāṭyam, as also several others, is treated as *yoga* and as ritual through which one offers the best of one's abilities to the gods. As among Tamil brāhmaṇas, to borrow words from Blacking (1977: 21, 23) that apply here,

> Curiously, for a society that believes in a mind superior to the body, we extol behaviour in which the mind is said to be absorbed in the body. Just as the ultimate aim of dancing is to be able to move without thinking, to be danced, so the ultimate achievement in thinking is to be moved to think, to be thought. It is sometimes called inspiration, insight, genius, creativity,

> and so on. But essentially it is a form of unconscious cerebration, a movement of the body. We are moved into thinking. Body and mind are one.

The total involvement of both, the body with all its senses and the mind in imaging the divine, is a major step in inculcating inner harmony and poise beyond the fragmenting dualities of the subject and object, thought and action, and inner and outer. An inspired actor and spectator transcends physical time and space, and in so doing reaches a state in which there is confluence of the imagery with the imaged, the dancer with the danced, and the self with the Self (Mathur, 2002). The gestures emotions and narratives accompanying the performance deal with cosmology and cosmic unity of different elements of the universe at many levels. This is replayed several times in the lives of Tamil brāhmaṇas as in daily rituals, incantations, readings from scriptures and prayers. The gestures used in the dance situation are also employed in ritual and non-ritual contexts though divested of the stylization that invariably comes with performances.

Some of the *mudrā*s most clearly common between dance and mundane, rather, "non-dance" situations are those of *pāśa* (in which index fingers of both the hands are interlocked while the others are folded), *kaṭaka-mukha* (in which index and middle fingers are extended to touch the thumb while the other two fingers are stretched out), *mukuṭa* (in which the fingers and thumb are extended to touch each other), and *arāla* (in which the index finger in the *patākā-mudrā* bends to touch the thumb) that denote, among others, enmity, picking and smelling of flowers, eating, and receiving holy water respectively. Admittedly, these *mudrā*s are also used to denote a wide array of activities that are not possible to list here exhaustively. What is important to note at this stage is that the Tamil brāhmaṇas employ these *mudrā*s, as also several others, in their daily lives for the same purpose as they would do in dance performances. The chief purpose of drawing out the similarity, in the use of gestures in dance and "non-dance" situations, though in a limited way, is to demonstrate the commonness in the articulation of knowledge in the two situations and to establish that dance may be viewed as extreme stylization of the lived lives of Tamil brāhmaṇas and conversely that the lived lives of Tamil brāhmaṇas are inspired by the fundamental philosophy and content of the dance. A logical concomitant of the continuity between the two is the exchange of ideas and ideals that accompany the use of gestures and since the life of Tamil brāhmaṇas revolves around pursuance of religiosity and piety, dance becomes an important medium through which these are fostered.

Dance mediates between the world of human beings and that of the supernatural beings operating as a conduit of divine beneficence. Importantly, for the Tamil brāhmaṇas, Bharatanāṭyam consists of stylization of the actions they perform as part of daily worship. The act of offering flowers to deities or putting children (whom they regard as representing Kṛṣṇa) to sleep are cases in point. There is demonstrable similarity in their enactment of Yaśodā (Kṛṣṇa's foster mother) putting her son to sleep in a dance sequence and the way they do it in a real life situation with their own children. This is also true of the gestures that are used to depict gods and goddesses in conversations. There are distinct gestures to denote the conch and discus of Viṣṇu, the trident of Śiva and the *Śivaliṅga* — his phallus symbol. What emerges from these examples is the semblance of unity between the dance and religious life of Tamil brāhmaṇas leading to spiritual fulfilment at different levels. The dancer invokes the attributes of brilliance and wisdom as also passion that are usually associated with the sun and moon respectively by wearing their diadems on her head as part of the costume of dance. In enacting deities, she radiates spiritual values and eternal poise (Mathur 2002).

The religious element in Bharatanāṭyam lies in the themes and narratives to which the dance is performed as also in the life philosophy from which it derives. Each one of them is drawn from the myths relating with deities (Mathur 2007).

Since repeating the name of gods and visualizing them in the mind's eye (*nāma-rūpa*) is considered the best form of worship, in dancing such sequences, performers are actually rendering worship. Those who dance say that a transformation in the psyche sets in when they perform the lives and deeds of deities. The transformation suggests alternation, if nothing else, in consciousness, perception and experience of reality. Meyerhoff (1990) stresses the aspect of overcoming barriers between thought, action, knowledge and emotion in the course of transformation. Performers embody the enacted character(s). Audience, on the other hand, feels the surge of joy on seeing the most revered deities before them. A successful performance is said to be one that uplifts both the dancer and the viewer(s). It is also true, however, that the laying of the identity of the imaged character over that of a dancer is purely temporary and that there is always a minimal distance between the two. This makes it possible for the actors to own their individual identity after the performance. So, while the dancers do not lose individual identity, the inner self becomes more and more cleansed, refined and elevated after each performance. This is also true of those who watch the performance with devotion and faith.

Dancers say that the transformation in the cognition, thought processes and psyche arising out of enacting the lives of deities is deep and more lasting in nature. The perception and world-view of dancers, like non-dancer devotees, rests on intense devotion to the gods and deep admiration for their creation. There is flux between the dancing image and its interpretation and personal meaning for dancer and audience. In suggesting a vision of the Universal Being, the dancer seeks to reach out to a heightened plane of consciousness, of psychic integration and homeostasis at which human imperfections, limitations and personal histories cease to define identity. This state of *ānanda* or tranquillity is said to be the fruition of austerity and virtues towards which discipline in religious life is geared.

References

Avtar, R., 1984, *Indian Dances: History and Technique*, New Delhi: Pankaj Publications.

Blacking, J., 1977, "Towards an Anthropology of the Body", in *The Anthropology of the Body*, as a Monograph is edited by J. Blacking, London: Academic Press.

Bosch, F.D.K., 1994, *The Golden Germ: An Introduction to Indian Symbolism*, New Delhi: Munshiram Manoharlal Publishers.

Chakrabarti, S.C. and Frits Staal, 1996, "Agni", in *A Lexicon of Fundamental Concepts of the Indian Art*, vol. III, ed. Bettina Bäumer, New Delhi: Indira Gandhi National Centre for the Arts and Motilal Banarsidass Publishers.

Coomaraswamy, A.K. and G.K. Duggirala, 1997, *The Mirror of Gestures*, New Delhi: Munshiram Manoharlal Publishers.

Dalmia, Y., 1988, *The Painted World of the Warlis: Art and Ritual of the Warli Tribes of Maharashtra*, New Delhi: Lalit Kala Akademi.

Das, V., 1977, *Structure and Cognition: Aspects of Hindu Caste and Ritual*, Delhi: Oxford University Press.

Durkheim, E., 1965 (orig. 1915), *The Elementary Forms of Religious Life*, tr. J.W. Swain, New York: The Free Press.

Filliozat, Pierre-Sylvain, 1996, "Jyotis/Tejas/Prakasa", in *A Lexicon of Fundamental Concepts of the Indian Art*, vol. III, ed. Bettina Bäumer, New Delhi: Indira Gandhi National Centre for the Arts and Motilal Banarsidass Publishers.

Ghosh, M.M., tr. 1950, *Nāṭyaśāstra*, vols. I, II, Calcutta: Asiatic Society of Bengal.

Gold, A.G., 1988, *Fruitful Journeys: The Ways of Rajasthani Pilgrims*, Berkeley: University of California Press.

Irschick, E., 1986, *Tamil Revivalism in the 1930s*, Madras: Cre-A.

Kersenboom-Story, S.C., 1990, "Devadasi Murai", *Sangeet Natak*, April-June.

Kothari, S., 1988, "History: Roots, Growth and Revival", in *Bharatanāṭyam: Yesterday, Today and Tomorrow*, ed. Dinesh, New Delhi: Sujata Dinesh.

Kuppuswamy, G. and M. Hariharan, 1982, *Bharatanatyam in Indian Classical Music*, New Delhi: Cosmo Publications.

Lewis Paul and Elaine, 1984, *Peoples of the Goddess Triangle: Six Tribes in Thailand*, London: Thames and Hudson Ltd.

Madan, T.N. (ed.), 1991, "Introduction" in *Religion in India*, Delhi: Oxford University Press.

Mathur, N., 2002, *Cultural Rhythms in Emotions, Narratives and Dance*, New Delhi: Munshiram Manoharlal Publishers.

——, 2007, "Dance Ethnography in the Anthropology of India: Prospects and Possibilities," *Eastern Anthropologist*, 60, 3-4.

Meyerhoff, B., 1990, "The Transformation of Consciousness in Ritual performances: Some Thoughts and Questions", in *By Means of Performance: Intercultural Studies of Theatre and Ritual*, ed. Richard Schechner and Willa Appel, Cambridge: Cambridge University Press.

Mushir-ul-Haq, 1972, *Islam in Secular India*, Shimla: Indian Institute of Advanced Study.

O'Shea, J., 2003, "'Traditional' Indian Dance and the Making of Interpretive Communities," *Asian Theatre Journal* 15(1).

——, 2009, *Bharatanāṭyam on the Global Stage : At Home in the World*, Delhi: Motilal Banarsidass.

Ostor, A., 1980, *The Play of Gods: Locality, Ideology, Structure and Time in the Festivals of a Bengali Town*, Chicago: University of Chicago Press.

Saraswati, B.N., 1975, *Kashi: Myth and Reality*, Shimla: Indian Institute of Advanced Study.

Sathyanarayana, R., 1994, *The Nartananirnaya of Pandarika Vitthal*, Critically ed. and tr. with commentary, New Delhi: Indira Gandhi National Centre for the Arts and Motilal Banarsidass.

Sivaramamurti, C., 1974, *Nataraja in Art, Thought and Literature*, New Delhi: National Museum.

Srinivas, M.N., 1952, *Religion and Society among the Coorgs of South India*, Oxford: Clarendon Press.

Stanner, W.E.H., 1967, "Reflections on Durkheim and Aboriginal Religion", in *Social Organization*, ed. Maurice Freedman, London: Frank Cass.

Subramanian, L., 2006, *From the Tanjore Court to the Madras Academy: A Social History of the Music in South India*, Delhi: Oxford University Press.

Subramanian, P., 1982, "Dance Notation of Adavus", in *Bharatanatyam: Indian Classical Dance Art*, ed. Sunil Kothari, Bombay: Marg Publications.

Turner, V., 1967, *The Forest of Symbols: Aspects of Ndembu Ritual*, Ithaca: Cornell University Press.

———, 1969, *The Ritual Process: Structure and Anti-Structure*, Chicago: Aldine.

Vatsyayan, K., 1993, "Indian Art: The One and Many", Jawaharlal Nehru Memorial Lecture delivered at The Nehru Centre, London (unpublished).

Vidyarthi, L.P., 1961, *The Sacred Complex of Hindu Gaya*, Bombay: Asia Publishing.

Visvanathan, L., 1984, *Bharatanāṭyam: The Tamil Heritage*, Madras: Sri Kala Chakra Trust.

Walker, A.P., 1986, *The Toda of South India: A New Look*, Delhi: Hindustan Publishing Corporation.

Walker, B., 1983, *Hindu World: An Encyclopedic Survey of Hinduism* 2 vols., New Delhi: Munshiram Manoharlal Publishers.

Weber, Steven A. and P. David Seaman, 1985, *Havasupati Habitat: A.F. Whiting's Ethnography of a Traditional Indian Culture*, Arizona: University of Arizona Press.

Zarrilli, P., 1990, "What does it mean to 'become the character', power, presence, and transcendence in Asian in body-disciplines of practice" in *By Means of Performance: Intercultural Studies of Theatre and Ritual*, ed. Richard Schechner and Willa Appel, Cambridge: Cambridge University Press.

Contributors

Amit Kumar Sharma, Assistant Professor, CSSS, JNU, New Delhi.

Anand Kumar, Professor, CSSS, JNU, New Delhi.

Avijit Pathak, Professor, CSSS, JNU, New Delhi.

C.N. Venugopal, Retd. Professor of CSSS, JNU, New Delhi, settled at Bangalore.

Nita Mathur, Reader, IGNOU, New Delhi.

Rabindra Ray, Reader, Department of Sociology, Delhi School of Economics, New Delhi.

Roma Chatterji, Professor, Department of Sociology, Delhi School of Economics, New Delhi.

Satish Jain, Professor, CESP, JNU, New Delhi.

Susan Visvanathan, Professor, CSSS, JNU, New Delhi.

Tiplut Nongri, Professor, CSSS, JNU, New Delhi.

Vinay Kr. Srivastava, Professor of Sociology, Principal, Hindu College, Delhi University.

Wagish Shukla, Professor, Department of Mathematics, IIT, Delhi.

Index